-75 Riverside IDrive, New York, NY 10115.

FROM
EVE
TO
DAWN

FROM
EVE
TO
DAWN

A HISTORY OF WOMEN

VOLUME 1: ORIGINS

MARILYN FRENCH

McArthur & Company
Toronto

First published in Canada in 2002 by
McArthur & Company
322 King Street West, Suite 402
Toronto, Ontario M5V 1J2

Published in Dutch by Meulenhoff Amsterdam.

National Library of Canada Cataloguing in Publication Data

    French, Marilyn, 1929-
      From Eve to dawn: a history of women

    Contents: v.1. Eve to the Middle Ages.
    ISBN 1-55278-268-9 (v.1)

    Women-History. I. Title.

    HQ1121.F74 2002   305.4' 09   C2002-900455-1

Design & Composition: *Mad Dog Design Inc.*
Jacket Design & f/x: *Mad Dog Design Inc.*
Interior Maps: *Jamie French*
Cover photo copyright: *Erich Lessing/Art Resource, NY*
    The Three Graces, Euphrosyne (Joy), Thalia (Bloom) and Aglaia (Brilliance).
    Fresco from Pompeii.
Endpapers (Peters Projection): *Akademische Verlagsanstalt FL-9490 Vaduz, Aeulestr. 56.*

Editor: *Rosemary Shipton*
Proofreader: *Pamela Erlichman*
Printed in Canada by *Transcontinental Printing Inc.*

The publisher would like to acknowledge the financial support of the Government of Canada through the Book Publishing Industry Development Program (BPIDP) and the Canada Council for our publishing activities.

10 9 8 7 6 5 4 3 2 1

To Barbara Greenberg and Margaret Atwood

CONTENTS

PREFACE

I WROTE THIS HISTORY because I needed a story to make sense of what I knew of the past and what I saw in the present. Other approaches to history took for granted many elements that seemed odd to me. Why, for instance, were children named for their fathers, when fatherhood was always uncertain until the present and, among animals, often does not exist. Long before I read Virginia Woolf I wondered why men owned everything. From what I saw around me, women worked harder than men, yet nothing belonged to them. I wanted to discover what was known about our origins that could make sense of our current situation. I wanted to find a non-patriarchal past, but I did not want to invent one.

A narrative, a story of human development, I felt, would offer me, and other women, hope for the future – that the world could maintain itself in a non-patriarchal way. Most people, women and men, know nothing about women's history, and perhaps not much about men's. When I began this book, people (both women and men) scoffed at me: women had no history! But as you can see, they do.

This book arose from a contract to provide material for a British television series based on the history chapter of my book, *Beyond Power*.[1] The TV series fell through, but I was hooked and stayed committed through ten years of research and writing, and five more of revision and addition.

This book is written from my perspective, the point of view of a feminist. But I have tried to be scrupulously true to my sources. From the beginning of history (as opposed to prehistory, which can only be deduced), women have been suppressed, rendered unfree, made men's property. It is astonishing how, in state after state, men pass laws repressing women, limiting them in every possible way, and how each state, no matter how distant from others in time and space, constrains women in exactly the same way. The people who oppressed women were men. Not all men oppressed women, but most benefited (or thought they benefited) from this domination, and most contributed to it, if only by doing nothing to stop or ease it. Men's responsibility for women's oppression is faced openly in this book, although many men today would happily see women's situation change. I would like men to take responsibility for what their sex has done, agree that it was unfair and unpleasant, and move forward into the new century with a new ethos.

Men most often justified their oppression of women by claiming that women were *by nature* weak in body or mind or both, that nature fitted women but not men to raise children, and that women belong in the home or domestic compound for their own protection. But who do women really need protection from? Men as a caste are predators on women as a caste. No woman fears another woman walking behind her on a street at night, but many women do not even go out at night because of men. Still they are battered, tortured, and killed at home – by men. I believe most men would be appalled if they realized how women feel about their sex. And vice versa.

Most people believe that only men hunt and soldier, that children were always named for their fathers, and that men always took care of women, and so it makes sense that, in many states, only men own property or most of the property. Yet all these statements are false. To trace their origins, we have to resort to non-historical studies. Therefore, the first two chapters of this three-volume work use ethnological, anthropological, archaeological, and microbiological data. One root of oppression is loss of memory.[2]

Although only I bear responsibility for the statements and point of view of this book, as well as the errors it must contain, I have not written it alone. Tens of scholars helped me, with essays summarizing the important points about their periods, bibliographies, and in some cases, articles or books. They helped me generously, even when they disagreed with my approach to historiography or disapproved of using anthropological information in a history. I thank them all.

First, I thank Claudia Koonz, who helped organize the subject matter and found most of the historian contributors. Jo Ann McNamara gave me information about Europe over an amazing period – from the Roman Empire all the way through to the late Christian period; Marcia Wright and Susan Hall patiently guided me through the thicket of

Africa, the history of a continent. In addition, I thank Françoise Basch, Jon-Christian Billigmeier, Charlotte Bunch, Rebecca Cann, Blanche Cook, Elizabeth Croll, Ann Farnsworth, Kirsten Fischer, Jean Franco, Martha Gimenez, Karen Gottshang, Carol Hochstedler, Anne Holmes, Nikki Keddie, Renate Klein, Johanna Lessinger, Susan Mann, Marjorie Mbilinyi, John Mencher, Carol Meyers, Marysa Navarro, Karen Nussbaum, Veena Oldenburg, Leslie Peirce, Cathy Rakowski, Nan Rothschild, Kumkum Roy, Karen Rubinson, Irene Silverblatt, and Stephanie Urdung. Help was also given by Alice Kessler-Harris, Catherine Pellissier, Carroll Smith-Rosenberg, Ann Snitow, Amy Swerdlow, Romila Thapur, and Alice Valentine. Researchers included Judith Byfield, Binnur Ercen, Tikva Frymer-Kensky, Rivka Harris, Kathi Kern, Stella Maloof, Linda Mitchell, Lisa Norling, Claire Potter, Gisela Shue, Temma Kaplan, and Tracey Weis. Other notable assistance came from Fadwa al Guindi, Beatrice Campbell, Donna Haraway, Barbara Lesko, Lynn Mally, Rayna Rapp, Judith Tucker, and Ann Volks. My incalculably important assistants over this fifteen-year period were Betsy Chalfin, Isabelle de Cordier, Hana Elwell, and Judi Silverman.

VOLUME 1

ORIGINS

PART ONE

PARENTS

THIS BOOK DESCRIBES THE EARLIEST EXPERIENCES of our species, insofar as we know them. It outlines the way the hominids – humanlike creatures – probably lived, the customs and social arrangements that the species followed for roughly 3.5 years. At some point in the distant past, but probably not much further back than twelve or ten thousand years, men rose in rebellion against women. They felt dominated by women, even though there were probably no political structures of domination. Women were central to society and they supported men; men may have felt marginal or left out, but they wanted children to be theirs instead of women's. To accomplish this transfer, they had to push aside mother-right (the right to name the child and control its labour) and so they invented patrilineality, naming the children for their fathers. But this connection is tricky, since fatherhood, before DNA testing, could never be assured. To guarantee paternity they had to control women, keep them under surveillance, and, in effect, own them. The revolution was a violent one, with women kidnapped and made part of their husbands' lineage (patrilocality). Women lost their previous rights.

In time, men devised a structure to incarnate patriarchy: the state. The earliest states – Egypt, Mesopotamia, China, and India – are discussed here along with Mexico, Rome, and Greece. States had rulers, kings who were often priests and military leaders as well. And with the rise of the state came war, slavery, and law, superseding custom, which had previously sufficed. The first codes of law we know about had special laws for women, who were more limited in their rights and actions than men. A new crime appeared, adultery, which only women could commit. Infanticide, the prerogative of fathers, was legal, but abortion performed by women was treason. Priests of the first state, Sumer, invented female prostitution.

The second structure to spread and strenghthen patriarchy was religion. This book concludes with discussions of the origins and attitudes towards women of Judaism, Christianity, and Islam.

CHAPTER 1

THE MOTHERS

H UMANS ARE PRIMATES, kin to monkeys and lemurs, and cousins of the great apes – gorillas, gibbons, orangutans, and chimpanzees. Our muscular and skeletal structure, nervous systems, teeth, and blood types resemble those of chimpanzees, whose DNA is almost identical to ours. Humans and apes descend from a common ancestor and diverged five to six million years ago. Different enough that we distinguish each other instantly, we were once so similar that our fossil remains can confuse archaeologists.

For primates to evolve to hominids, major changes had to occur to the skeleton: the pelvis grew shorter and broader, the legs longer; the feet became less flexible; and tooth pattern altered. Essential changes occurred in women. Both higher primate females and women have clitorises (the only organ in nature dedicated solely to sexual pleasure), but women's pelvises widened considerably to permit the birth of babies with large skulls containing a large brain. Women lost estrus – they can be sexually receptive at any time – and, unlike other mammals, do not have "heat," or periods of sexual receptivity. Some scholars think that changes in female bodies alone triggered the "hominization" of earlier species.[1]

Hominid Life

Fossil remains of a hominid, genus *Australopithecus,* that walked on two legs 4.4 million years ago were found in Ethiopia. Lucy, 3.9 million years old, was around 1.2 metres tall, weighed about 27 kilograms, and had very long arms and a massive jaw. Her brain was not much larger than an ape's.[2] *Homo,* our genus, evolved or diverged from *Australopithecus.* The first toolmakers *(Homo habilis)* lived about 2.6 million years ago. One to 1.2 metres tall, with long apelike arms and slightly larger brains, they made at least eleven different types of tools, rough flakes for hacking roots and vegetables and for scraping meat from bones (probably from dead animals or from small ones trapped in the hands). About 2 million years ago, *Homo* began to wander from Africa to southern Asia and northern Eurasia.[3] Our genus, *Homo sapiens,* emerged 200,000 to 100,000 years ago with a brain almost four times larger than Lucy's, a thick-boned skull, and a robust body. A 120,000-year-old slender-bodied species, *Homo sapiens sapiens,* had the same brain capacity, but while *Homo sapiens* was making flake tools in Europe and Asia 90,000–80,000 years ago, *Homo sapiens sapiens* (our species) was making sophisticated blade tools from selected fine-grained rock, building windproof shelters and watercraft, tailoring clothes, and perhaps hunting stealthily in Africa.

Hominids and early humans lived differently from us, but the way we live now is rooted in their ways. We are not, so far as we know, imprinted with behaviours as, say, bees are; but the limbic brain probably retains a memory of behaviours that fostered our survival, just as our values are a heritage from and reaction against the values and ways of our forebears.[4] This chapter describes that early life, an economic and political structure called matricentry, or life centred around mothers.

About forty years ago biochemists began to study genetic material to learn how life evolved. Studying DNA, the nucleic acids that transmit characteristics from parent to child, they found that most evolutionary change is caused by mutations in genetic molecules. Complex measurements of human, monkey, and ape DNA showed that humans diverged from African apes about 5 million years ago. DNA was also found outside the cell nucleus in the mitochondria – organelles found in all multicelled life, the engines of cells, metabolizing food and water into energy. Once probably separate bacteria, engulfed by larger ones with which they began to live symbiotically, mitochondria still retain their own DNA code for the proteins needed in metabolism.

Mitochondrial DNA is, uniquely, passed on only by mothers. Researchers at the University of California at Berkeley studied mitochondrial DNA in 147 people from different parts of Europe, Asia, North Africa, and the Middle East, with ancestors from sub-Saharan Africa, Australia, and New Guinea. Mutations in these samples showed that the entire human race is descended from a single woman: there was an Eve! The Berkeley group estimates that she lived in Africa 285,000 to 143,000 years ago, that human *(Homo sapiens sapiens)* life began in Africa, and that the species left Africa, at the earliest, 135,000 years ago.[5] A later researcher challenged this chronology, arguing that our foremother could have lived anywhere between 100,000 and 1 million years ago.[6] "Eve" was not the first woman in the world, but the first whose daughters gave birth to daughters who transmitted their DNA. The new species coexisted for eons with other species that eventually died out. We who live today, whatever our colour, stature, or body type, are truly siblings, descendants of a woman who was the mother of us all.

History is the written record of the past, but writing did not begin until the third millennium Before the Common Era – about 3000 BCE. By then, hominids/humans had existed for over three million years. History records only a fraction of the human past. To discover how humans lived during earlier days we must turn to archaeology, anthropology, and paleontology. Some stone buildings, monuments, and artworks remain; some myths hazily reflect early attitudes. To some degree we can extrapolate from the behaviour of higher mammals, especially chimpanzees, and from groups that retained Stone Age customs into this century.

For most of our past, people did not recognize paternity. Just as animals recognize their mothers (who know their young) but not their sires (who do not), early humans did not connect the sex act with its delayed and random consequence. Cave paintings and carvings from around 5000 BCE depict animals copulating in spring and females pregnant in the summer, so the male role in procreation may have been known for 10,000 years. But for 125,000–275,000 years of *Homo sapiens sapiens'* existence, females were seen as solely responsible for life. If paternity is not known, the mother is the only parent. Early people revered the female power to reproduce and to ensure the continuity of the community.

Females raise the young in all mammal species. This caretaking is not instinctual but learned. Experiments show that there is no biological "maternal instinct" except just after birth; animals taken from their mothers at birth do not mother their own young.[7] Animals learn to mother: the female characteristic that most people believe is innate is learned. Early human females probably acted like other mammals, like chimpanzee mothers, carrying their babies with them, feeding them from their breasts and sharing solid foods with them. They taught the young survival techniques – which foods were edible, which animals were friendly, and where to sleep. Hominid mothers probably made a nest each night to sleep in with their young. Chimp mothers socialize the young, teaching males to share food with adults of both sexes and females to feed their offspring. The mother-child bond constitutes the base of all mammal society, and in some species it is the only society. Prides of lions and herds of elephants are generations of females and their young. Male mammals leave the group voluntarily or by force in adolescence. Some baboons and macaques live in all-male troops; other males live on the fringes of the group, isolated. Monkeys and chimpanzees, social and gregarious, live in close bisexual communities; humans probably did too.

Hungry hominids went out during the day when the forest was relatively safe: predatory animals hunt at night. They knew all the plants and herbs; they picked fruit, nuts, and vegetables and dug roots, eating as they went, foraging. They probably had some system of communication, sound patterns that meant "here are mushrooms" or "stay away from that," just as chimpanzees convey information about their environment to each other.[8]

Walking miles each day kept hominids thin. But if food was sparse or had disappeared, they had to walk very far to find small quantities; in such cases, females lose weight and stop menstruating. Thus, in times of scarcity, no children are born: it's a form of natural birth control. Women in simple societies today know roots deep in the ground that can sustain them until they find better terrain in a new area. When food becomes plentiful again, women gain weight, resume menstruating, and conceive young.

One problem was babies, who have to be carried, grow heavy, and occupy at least one arm. Women may have invented the container, which could hold a baby on their backs or chests. They had tools – cutting and chopping flakes and digging sticks – with which they could cut leaves and bark to weave together into a carrier. They laid the baby in the holder, lifted it across their chest, and fastened it over their shoulders and around their waist with twisted vines. Then, unless a woman had to help a four year old across slimy rocks fording a stream, her hands were free.

Containers opened up opportunities. Foragers must stay near water or risk being parched. With a container of water on their heads, they could travel in search of novelties. They could collect food for more than one day – gathering, not foraging – and they could rest some days. This enlarged range improved their diet, and the rest days freed them to invent activities like weaving.

The sexual division of labour found in every society may have originated with the container, since, in extant simple societies, men rarely gather. Women take the responsibility for others, feeding the entire group. Men may occasionally share an animal or bird, and sometimes hunt, but they depend on women for 80 percent of their diet. Women also take responsibility for processing the food, chopping and cooking the vegetables and herbs.

Between 100,000 to 200,000 years ago humans built shelters in a circle, with a fire in the centre to keep lions and jackals away. They roasted meat and vegetables until they were tasty and tender, and they gradually lost their large rear grinding teeth. They began to hunt. When game was running, the adults in a band picked up stones and fronds and surrounded an animal. Clacking the stones together and waving the fronds, they made loud noises to frighten the animal into a corner, then moved in, driving it towards a gully. After the terrified creature leaped or fell into the gully, the band rushed to kill it. For small animals and birds, they used a sling shot. They begged forgiveness of fallen creatures for killing them, their siblings.

With tools, they made garments and baskets out of leaves, bark, woven reeds, and animal skins. They strung necklaces from small stones and shells. Most important, they spoke. We do not know when people began to speak, but they must have begun with the sounds creatures make – birdsong, monkey cries, chimpanzee vocalization – with particular meaning in each band or locality.

Half the children born died in infancy. Men often tended children when the women gathered, but children were women's responsibility. Mothers taught them about plants and animals, the trails, and how to dispose of their body wastes in the forest. The clans survived by sharing and cooperation, but women did most of the work.

No people today lives exactly as its ancestors did thousands of years ago – all have been exposed to modern ways. But isolated groups in Africa, Australia, New Guinea, and South America maintained Stone Age culture into the twentieth century, and a few gathering-hunting societies still exist.[9] They have customs we share and customs we have renounced, in which we can see our origins.

The !Kung of the Kalahari Desert

The !Kung (the ! represents a click) live mainly on high-calory mongongo nuts (300 have the protein of 400 grams of lean beef). Two or three days a week the women, who can discriminate among hundreds of plant species and recognize each stage of plant growth, gather the nuts and eighty-nine other roots, fruits, and berries, 70–90 percent of the !Kung diet. !Kung men work only twelve to nineteen hours a week: they forage and sometimes hunt or trap small animals. No one works until marriage: children, adolescents, and old folk do not work. Ten percent of the !Kung are over sixty, yet everyone is cared for, even the impaired.[10]

Girls marry between fifteen and twenty, boys between twenty and twenty-five. First marriages are usually arranged by parents; adultery on either side can cause divorce. !Kung men live with their wives' kin after marriage, remaining for five to ten years, doing bride-service for the family. Men who kill an animal in the hunt divide it in an elaborate ritual: first it is shared by the hunters; then the man who killed the animal gives some to his wife's parents, his wife and children, and his own parents, if they live nearby.

Only men can be healers, going into trances during dance ceremonies and claiming to cure the sick. Only men head bands or claim to "own" water holes and the vegetation around them. But both !Kung women and men are autonomous, with high self-esteem. They are opinionated and express themselves freely. They live in anarchy – that is, without leaders – in small groups. If a quarrel cannot be resolved, one member will leave. The Hadza, Ik, Dogrib, Netsilik Eskimos, Gidjingali, Mbuti, and others live in similar "anarchic" societies.

The Mbuti of Zaire

Colin Turnbull has written lovingly about the Mbuti, a people under 1.5 metres feet tall who live in the forest.[11] Their egalitarian society centres on motherhood and hunting. "Real" men hunt – others are "clowns," a respectable occupation. Women gather and go net hunting with men. The Mbuti have only one word for elder *(tata)*, one for child *(miki)*, and one for peers *(apua'i)*.

Sex is unimportant, except in adulthood, but Mbuti sexual arrangements are unusual. Once a girl is sexually mature, she can sleep in an *elima* house. Boys come to its door every night, begging entry. The girls and their chaperons stand in the doorway teasing, mocking, and hitting the boys. Some girls flick boys with a whip and let them enter. The youngsters spend the night together in an "embrace." The embrace is said to be ecstatic, but less so than the embrace of marriage. Intercourse is permitted with certain restrictions, yet no girl ever gets pregnant in an *elima* house.

Marriage is by choice and patrilocal, but the group a woman joins must replace her in the group she leaves. After giving birth, a woman rests for three days, then resumes her usual work – the hunt or gathering expeditions – taking her baby with her or leaving it in camp. But sexual intercourse is taboo for three years after a birth, guaranteeing babies three years of mother's milk. Husbands may go to the girls' hut or have an affair with a married woman, though sometimes this dalliance causes trouble. The men do not like the arrangement; Turnbull did not know how the women liked it.

The Mbuti have a lovely fatherhood ritual. When a baby is two years old the mother carries it into the centre of the compound, where the father sits with some food. The mother hands him the baby, and the father puts the child to his breast. The child tries to suck, gets nothing, and cries "mother" (ema). The father then puts solid food in the baby's mouth and teaches it to say "father" (eba). The baby learns that fathers too nourish and cherish. The Mbuti foster harmony, teaching cooperation, not competition. It is unacceptable to win, for winning isolates the winner and saddens losers. Those who excel at something encourage and help others. This harmony extends to nature. The Mbuti, the children of the forest, see animals as fellow creatures. They believe that people were immortal until one of them killed his brother antelope. They will continue to die until they stop this slaughter. They kill animals only when they must, but never each other.

Conflicts between Mbuti women and men inform some of the rituals. One flute ceremony, called the molima, is for men only. The women intrude on it, claiming that the men stole the flutes and the ceremony from them. They dramatically mock the male penis, and the men in turn mock their menstruation. They regularly banter and tease each other, often about sex. (The !Kung, too, tease each other about their sexual organs, with men suffering most of the mockery.)

Australian Aborigines

The Aborigines of coastal Australia, like native Americans, were killed by disease, exploited, and pushed farther and farther inland by white settlers. By the late nineteenth century they were confined in the arid centre of the continent, one of the harshest environments on the planet, yet they remained healthy and vigorous. Aborigines live by religion, a complex structure revealed to them by "the dreaming." They believe the physical world was created by gods who transmitted spiritual powers to rocks, sand, streams, and plants. Dreaming rituals tell the present or the future and are led by women or men, who may welcome the other sex.

Semi-nomadic Aborigines live in settlements. Women do most of the work – socialize children, gather, hunt small game, process food – and provide most or all of the group's food. In the mornings the women fill deep wooden bowls with water, and a twist of grass to keep it from sloshing. They place them in a loop on their heads, pick up their digging sticks, and set off with the children, the trained dogs, and a lighted firestick for communication.[12] They walk miles, gradually drinking the water, and gather whatever food they find, anxious to get back to camp before the hot winds spring up. The children help and are praised generously. When food is scarce, the woman go out again after the sun cools. On the way, the dogs may help them kill small game or a kangaroo, which they carry to camp. They spend the rest of the day grinding vegetables and cooking food.

The men do far less: they gather and somewhat unreliably hunt larger game. With spear and spear thrower they go separately, but not far, and often come back empty-handed. A man who returns with something – a lizard, say – is triumphant and spends the rest of the day bragging of his prowess and knowledge of hunting. When the women return, the men go to the place where they hide their sacred totems – cult symbols they conceal from the women.

Richard Gould says that both sexes are content, proud of sustaining themselves by their knowledge and skill, believing they are part of a harmoniously ordered universe. They think that marriage is a mutual economic arrangement and that cooperation is essential to survival. Men have more prestige, but women know they are necessary. Both derive satisfaction from their roles.

Accounts of Australian Aborigines conflict, especially on the status of women. Early observers reported that woman, because of the marriage rules, had a low position in society. When a Warlpiri boy reaches maturity and is to be initiated, his mother chooses a circumcisor, who is obliged to find him a wife.[13] Marriage partners are chosen primarily on the basis of kinship, with preference for cross-cousin marriage – the child of the mother's great-uncle's daughter. Once, no other choice was acceptable. But the pivot of the process is the circumcisor: during the pre-initiation ceremonies, the mother passes the firestick to the woman whose husband she wishes to be the circumcisor. All the women of the kin-group are involved and are consulted by the men.

A boy is betrothed to an infant girl: neither has free choice. Both are sexually free before and after marriage, and young women may abort themselves to postpone motherhood and to keep sexually active. After marriage, free sexuality is common, but some men beat their wives for it. Wives, however, hit back at their husbands with their digging sticks and, if the original beating was too severe, they may leave the man. Women have a refuge, the jilimi. Any woman may visit or live at the women's camp, but men may not enter or pass near it and must take roundabout routes when travelling. The camp is a haven for single women, widows, estranged wives, visiting or sick women, and dependent children. It lets married women come for a day or for a longer period of time, and they may go home occasionally to spend time with a man or with several men.

The ideal marriage progression has a young man first marry an older widow, who teaches him the art of love before she dies. He then marries the young promised wife. Young women marry experienced husbands and learn wifely tasks from co-wives. Most older husbands tolerate their wives' affairs; older wives are grateful for help in child-raising and in providing food. Co-wives may become close and remain friends, even after a husband dies. Men, usually fifteen to twenty years older than young wives, die sooner.

Women have freedom to manoeuvre in second marriages and may choose a husband who raises their status. If he dies, they often marry very young men, completing the circle. Elaborate mourning rituals place taboos on some speech and heterosexual contact. A widow needs a husband's brothers' permission to release her from the last stages of mourning, but it is not always given. Polygyny, the ideal, is rare now. Since European contact, the Warlpiri have tried a new kind of marriage between young men and women: it is the most fragile form they have known.[14]

Farming Societies

Humans began to bury the dead in stone enclosures, perhaps ceremonializing death, about 70,000 years ago. By the later Old Stone (Paleolithic) Age, about 40,000 years ago, they had refined stone and bone into projectiles (spears) to hunt large mammals. But there is no evidence of war – large-scale killing of humans with weapons – until the Magdalenian Age, about 12,000 BCE. About 100,000 years ago, people began to measure time: rocks are marked like calendars. It is thought that women devised calendars and measurement by timing their menstrual periods with phases of the moon. Early horticulture was timed to moon phases. In some extant societies, women keep lunar calendars; Yurok women's tally systems let them predict a birth within a day.[15]

Archaeologists think that, in some regions, groups settled in relatively permanent villages about 35,000 years ago, building sturdy shelters and making pottery and jewellery. They gathered and hunted, but gathered more than they needed, storing the surplus against barren seasons. A surplus can also be traded for things a group does not produce, so the members can enjoy a richer standard of living. Societies in which people do not produce more than they need to live are called "subsistence cultures."

The first farming we know of, Nile Valley cereal cultivation, began about 15,000 years ago and became widespread around 9000 BCE. "Horticulture" is farming with hand tools (done mainly by women); "agriculture" is farming by machine (done mainly by men). Both types feed more people than gathering, but require much more labour and some settling. In time, farming revolutionized human life and altered divisions between the sexes. At first, when land was plentiful, some groups used the slash-and-burn technique, a type of horticulture in which they clear land by slashing, then burn the vegetation for fertilizer. Because this method depletes soil quickly, slash-and-burn farmers move every few years, leaving plots fallow for eight to ten years so nutrients return to the soil. Some groups combined this rude farming with gathering and hunting.

The Bari of South America

The Bari once populated northeastern Colombia to north-western Venezuela, but they were destroyed by Spanish and German colonial policies and diseases. Fewer than 2000 Bari remain today, confined in 1000 square kilometres of mountainous, wooded, inhospitable land. They strongly re-sisted Western ways, but they were overwhelmed and remain egalitarian only in isolated regions. They remain harmo-nious, but their grim history has made them hostile towards usurpers. Some members have influence, but they have no leaders, no slaves, and no word for "chief," despite colon-ialists' and missionaries' efforts to get them to name one.

The Bari fish, farm, gather, and hunt but have no con-cept of land ownership. They live in groups of approximate-ly two hundred, in communal houses for forty to eighty peo-ple, with several hearths each used by a small group that shares and cooks together. Groups usually contain one or more nuclear families, along with intimates not related to them. They all have allotted space in which to hang their hammocks and store their belongings, and they all respect the others' rights. Despite their slash-and-burn farming, they are careful to avoid depleting the resources of a region and they keep things sanitary. Groups often move, and members may shift groups during moves.

Their division of labour is flexible: together, they build dwellings, fish, and plant, cook, gather, carry loads, and tend children. No work has more status than any other. Sex is free and unbound, as long as the partners are not kin, both before and after marriage, and there is no sexual jealousy. Marriages, which are usually stable, are easily dissolved. Like their parents, children are responsible and autonomous. Parents are never harsh towards a child who refuses to do something. Men and women are extremely affectionate with children; mothers may carry their babies with them or leave them with their hearth group.

The Bari have no religion and few rituals, though they have one wonderful celebration, the song-fest. A group invites another to visit, often from far away. The guests climb into hammocks – the men into high ones, the women into low ones – and lie back. Each host sits on a hammock facing away from a guest of the same sex and they sing together. When they finish, they exchange gifts. The pairs stop when they want to and change partners. They continue for days or weeks, until every host adult has sung with every visiting adult of the same sex.[16]

Native Americans

Grave goods and skeletons show that early Native Americans had no strict division of labour. Muscle attachments on skeletons in the 4000-year-old Indian Knoll burial ground in Kentucky showed that both sexes performed similar muscular activities.[17] Both men and women gathered and hunted; female graves contained projectile points used in hunting and war, although male graves contained more. Aside from one cemetery where women were buried with more objects than men, in the oldest sites (3000–4000 years old, called Archaic) the sexes (but not the aged) were buried alike. In 1000-year-old Mississippian cultures (farmer-gatherer-hunters), some children were buried with conch pendants, perhaps a sign of rank. Children do not hold rank in egalitarian societies, where status or prestige is earned. If certain Mississippian children were ranked, the society may have been stratified. The distinction was not economic, however, for the actual burials were similar. Some of the graves held more objects than others. A few people in the gravesites had lived to their sixties, which was rare in Europeans at that time.[18]

The Montagnais-Naskapi of North America

A seventeenth-century Jesuit, Father Paul Le Jeune, recorded his impressions of the Montagnais-Naskapis in eastern Canada and Labrador. Moving between winter and summer camps, gathering in summer and hunting in winter (everyone worked), they dwelt about eighteen to a tent. They cherished all their children, and both sexes tended children and handled traps. Couples chopped and hauled logs together, a man and his daughter sawed wood. Canoeing families hauled in fishnets. Young women hunted rabbits alone, and men in camp cooked for themselves. Only a few jobs were sex specific: men did woodwork, carved canoes, and made snowshoes; women scraped, tanned, worked, and sewed skins.

Marriage did not imply dominance: partners were sexually free. Women decided when and where to go to winter campgrounds. Both sexes were shamans (priests or healers) and fierce leaders in wars. The sexes were interdependent and valued generosity, cooperation, patience, and good humour; they hated coercion and despised anyone who tried to dominate others. They might tease, ridiculing someone who refused to accept a group decision, often in bawdy ways, but they never coerced anyone into compliance. Both the male and female elders made group judgments. Leaders were pro-tem for one activity and never tried to stay in charge.

The Jesuits tried to "improve" Montagnais-Naskapi morality: they demanded that they discipline their children harshly, establish an elite with formal authority, and create a hierarchy where men assumed authority over women and forced them into sexual fidelity. They removed children from the family to educate them. Unfortunately, they had some success: Christian converts treated others with great cruelty.[19]

The Iroquois of North America

Sixteenth-century Iroquois lived by horticulture and hunting in villages of longhouses – semi-permanent bark-shingled frame houses. Several hundred people could dwell in each longhouse, about twenty-five families, each with partitioned sleeping quarters and a hearth shared with the family opposite. The Iroquois traced descent matrilineally, and women had usufruct rights to use particular plots of land, rights they passed on to their daughters. (Usufruct rights appear mainly in matrilineal societies which believe not in land ownership but land use.) Marriage was matrilocal – men lived with their brides' families – as is usual when women own usufruct rights to land.

The women farmed with digging sticks and hoes, made of deer shoulder blades. They stored food in anterooms at both ends of a longhouse and controlled food distribution. Equal numbers of women and men made up the Keepers of the Faith, the moral overseers; each nation sent a representative to the Council of the Confederacy, which determined group policies but lacked any power to coerce. Historian George Bancroft has written that the United States form of government was based on that of the Six Iroquois Nations.[20] The council sachems among the Iroquois were all male, but women could depose any chief who displeased them. Chiefs could not make war without the consent of women, who controlled the food.[21]

The social arrangements of many Native Americans are like those of the Iroquois and Montagnais-Naskapi, who lived by rules that fostered harmony, cooperation, and sharing, the values necessary to their survival. Some simple societies are stratified, with men enjoying prerogatives or authority over women or dominating them. In general, men have higher status than women in most simple societies. The groups discussed above, in which the sexes are relatively equal, do not believe in private property. Australian Aborigines believe the land belongs to their clan or moiety but generously let others hunt or gather on it.

The Tlingit of Alaska

The Tlingit of Alaska are a rarity – a gathering-hunting society with private property. Hunting men have status and power in northern regions with little vegetation, where the people depend on meat for subsistence. The Tlingit and similar groups say that women once hunted and fished along with the men, but they no longer did so by the time of European contact. By then, men, who provided most of the food, were dominant. The Tlingit were more competitive and male-centred than other Native Americans, yet women had a lot of power.[22] They guarded the family wealth, which the men gave away in competitive parties called potlatches: these lavish entertainments earned men prestige and put pressure on other men. The quarrelsome and competitive Tlingit, obsessed with rank and status, were fiercely male dominant.

Complex Societies

Humans probably made art out of fragile materials that decay until about 30,000 years ago. Pottery, invented at different times in different places, was widely known by 12,000 BCE. Many scholars believe that women were the first horticulturalists and pottery makers, and both tasks remained "women's work" for millennia, as they still are in simple cultures. Metallurgy was discovered, at the latest, about 7000 BCE, first copper, then bronze. The difficult, complicated process for smelting iron was discovered in approximately 600 BCE in Africa. People were painting rocks and cave walls in France, Iberia, Russia, Italy, and Mongolia 30,000 years ago. Women were the early cave painters in India, and a decorated cave at Pech Merle, France, holds the footprints of a woman and a child.

Paintings from 8000 BCE to 2500 BCE were found on a thousand rock shelters in a remote area of central India.[23] The paintings show a gathering-hunting culture: the area still has a tribal population, rich forests, and animals roaming wild. Easily visible from down below, the paintings, on hard-to-reach surfaces, depict animals, humans hunting and dancing, and symbolic designs. There are more women than men and they are more fully and carefully drawn, even to painted body decorations. The men, in comparison, are stick figures.

Women, pregnant or suckling babies, gather fruits and vegetables in baskets or string nets, grind grain, prepare food, and kill rats and fish. Their strength is emphasized: they stride purposefully and work with energy. A woman with a basket on her shoulder holds two children and carries an animal on her head; a woman drags a deer by its antlers. Two figures that a male archaeologist dubbed "hunting chieftains" are women.[24] In one site, nine hunters armed with sticks, three of whom are possibly women, surround a buffalo.[25] South Bihar tribal women still hunt on festive occasions, re-enacting an old custom.[26]

A spider-shaped figure much larger than the figures surrounding her, with raised hands, thighs opened sideways, and a tiny baby below her genitals, has been called a mother goddess. There are also realistic portrayals of women and sexual activity. In some sites, women and men are shown embracing closely, neither dominating the other.[27] Depictions of sex from patriarchal cultures, in contrast, rarely show mutual sex. Rather, they show women in forced submission to men, in degrading positions, naked while men are dressed, or much smaller than men (see chapter 3). In the groups in India, women are central. A pregnant woman is surrounded by two large women, one playing with a child; a man with a stick and two children are marginal. Three women dance while others grind corn, put a digging stick into a basket, suckle a baby, and fornicate in a cave.

The vivid paintings are drawn with a few simple, strong strokes in dyes (mainly red, white, black, yellow, and green) made from local elements. Until recently, female peasant artists of Bihar used soot for black, clay for red, and carnation pollen for yellow, mixing the pigment with goat's milk or bean juice. The ancient artists were also probably women:

today, caste-stratified peasant and tribal women do home wall painting. In Mithila, techniques and symbols of Indian painting have been handed down from mother to daughter for generations. A frequently used motif, the handprint, often a child's handprint on a mother's breast, is also found in Neolithic cave paintings in Europe, at Catal Hüyük and elsewhere. Paintings hundreds of kilometres apart share style, theme, and method of execution and reflect a gathering-hunting matricentric society dedicated to life and fertility, egalitarian but with women considered more prestigious than men.

The corpses in Neolithic graves elsewhere are painted with red ochre and have cowrie shells (shaped like the female vagina) arranged on the body in a vaginal pattern. Archaeologists have unearthed thousands of sculptured figures of females or females-cum-animals in China, the Middle East, Europe, and Mesoamerica. Made from about 25,000 BCE into the Bronze Age and the Classical period, they are still common at the beginning of the Common Era.

Many researchers believe these art works testify to worship of a female principle – that women's ability to produce life from their bodies indicated a special connection with nature. Associating female and nature's fecundity, people prayed to a female procreatrix for healthy crops, pregnancies and births, or other material benefits. Believing that animals, who died yet reappeared the next season, were reincarnated, people thought that humans also went through a cycle of birth, death, and resurrection. The gods people worship always embody the qualities they most value. Worshipping natural bounty in plants, animals, and women, Neolithic peoples may have worshipped a goddess associated with fecundity and rebirth.

Scholars question whether worship of a female principle meant that women had high status in the Neolithic era. Almost no images of males exist from the Neolithic era, and those that do show men as somewhat lesser than women. Excavating Upper Paleolithic chambers, French historian André Leroi-Gourhan saw female figures and symbols placed centrally, with males set peripherally around them. In a painting in the Cogul rock shelter in Catalonia, women dance in what may be a religious ceremony around a smaller nude male. A North African rock painting of a man about to shoot an arrow into an animal shows a line to his penis from the vulva of a naked woman who stands behind him, hands outstretched as if she is transmitting energy to him.[28]

Catal Hüyük and Other Towns

Catal Hüyük, a town in Anatolia (Turkey), flourished from 7000/6500 BCE to around 5650 BCE and was home to about 5000 people who farmed, kept animals, wove wool and flax, chipped and polished stone tools, and made beads, fine wooden vessels, simple pottery, and copper and lead jewellery.[29] They travelled long distances for materials and traded local products for obsidian from nearby volcanic mountains, timber from the Taurus Mountains, flint from the south, and shells from the Mediterranean.

Catal Hüyük has no streets, plazas, or public buildings. Its beehive-shaped, one-room, mud-brick houses, entered through the roof by a ladder, are all the same size. Immaculate, each held a hearth, an oven, and, along the east wall, a large sleeping platform with red-painted wooden posts. Beneath it, the women of the community were buried, some with children. Sleeping platforms elsewhere in the room held men's or children's graves, though never together. About a quarter of the houses were shrines, recognizable by wall paintings of bulls' horns and heads, plaster reliefs of goddesses and religious statues, and elaborate burials.

For over a thousand years the town built on itself twelve times. In this period there is no sign of war or animal sacrifice and no weapons, yet the earliest wall paintings show animals and bulls' horns. The first paintings of goddesses date from about 6200 BCE, in shapes connoting birth, death, and crops: hunting may have been waning, and horticulture was the primary source of food. One shrine, decorated with textile designs, hints at a goddess of weaving. In the last period, hunting murals in a shrine were painted over and replaced with images of horticulture and weaving and with nine statues of the goddess. A figurine of a woman and a man embracing is backed by a woman holding a child: the connection between sex and procreation may have been recognized.

The lack of a public hall or space and the similarity in the dwellings suggest there was no authority or leader.[30] The placement of the sleeping platforms and graves indicates that women "owned" the houses and the children. Since they also had somewhat longer lives than contemporary women elsewhere, they may have had high status. Their wall paintings show women and men dressed in leopard skins dancing around deer and bulls. People buried in the shrines have finer grave goods than others, and archaeologist James Mellaart hypothesized that the residents may have been priests-priestesses. Men have belt fasteners, perhaps for the leopard-skin garments. But most shrines hold female skeletons painted in red ochre, buried with precious obsidian mirrors. For a thousand peaceful years Catal Hüyük was a society, rich spiritually and materially. If the women had more prestige than the men, they did not have authority over them or each other.

A common art object here and in other Near East villages was the female figurine.[31] Most figurines found in these villages were objects used in religious supplications, probably made and used by women. Some are anthropomorphic but sexless; others represent animals the women raised. Most of them were of women and children and may have been used to appeal for pregnancy or good health. The most beautiful representations by far come from Catal Hüyük. Hacilar, the Turkish site of a later society, contained statuettes of women realistically portrayed at every age – young girls with pigtails, women with children, and women with aging bodies. Sexually explicit figurines may have been used as teaching aids.

Some scholars, confronted with the idea of egalitarian or woman-centred societies, deny they ever existed or scorn them as primitive, "uncivilized" clans practising savage rites of human sacrifice and bloodletting. Although human sacrifice does occur in early states, Catal Hüyük and similar towns prove that this view is false. Marija Gimbutas studied ruins in Old Europe (the Aegean and Adriatic coasts, Czechoslovakia, southern Poland, and western Ukraine) of villages settled about 7000 BCE in fertile river valleys. They lived in peace and stability for thousands of years, farming, raising animals, making pottery, and crafting bone and stone implements.[32] Set in beautiful, accessible, unfortified sites with good water and soil, none of these villages show signs of war, nor do the graves show stratification.

From 7000 to 3500 BCE these towns developed complex governing, social, and religious institutions, specialized crafts such as goldsmithing, and perhaps a rudimentary script. By 5500 BCE they knew copper metallurgy and depicted sailing boats on their ceramics. Their houses hold altars similar to those in Catal Hüyük, devoted to female images: there are statues and paintings of women alone, women with animals, or merged female-animal shapes emphasizing fertility (a woman's head on a chicken's body containing an egg); there are also images of rebirth, such as a woman with a snake or a butterfly, like creatures associated with regeneration – butterflies metamorphose from pupae, snakes shed old skins. Some of these images bear inscriptions with, perhaps, symbolic meaning and designs that may be writing: spindle whorls (used in the new art of spinning) and chevrons (inverted Vs, always placed near breasts, which may symbolize rain, the earth's "mother's milk").

Scholars attacked Gimbutas' second book for advancing the theory that people from southwestern Russia domesticated the horse, migrated across Europe 6000–4000 years ago, spread the root of Indo-European languages, and destroyed the old matricentries.[33] But geneticist Luigi Luca Cavalli-Sforza recently found DNA evidence strongly supporting her theory.[34]

Female figurines from 2000 to 600 BCE are the major ancient artifacts unearthed in Palestine, Assyria, Babylonia, in eastern Europe as far north as Denmark, and in Mesoamerica. Almost no male images in Mesoamerica date from 3000 to 300 BCE, although there are male skeletons. A society flourished in Thrace from around 6000 to 4000 BCE that built its walls of lath and plaster, made brightly coloured graceful pottery, and left many clay or bone female images and goblets decorated with the heads of women warriors.

Dwellings shaped like those at Catal Hüyük were built in

other parts of the world after 4500 BCE. On Malta and Gozo, in the Mediterranean, archeologists found female figurines and stone temples built so that cave, tomb, and temple make up a huge female body. The temples were sacred healing centres into historic time. Neolithic villages exist on the Orkney Islands; Skara Brae contains about sixty beehive houses with tunnel entrances resembling the vaginal passage to the uterus. The houses are all about the same size and contain altars (although a guide called them "dressers"!). Skara Brae is set on a very windy coast, and the tunnel entrances may have been intended to keep out wind. The beehive shape is striking, however, and the villages contain no public space.

Even more astonishing are huge "mounds" containing or connected to chambers and passages. Some were built as early as 4500 BCE in central Bulgaria and in Silbury Hill, Avebury, and West Kennet in England (which has 1500 such earthworks). From the air they look like large seated women. West Kennet Long Barrow, Medamud Temple in Egypt, and Bryn Celli Ddu mound in Wales are shaped like high round bellies (or uteruses) entered through wide stone "thighs." Michael Dames, who studied the British sites, believes that Silbury Hill is part of a huge complex centred in Avebury, built between 3250 and 2600 BCE for use in sacred rites.[35] Neolithic horticulturalists built similar mounds in North America. The earliest, from 1000 BCE, are in the southeast. The Serpent Mound of the Adena culture in Ohio is 425 metres long and shaped like a snake curled around a cosmic egg, the maternal ovum.

People who move constantly share resources and do not argue about territory. When people become sedentary, however, the population usually grows, bringing conflict about territory and resources. Settlers need social structures to mediate conflict. The community assembles to discuss the problem, a public sphere is born, custom gives way to law, and, eventually, simple society becomes complex.

Historians reserve the accolade "civilization" for societies with attributes like pottery, cities, or writing. The discovery of complex Neolithic societies without pottery (Jericho), cities (the Maya), or writing (the Inca) forced reconsideration of the term.[36] Some scholars believe the hallmark of civilization is war, which seems paradoxical. Tacitly, "civilized" seems to mean "patriarchal." I believe that all human societies are civilized and prefer to distinguish between simple and complex: simple societies are small, relatively egalitarian, communal (sharing resources), and live by custom; complex societies are stratified (groups vie for resources), live by enforceable laws, and create institutions.

The earliest complex society we know of was in India, a sophisticated society made up of a series of cities (seventy have been found so far) which flourished in India on the Indus River and the Arabian Sea around 3000 BCE. Its two major cities were Harappa and Mohenjo-daro.[37] The most elaborate and luxurious Neolithic society found so far is on Crete. A colony of goddess-worshipping immigrants, perhaps Anatolian, settled on Crete around 6000 BCE and farmed, developing over the next 4000 years considerable skills in architecture and trade, pottery making (it is believed they invented the potter's wheel), weaving, and metallurgy, engraving, and a brilliant style of art. Their cities had multistoried palaces, villas, residential districts, harbour installations, aqueducts, irrigation and drainage systems, roads, temples, and burial sites.

Around 2000 BCE, as gods were replacing goddesses elsewhere, Cretan society entered a phase called Mid-

Minoan (after a mythical king of Crete). Originally based on a matrilineal *genos* (clan), this society seems in this period to have become a state with a central government. The governments may have used tax revenues to benefit the whole population, for it built drainage systems, sanitary installations, viaducts, paved roads, lookout posts, and roadside shelters. Hieroglyphic writing evolved, then a script (Linear A), though neither has been deciphered.

Knossos, the main city, had about 100,000 residents. Connected to southern ports by paved highways (the first in Europe), its streets were paved, drained, and lined with neat two- or three storey houses with flat roofs – some with penthouses for hot summer nights. Houses had toilets and baths, with clay pipes to drain sewage and carry running water indoors. Designed for privacy, they had good natural light and were surrounded by gardens. Stratification seems to have coexisted with sharing – no home found so far looks poor or has poor living conditions. Walls were plastered or marble-faced, and murals on the walls, floors, and ceilings in every class of dwelling depict sea life, plants, ceremonies, and social life.

Scholar Sir Leonard Woolley called Cretan art the most inspired in the ancient world. Wall paintings, figurines, and jewellery show priestesses central in rituals, holding serpents or butterflies (described as double-axes). Young men and women together jump the bulls – a dangerous sport in which one person grasps the bull's horns, another somersaults on its back, and a third receives the jumper. Scholars think there were no gods, only goddesses, in Cretan culture or that goddesses far outnumbered gods. Depictions of ceremonies always put priestesses in the foreground, with male assistants behind them. Goddesses, priestesses, and court ladies wear the same sexy costume – jackets exposing the breasts, and long sheepskin skirts with a tight waist emphasized by a metal belt. Men's outfits were sexy too, accenting the penis. Both sexes wore jewellery – bracelets, armbands, collars, headbands – and had hair falling down the back, curling over the ears; both wear loincloths and codpieces in bull-leaping scenes.

Depictions of women show them working as merchants, farmers, chariot drivers, and hunters; on a signet ring, a woman (perhaps a long-distance timber trader) disembarks from a ship, carrying a tree. The Ring of Minos has a woman steering a ship. In many wall paintings women perform religious rituals. In a scene of people watching female dancers, the sexes are segregated, but the women have the better seats. Several women's tombs were filled with jewellery and gold, precious stones, and copper (one grave has 140 such pieces); no male grave has equal valuables.

The rich, stratified, female-centred Cretan world seems to have developed technologically without abandoning the old values of sharing, peace, pleasure, nature, and sex. Later, Crete had a division of labour: men were soldiers, farmers, and metalworkers; women worked indoors, made textiles, and controlled religion. Both may have been potters and artists. In Minoan Crete, unlike Greece, women lived longer than men.[38] This society was wrecked, probably by a volcano erupting on Santorini (Thera) in 1626 BCE. Later, Crete was overrun by Myceanean invaders from Greece and by Dorians. Similar invasions during the third and second millennia BCE in Europe and the Middle East, though not in sub-Saharan Africa, the South Pacific, or South and North America, overthrew matricentric societies and installed patriarchy.

CHAPTER 2

THE FATHERS

MATRICENTRY, SMALL SIMPLE SOCIETIES centred about mothers, was supplanted by a different moral, economic, and sociopolitical structure. Male-dominant patrilineality, later with stratification, gradually destroyed anarchic egalitarianism and women's high status. But old ways lingered, and they still pervade our consciousness. Everywhere, even in patrilinies in which fathers "own" children, women were expected to raise them and to feed the family (as they do in parts of Africa today). Moreover, women accept these responsibilities almost automatically. Because they do, men take little responsibility, especially in Africa and India, despite a contradictory tradition that granted men the rights to private property and responsibility for it.

In the shift from matricentry to patrilineality, women lost status and their rights to children and to land. "Status" means standing in a society: the body, work, and rights of a person with status are respected. People with status are valued and can walk among their kind without fear of violation; they are entitled to the same resources available to others and have the same obligations to kin and to the old, the sick, and the very young. People without status are "dependants," which really means without rights. It is assumed to mean that they are non-contributory, but most dependants work harder than those on whom they supposedly depend.

The shift from female centrality to male domination occurred before the development of writing, so its roots are hidden. Its consequences, and men's response over the millennia to all moves by women towards greater autonomy, suggest that it emerged from male hostility towards women and was imposed on them. The destruction of matricentry was the first and most important male war against women. We can only speculate about why men wanted the change, how they imposed it, and why women accepted it. My inferences on these questions are drawn from the shift from matrilineality to patrilineality that was occurring in Africa when Europeans invaded it in the fourteenth century, from customs in extant simple egalitarian and male-dominant societies, and from remnants in myth.

A Theory of the Origin of Modern Gender Roles

In matrilineal societies women had high status because they produced children, fed their communities, and possessed usufruct rights to land passed in the female line. The shift to patrilineality eradicated women's rights to land and to children, but it did not affect most women's willingness to care for their children. Because they continued to do this work even when they were deprived of their rights over the children, men assumed that women were biologically programmed to tend their offspring and needed no reward for doing so. Men believed that women were non-volitional beings, bound to their bodies and their instincts. But studies have shown that mothering is learned; it is not instinctive. We learn to mother by being mothered, and creatures who are not mothered cannot do it. Taking care creates love, for a baby, a piece of land, an animal. Men devalue this work, attributing it to mere instinct, ignoring the many women who abandon children or raise them cruelly. Taking responsibility is not instinctual in human beings as it is in other mammals. It is a choice.

This issue is the basic division between the sexes. The desire to own children is the root of male dominance, the first aggressive act in the drive towards patriarchy. Men usurped women's right to name their children for themselves, an act inconceivable for the hundreds of thousands of years when the male contribution to procreation was unknown. But long after men recognized their involvement, they did not try to "possess" children. Statuettes in Catal Hüyük made between 7000 and 5600 BCE show awareness of a link between heterosexual embrace and the birth of babies, but the recognition of paternity did not suffice to inspire a shift to male dominance until two further steps had occurred: the creation of male solidarity and the invention of patrilineality and patrilocal marriage, both appropriations of traditional customs.

The Creation of Male Solidarity

Men may have seen women as having natural solidarity, but,

historically, women had little common cause, even before the rise of the state. Women gather alone: members separate so each can cover a swath of terrain. In food preparation, women may work near each other but they remain separate. Women who smoke meat or hides work separately, sitting near others. And they bear children alone, although others may assist. Before they give birth, women's primary bond is, like men's, with their mothers. Afterwards, it is with their children. Females have historically united only when their children's or men's survival was endangered. Female solidarity was traditionally aroused by forces threatening community survival, not by men as a caste. The only thing women had in common was the ability to bear children and a willingness to take responsibility for them.

This alone, however, amounted to a natural role, something men did not possess, and it may have infantilized them. When large game hunting began, men may have felt they had found a function: they are the main hunters in all hunting societies. Male anthropologists have claimed that women, always pregnant or nursing, did not hunt because of danger and exertion. But women did go large game hunting, which is done in groups, and gathering is just as dangerous as hunting. Still, men usually killed the animal. There may be a symbolic element in hunting: some Native American groups saw females as responsible for life (children) and males as responsible for death (hunting and, later, war).

Perhaps hunting, on which male anthropologists place so much weight, gave men a sense of identity, responsibility, and power. During the hunt, a group activity requiring cooperation and teamwork, fellowship had to supersede competitiveness for safety's sake. Participants in a project invariably develop a sense of "us versus them" and pride themselves on shutting out – "exclusive," after all means "shutting out." Who is included matters less to a group's image than who is excluded. The included are seen (by themselves and by outsiders) as superior because of their exclusions. If men had felt marginal, cooperation during hunts may have provided an exclusive sense of maleness and solidarity. They would have tried to exclude women, even though the women also went on hunts. And, indeed, hunting cults are exclusively male in all societies, involving rituals and objects women are forbidden to see or touch. The exclusion of women is the cult's purpose.

By 5000 BCE, however, horticulture was common and game was vanishing in populated areas. Men were losing the activity that gave them a sense of purpose, and boys were not developing a sense of solidarity. More men were farming now, an isolated activity rarely requiring teamwork and involving nothing essentially male. Indeed, horticulture was usually performed by women. To counter their loss and to indoctrinate boys into male solidarity, men devised a new ritual: group puberty rites. These rites had a dual purpose: to inculcate a sense of solidarity and to heighten boys in importance. The difference between the sexes is nowhere clearer than at puberty. Female maturity is evident in the onset of menstruation; nothing signals male maturity. When a boy becomes capable of an erection, he may or may not yet be able to father a child. The ambiguity of male maturity, together with the lack of a given role that it seems to indicate, is precisely the problem male solidarity is intended to counter.

Puberty rites did not arise in gathering-hunting societies but in horticultural ones. Except for some Australian Aborigine groups, gathering-hunting people do not initiate boys in groups. Single rituals differ profoundly from group rituals: boys initiated singly are taught the essentials of survival; group initiations teach gender roles. Men began to educate boys in maleness after they had lost what felt like a naturally given role and they needed to create a male identity.

Male solidarity was and remains a mobilization against women. The first political movement, it arose, like all solidarity movements, to counter a sense of powerlessness and oppression. (The notion that men suffer from envy of female procreativity has long been a theme in psychology.)[1] The main thrust of group initiations is denying the mother and all the qualities associated with her: nutritiveness, compassion, softness, and love. Boys are taught to scorn "feminine" emotions, replacing them with hardness, self-denial, obedience, and deference to "superior" males, creating a bond not of love but of power directed at transcendent goals.

Initiations

Puberty rites are specifically designed to coerce boys to reject their primary and deepest bond, to their mothers. Male initiations emphasize that men must be born twice, once through the mother and a second time through men. Initiation rites vary, but the most brutal initiations occur in polygynous patrilineal societies (which are extremely male dominant) with a long postpartum sex taboo. In such societies, men and women usually live separately. Men may not have sex with their wives for a long time after the birth of a child; children are nursed for many years and live almost entirely with their mothers, developing deep ties to her. At puberty they are taken to be made into men.

To wean a boy from his beloved mother and teach him to dominate women, men brutalize him: they take boys away

from society for weeks or longer, subjecting them to pro-
longed humiliation and mutilation. Austro-melanesians
wound the penis to make it bleed in imitation of women's
menstruation; other groups wound other parts of the body for
the same import. Men feed boys to a symbolic crocodile from
which they emerge newborn, or house them in a symbolic
male womb tended by male "mothers." The Gimi claim the
penis is a gift adult men create and confer on initiates, called
"new vaginas." Some groups let blood from the penis periodically. The Fore of New Guinea say "women's menstruation
has always been present; men's bleeding – that came later."

Boys, told they are "women" to older men, learn first-
hand how men treat women. Taught to act not on feelings
but on an external standard of maleness that prizes control
of self and others, boys are terrorized into living up to the
code of the elders because men must control the "woman" in
themselves and their lives. The Gelede society in Yoruba culture mocks men who are easily seduced by women as pup-
pets in female control.[2] The reward for their pain, humiliation, fear, and obedience is admission to manhood, the fellowship of men, and the pleasures (such as they are) of domination. They learn solidarity with other males vis-à-vis
women. But only women unite men; their solidarity fades
easily in other conflicts. Men who conflict with each other
on other grounds must defer to "superiors" and stand
together against women. In such societies, adult men usually live in men's houses, in a hostile, competitive, and con-
tentious atmosphere, but whatever rivalry or dislike men
may feel for each other fades in the face of the other sex.

Girls too are initiated in these societies. Because female
maturity is obvious, girls are initiated individually and are
not taught female solidarity. Gatherer-hunters (especially in

North America) hold public initiations to celebrate woman-hood, which is regarded in high esteem, but in male-dominant societies girls are humiliated. Isolated, confined, allowed only small amounts of certain foods and drink, taught that her body is powerful but contaminated, a girl learns she has power – to pollute: in such cultures, menstrual blood is a source of horror and fear. Menstruation symbolizes female power, considered destructive to men. If female power can destroy men, women are men's enemies, and the condition of the sexes is a state of war.

The Papagoes believe that all women are born powerful, but only some men achieve power; Chipewyans believe that to be female is to be power, but men must acquire power. Womanhood is the realization of a biological capacity; manhood is devised, created, manufactured. A girl becomes what she was born to be; a boy must become something more. Even today some men see maleness as an acquired identity that makes them superior to women, who are what they are by nature. Men take an extra step. Whatever you think about these ideas, they continue to have great power. The "fragile" male ego, "natural" male aggressiveness, the insistence that men must see themselves as superior or they will disappear into their mirrors: all these notions express the sense that maleness requires extra effort to achieve, and that it must be learned and therefore taught, or indoctrinated, in schools, the military, or gymnasia. People still feel that boys need to be made into men. Initiations like bar mitzvahs or fraternity rituals remain popular. And initiation still constitutes a second birth of a male by males.

Perhaps one reason group puberty rites emerged in horti-cultural societies is that farming, a revolutionary event, frightened people. For millennia, humans had considered the earth sacred, collecting its fruits with no attempt at control. But horticulturalists dig open the earth's body to plant seed; they exercise control and domination, violating their ancient attitudes of awe and reverence for the earth. Ceremonies like those Michael Dames describes at Silbury and Avebury may have been efforts to mollify the goddess whose body they were raping.[3] People in simple societies beg pardon of animals they kill in the hunt, or for the "mana" of a tree before they cut it down to make a dugout canoe.

The job that offers the greatest violence to earth – clearing the land – is mainly done by men, who may have seen this task as naturally theirs because of their upper-body strength. In any case, they saw it as a masculine job. To clear a plot in earth traditionally seen as sacred and female felt violent. Ploughing it, ripping up earth, an act associated with violent male sexuality, may have made men frightened, proud, or both. Metaphors associating ploughing with rape abound in ancient literature. When, thousands of years later, machines were invented for ploughing, men would not let women work the plough: at most they could guide it. Rituals were designed to protect men from earth's retribution, and it has been suggested that after the invention of horticulture, humans began to attribute creation to a deity *above* nature, rather than within it, to a male god rather than a female goddess.[4]

In most horticultural societies men raise different crops from women, and theirs is the prestige crop. Entering an activity women had invented, men managed to dominate it. Although women in all horticultural societies do far more work than men, they always have less status than men, even if they control the distribution of their produce. This inequality is inexplicable on any but political grounds. Their dangerous work gave men status.

The Shift to Patrilineality

In matrilineal societies men are responsible for their sisters' children – their closest genetic kin if paternity is unknown. Matriliny reflects the mother-child bond: it arose when the first speaking human gave birth to her first baby. The baby was referred to as hers – Eve's. Patriliny was invented by men who wished to own children, not raise them; the form was invented out of love not of children but of power. But these children are referred to by their father's names: they are Adam's.

Many Native American, Aboriginal, and African societies are still matrilineal. Matrilineality differs profoundly from patrilineality – it is not just that the child is named differently. Matrilineality and patrilineality are not morally neutral forms: they create different societies, with different ambiences. Anthropologists write that people in matrilinies are more contented, easier with themselves and with the other sex than in patrilinies.

Most matrilineal societies are matrilocal – couples live with the bride's family after marriage because women inherit rights to land use. As "owners," they have a voice in group decisions but do not deny men a voice: men are politically dominant in most extant matrilinies. But women own their own bodies: their sexuality is their own affair. Men do not lock up their wives. And all children are raised affectionately as members of the group.

Patrilinies are founded on domination. To own children, men must guarantee their paternity, which requires them to guard women's bodies, claiming to own them. This claim turns women into men's possessions. Controlling another requires force, so patrilineality permits or encourages brutality towards women. Such behaviour makes for bad relations between the sexes. Brutality is rare in matrilinies, where women are surrounded by kin; men invented patrilocality to control women. In patrilocal marriage a woman lives with strangers, isolated from any who love her or will protect her, sometimes even from any who share her language. Often abused and exploited by husbands and their families in patrilocal groups, women do not possess their bodies, their labour, or their children, who belong to their husbands' lineage. Some patrilocal societies allow wives to leave, but they can never take their children with them. Therefore, most women remain.

Matrilocal marriage does not isolate men from kin and those who speak their language because matrilocal societies are usually endogamous. All known societies have rules about marriage. Most simple societies permit only one form of marriage – endogamy or exogamy. Endogamy is marriage inside the group; exogamy, outside it. They are mutually exclusive. In endogamic groups, people marry within their clan, subject to incest controls. Both partners live among kin after marriage. But exogamic groups exchange marriage partners with groups that may live far away, estranging the ones who must leave (always the women) from their families and childhood friends. Exogamy occurs only in patrilocal societies. Men in patrilocal societies remain at home after marrying women from outside; they retain solidarity with the men of their lineage, but their sisters must marry out. Exogamy, designed to bolster male solidarity, weakens women by making them aliens and turning them into objects of exchange among men. They come to be viewed not as persons but as commodities. Even in matrilocal marriage, women are paid for by bride-service.

In no society have women constricted men within the domestic compound or regularly battered or raped men. In no known culture, no matter how high women's status, have women as a caste locked up husbands, limited their bodily freedom, or denied them a voice in group decisions. Men in matrilinies do not suffer as women do in patrilinies. Matrilineality is rooted in the bond between mother and child; patrilineality is rooted in dubious assertions of ownership of women and children.

Patriliny, being, first, uncertain (at least before DNA testing) and, second, a usurpation of women's ancient rights, had to be imposed by force. Its violent origins became visible during the European invasion of Africa, when many African societies were still matrilineal. Men in matrilinies could add to their lineage only by abducting and enslaving women, which they regularly did. Enslaved women's obligations to their lineages and their rights were annulled: they were totally owned – labour, body, and childbearing capacity – in contrast to male slaves in Africa, who owed their owners only labour. Women farmed, so men gained a sexual slave and a food producer. Slave women's children bore their fathers' names. Women were forced to accept the new ways – kidnapped, taken from their people, and settled in a society that granted them no rights or voice. Entire clans were formed this way, as the founding myths of Athens and Rome attest; other myths also suggest that men usurped women's rights by violence. It is only just that men should share those rights, but men denied women all rights, even bodily safety.

Many myths intimate some violent conflict between the sexes. It underlies some of the tales in early books of the Bible, such as the Jacob cycle. Isaac and Rebekah have two sons, Jacob and Esau, fraternal twins. Isaac loves Esau, the hunter, who brings him meat; Rebekah loves Jacob, the herder. The elder son, Esau, is entitled to the patrimony – a blessing. But Rebekah, asserting mother-right, orders Jacob to deceive Isaac and take it in Esau's place. The blessing accurately promises domination to the settler, not the hunter; Rebekah's and Isaac's struggle reflects a cultural war between mother-right and father-right.

Esau treats his traditions carelessly, trading his birthright for a bowl of lentil stew and marrying outside the group, but he is outraged by Jacob's deceit. Rebekah sends Jacob to her brother, Laban, for safety, hoping Jacob will marry in her clan. Such an endogamic marriage indicates that this tale was probably told in a transitional period, for Rebekah does not live with her clan. In Syria, Jacob marries his cousins Leah and Rachel. He is deceived by his uncle Laban, who substitutes Leah for Rachel, the sister Jacob desires. The marriage is matrilocal – Jacob does bride-service, living with his wives' clan, and when he wants to return to his own kin he must get Laban's permission. The mothers, not Jacob, name their children, and Rachel takes her father's household gods when they leave, as if they belonged to her. Yet the men have multiple wives.

Jacob, the major transitional figure, represents the shift from hunting to herding. His name changes from Jacob to Israel, to make him the father of his people. Some biblical scholars think Israel was originally named for Sarai and that Jacob's name change was invented later to give it a male root. Hebrew writing contains only consonants, and "Israel" was indicated by *S R*.[5] The story of Jacob trying to wangle a greater share of Laban's cattle displays a shaky sense of the facts of reproduction – the cattle get pregnant when they drink, he thinks, and the colour of their offspring depends on the nature of what they are looking at as they imbibe.

Many myths describe wars between the sexes, and men always win or take women's powers. Central and Western Desert Australian Aborigines say women once owned or controlled the sacred songs, rites, and objects, which men took through trickery, theft, or persuasion. The Papuans of New Guinea teach boy initiates that women were omnipotent until men stole the powerful snake grease from them and took over all the power.[6] Myth cycles reflect the gradual diminishment of females. The Sumerian Siduri is transformed from the high god of the culture into a lowly barmaid. The Babylonian/Assyrian creation epic describes how Marduk defeats Tiamat, the divine mother. In Greek myth the original creator of everything, Ge or Gaea, creates a son by herself, marries him, and produces the gods. Her name is often omitted from surveys of Greek myths, which portray males as dominant from the first.

Norse myths retain only traces of the Vanir, fertility gods who ruled the earth before the Aesir, the gods of war, conquered and almost obliterated them. The Aztec, too, worshipped violent gods, retaining a vague memory of a paradise that existed at the outset of things, ruled by Xochiquetzel, the Earth Mother or Precious Flower, until her son, Huitzlopochtli, destroys her and her daughter, the Moon. (There are several versions of this story.) Eventually, Earth Mother is distorted into Mecitli (whose name became Mexico, place of Mecitli), a hideous bloodthirsty goddess who is killed by fire but who survives, hungry and moaning for human hearts to be cut out and sacrificed to her. Later, Huitzlopochtli demands the hearts.[7]

"Social charter" myths, designed to justify male rule,

claim that women committed some sin or wrongdoing, or have some innate weakness that vindicated men's seizing control.[8] Myths rarely offer facts, only metaphors for political or social forces, but myths about former female powers would not exist if men had always controlled women. If men always controlled women, their domination would need no explanation or justification, but would seem natural. Myths of once powerful females are amazingly universal.

The Origins of Patriarchy

For 99 percent of hominid and human existence, people lived in egalitarian matricentry. At different times in different places, men used political solidarity to wrest control from women and forced a shift from matrilineality to patrilineality, matrilocality to patrilocality, endogamy to exogamy. Men gained prestige, some degree of domination, and authority. Not all simple societies became patrilineal; matrilineality still exists. Sometimes only part of a society changed: Australian Aborigines have both matrilineal and patrilineal moieties. In some societies the sexes are equal, but men and their activities have more prestige. In stratified societies the elite might remain matrilineal while commoner groups shifted, or shift to patrilineality while commoner groups remained matrilineal.

Once the mechanisms of patrilineality, patrilocality, and exogamy were in place, it was difficult for women to escape. In time, men in some groups raised vying for status to an organizing principle, competing to show their importance within the group and generating "big man" societies. These societies fostered the rise of the state and its sociopolitical form – patriarchy.

The term "patriarchy" denotes institutionalized male dominance, guaranteed by a set of interlocking structures that perpetuate the power and authority of an elite class of men over all other humans and grant all men power and authority over women of their class. Power is might – physical, psychological, or economic. Animals may dominate other animals by virtue of birth or charisma. But authority – a moral or spiritual right (tacitly backed by force) to judge others and coerce behaviour – does not exist among animals. Authority is insidious because we tend to internalize it: we feel guilt at performing acts called wrong by authorities, even if we ourselves do not believe them wrong.

Patriarchies are societies with institutions – hierarchical bodies of government, religion, law, education, commerce, and culture – designed to transcend individual lives, to endure over ages, and to maintain and transmit power from man to man, a practice called "passing the mantle." All institutions have customs or laws that give men prerogatives or advantages and that exclude or limit the participation of women and certain men. Patriarchies in different states disempower different male groups, but they all disempower women.

Matriarchy, if it existed, would be identical to patriarchy, with females dominant. Women have wielded great power in the world and have had personal authority over men in their families or communities. But no society has institutionalized female-dominance, a sociopolitical structure giving women authority over men and the right to use force against them. So entrenched is patriarchal thinking, however, that people commonly use the term "matriarchy" to describe women living free of male authority.

PART TWO

THE RISE OF
THE STATE

AT SOME MOMENT IN THE DISTANT PAST, an ancestor, probably a male in Egypt or Sumer, stood up and said, "I am superior to my fellows." Perhaps he was, in terms of bodily strength, intellect, political skill; and taking his talents as divinely given, he felt – or wished – that they made him utterly superior and not subject to the same natural laws as other human beings. He believed his superiority gave him the right to rule others. Since that time, earth has been the nursery of war, as one "superior" fights another for the right to claim championship of the world.

The superiority the man felt to others was perceived as power. The superior man tried to build a community transcending human families, more enduring, and offering him more control: a state. The state is built to incorporate power, maintain it, and pass it on to the chosen next in line. It confers symbolic immortality on a man and his descendants.

CHAPTER 3

STATE FORMATION IN PERU, EGYPT, AND SUMER

A STATE IS A TERRITORY WITH BOUNDARIES, which may be in dispute. In principle, what lies inside the boundaries is a group of people united by kinship, religion, language, or all three. States are built on the notion of private property: a person or a corporation claims to own the territory and the people inside it as well, people supposedly linked by a common heritage of language, customs, or blood. But creating states requires destroying, gutting, or weakening kin-groups linked by blood, customs, and language – like the peoples we have been discussing. There are thousands of peoples in the world, but only hundreds of states. States absorb, dilute, and eradicate peoples.

States are corporations masquerading as peoples. They encompass diverse peoples with varied customs, bloodlines, and languages, and they are ruled by an elite that imposes unity by force and asserts a bond of nationality that supersedes traditional blood or family ties. A state makes laws, claiming the right to punish infractions; it regulates what languages may be taught or spoken within it in public; it may decree an official religion and punish those who do not accept it. It regulates exchange, mints money, prints stamps, and forbids the use of others within its borders. If most of its people speak a common language and acknowledge the same laws, in time the unity of a state becomes real. Few states, and no large ones, begin unified.

States are not static monoliths. Even in totalitarian states, no dominant group (elite) possesses absolute power over all others. Rather, varied elite and non-elite groups interact dynamically, jockeying for their own goals; classes, ethnic groups, occupations, guilds, and other groups uneasily shift alliances. Contest for domination is constant. What is at stake is the power to determine the nature of institutions and their policies. The winners set the discourse of a culture.

Elites must possess not just armed might but legitimacy. Even with today's complex weapons, to maintain power a regime must gain acceptance by people in general, however grudging. A regime that maintains itself by armed force without creating a legitimating myth is easy to shake (like the regime of Shah Pahlevi in Iran). Most, perhaps all, states contain pockets of disaffected people, with their own customs or language, who resist conforming – like Muslims in the former Soviet Union, Sikhs in India, Kurds in Turkey and Iraq, and Basques in Spain. States experience constant eruption, as one man, elite, class, or group overthrows another. Some states exercise hegemony, or powerful influence, on the regions and states around them.

The great socialist thinker Raymond Williams compared life in a state to driving an automobile. As we drive, we are aware mainly of our own intention, direction, and self-determination. We know where we are going and why, and we feel we are moving freely. But the roads have been laid and the traffic is regulated by others; we can proceed only on those roads and only in obedience to the regulations. A sense of individual freedom and purpose blinds us to the way our course is determined and prevents us from seeing how larger social purposes may, in fact, be impeding us.

State formation did not occur until about 5000 years ago. Because it began before writing was invented, it is shrouded in mystery. (Writing was first used mainly for economic records and provides little information about events, customs, beliefs, and attitudes.) But oral literature (which was recorded later) does contain value-laden narratives. Although someone alive during a period of state formation might not be aware that a major shift is occurring, the myths of many cultures describe gigantic battles between forces perceived as masculine and feminine. The masculine inevitably wins and is vindicated. Art and literature were created to justify and exalt the winners and were sometimes obliterated when a new regime came to power. Egyptian rulers, for instance, regularly defaced the art commissioned by their predecessors, even that testifying to the supremacy of their own elite. Extant ancient literature justifies a ruler and a ruling class, presents their self-image, and records events exalting them.

Like humans, states are mortal: they have a lifespan. We tend to think there has always been a France, say, but it has existed for only a little over a thousand years; Sumer existed far longer, and few people today have even heard of it. Athens is remembered, but who knows of Ugarit or Byblos?

Powerful states like Assyria and brilliant ones like fifth-century Athens may disappear or decline in a century – yet people living there at the time might not have been aware of this course. Citizens of Great Britain, which for a century dominated the largest empire in history, have only recently realized that its prominence has faded. Citizens of the United States are reluctant to acknowledge its current decline, and its leaders persist in the militarist expansionism that precipitated the downfall of other states.

Graham Connah defines the state as a stratified society in which a governing body exercises control over the production or procurement of basic resources, and necessarily exercises coercive control over the remainder of the population.[1] Rulers' first concern is always to maintain their own power, never the well-being of their citizens. Ancient rulers regulated the raising of food, ordering monocrop agriculture (one region raises all the beans, another all the rice, a third the squash) so no region could be independent. West Africa is unique in that its people firmly resisted such pressures, refusing to give up their old ways of farming, and it has had few famines. If a people raises only squash and the crop fails, they starve. If they raise several crops and one fails, they have something else to fall back on.

Historians define a state as a society with centralized and specialized government institutions. Some claim that states arose from conflicts among unequal social classes, culminating in the victory of one class, which becomes the elite. This group must be physically repressive because it must constantly protect its privileges. Others hypothesize that the state evolved from a voluntary alliance of social groups, which submitted together to a governing authority to gain the military and economic benefits of centralization. This theory sounds like idealization, but we can only speculate how and why and even when states first arose. So far as we know, the state first arose either in Egypt or in Mesopotamia. We have information about the rise of one state, however, the Inca Empire. It did not imitate others, because it was isolated. The process of its state formation may be exemplary.

The Andean People

Andean society is famous for the Inca, whose complex civilization in the Peruvian mountains is known for its gold ornaments, which have been widely exhibited. Before the Inca conquest, the region was inhabited by disparate traditional egalitarian kin-group communities called *ayllus.* Each adult was entitled to land, animals, and access to water; each had the necessities of life and did tasks divided loosely by sex and age. The work of each sex was essential to the group and complemented that of the other, so all felt needed by their families and their *ayllu.* Identity was based on sex, and descent was assigned by sex in a parallel system. Lineage was traced through mothers, but women saw themselves as descendants of women, and men as descendants of men. Their place in these lineages gave them rights to resources.

Andean women spun and wove, cooked, brewed *chicha* (corn beer), planted and harvested fields, and selected and stored the seed for the following year. They herded, carried water, and raised children. Their work was seen as a contribution to the *ayllu,* not as service to their husbands. Men's main activities were ploughing and soldiering; they cleared the fields, weeded, helped in the harvest, carried firewood, built houses and terraces, constructed irrigation works, herded, and spun and wove when necessary. All were buried with the tools of their work. On ritual occasions, men were honoured as "first" for their victories in war, but they made no claims to the land, labour, or products of conquered groups.

Andean peoples spoke different languages and worshipped different gods representing similar concepts – earth, corn, and the heavens – in a religion structured by complementary spheres: the powers of heaven were masculine; the powers of earth, feminine. Interaction between the two was necessary for life. Gods, like humans, were interdependent: earth, needing rain to fulfil her generative powers, was married to thunder and lightning, the main heaven-god. Each sex worshipped divinities of its own sex, but both sacrificed to the Earth Mother, the primary deity. Some groups called her Pachamama; with her sacred daughters, she incarnated procreative forces. Others worshipped Saramama, the Corn Mother, Pachamama's daughter; every field had a stone in its centre as an altar in her honour. All *ayllus* worshipped the goddess as if she were part of the community. Male gods like Illapa, Thunder and Lightning, and his sons, the mountain gods, represented political entities, expressing the *ayllus* in relation to each other. Andean peoples did not separate private and public spheres: the *ayllu* together made decisions about domestic and political affairs. But religion distinguished internal (earth or corn mothers) from external deities (male heavenly powers). Andean life had no public-private split, but Andean thinking did.

The Inca of Cusco were simply one of many Andean peoples until the fifteenth century CE, when they set out to dominate the region by war and strategic alliances. In time, their empire stretched from southern Colombia to northwest Argentina. Inca gods were like other Andean gods, and their society was structured by gender parallelism. Before the

Inca began their conquest, however, they invented high gods, the Sun (male) and the Moon (female), placed them above the earth-and-heaven gods of the Andean pantheon, and claimed direct descent from them. Their transcendent gods gave them the right to dominate others. The Inca also worshipped Pachamama and included her image with those of their high gods in public ceremonies. A deity who symbolized procreative power and well-being to all Andeans was theirs too, and she bound the well-being of the *ayllus* to their own gods. From a local goddess tied to familiar soil, Pachamama became an emblem of empire.

In time, the Inca stole the attributes of local gods for Inca gods. Placing the Moon above all other female deities, even Pachamama, they gave her power over fertility, spinning, weaving, and food production, formerly other gods' spheres, and insisted that all women were her subjects. The Sun was given power over other male deities and control of all men. Claiming that an Inca queen, Mama Huaco, introduced the sowing of corn to the Andes, the Inca honoured her by reaping her field first during harvest rituals.

Political changes accompanied the new ideology. All non-royals (non-Inca) were now peasants, a new class. The Inca owned everything, although land was still communally owned. Peasants worked royal lands and herds and were granted other lands. Most people retained their old way of life, working the same lands and tending the same herds, but they now had to share the fruits of their work with the Inca. What changed was their sense of their lives: instead of working land owned by their *ayllu*, autonomously, they worked the land of superiors to whom they owed a share. This conceptual difference altered their sense of identity and their attitudes towards work.

The Inca divided the country into four provinces ruled from a capital. They expanded land by terracing, allotting a third of it to the *ayllus* for their subsistence and the rest to the state and to state religion.[2] The Inca enforced compliance ruthlessly. Refractory communities were punished by being moved to foreign regions; rebellious communities had their women taken from them. If that did not subdue them, the Inca executed their leaders, appropriated their land, and sometimes dispersed the people. The Inca required periodic rotating labour service, or corvée, for civil projects, state-owned mines, and the army. They fed workers who were assigned to royal properties or projects, but the families of impressed workers had to fend for themselves with the help of their kin.

The Inca claimed to own all the resources, including people, over whom they exercised absolute power. They purchased loyalty to their regime by appointing people within the *ayllus* to positions of prestige and rewarding them for cooperation by training their children in Inca thought and ideology in sex-segregated schools in the capital. Certain men were trained as Inca administrators and attendants. This process (co-option – buying loyalty by bribery) split the loyalties of both co-opted leaders and the community. Co-option, a tool used by every conqueror, successfully undermines and divides the tightest communities.

Discarding gender parallelism, the Inca designated men as the representatives of households and, in the imperial census, called married men "soldiers" and married women "soldier's wives." The association of men with arms bearing became fixed: men were soldiers because they were of use to the Inca in that capacity. Soldiers of noble (two Inca parents) or intermediate birth (an Inca father and a commoner mother) who did well for their masters were rewarded with positions as magistrates, overseers, judges, governors, and headmen as well as with land, produce, and women.

Women, not valued as soldiers, were not entitled to such rewards, but they still had to give their bodies and their labour to their superiors. The Inca chose women from the *ayllus* to become wives of the Sun god. Physically attractive and very young to assure virginity, these girls (*acllas* or *mamaconas*, some of whom were the daughters of *ayllu* headmen) were removed from their communities by imperial male agents and taken to Cusco or the provincial capital, where their bodies were guarded and they were taught "women's work" – to prepare *chicha* and other special foods and to spin and weave. Their fine weaving became famous. They were reserved for one of three roles: to be celibate servants of the gods and to officiate in rituals; to be second wives or concubines to royal or official men; or, if they were physically and morally perfect, to be sacrificed in important state rituals.

The institution of the *aclla* was intrinsic to the Inca maintenance of power.[3] The Inca gave *acllas* as second wives to elite men and commoner governors or to headmen in the *ayllus* as rewards for loyalty or accomplishment. This gift generated a debt of gratitude and reverence for the state, which alone could transfer women. (No woman, even in the Inca elite, had the right to more than one husband.) The Inca celebrated mass marriages in conquered villages once a year. Parents still married their children as they wished, but now had to have the king's permission. This system provided ritual affirmation of Inca control over all women and made marriage a metaphor for conquest. It politicized sex: the male elite treated all non-Inca as women.[4]

For pre-Inca Andeans, virginity had no advantage. Like most horticultural societies, they accepted or encouraged premarital sex, which proved a girl's fertility before marriage. But the state took control of the sexuality of the prepubescent *acllas*, who were guarded and forbidden to all men but the Inca and their beneficiaries. Selection as an *aclla* conferred prestige, so fathers wanted their daughters to be chosen. Girls too may have seen it as a high honour: they would live in luxurious surroundings and be liaisons between their families and the exalted Inca. Recruitment of *acllas* broke the natural tie of affection among families, for an *aclla* taken from her village might never be seen again and might even be killed. We have a description of such a sacrifice.

For the state festival honouring the Sun, *acllas* representing the four divisions of the empire travelled to Cusco with provincial officials. In elaborate ceremonies, they did homage to the Inca rulers and were honoured by them. A seventeenth-century observer, Hernandez Principe, described the procession, the four girls (ten to twelve years old), "without a blemish, of consummate beauty, children of the nobility."[5] He saw the golden Inca throne, statues of the gods, the pouring of *chicha*, and the slaughter of a hundred thousand llamas for the feast. Then the girls were lowered into a waterless cistern and walled in alive.

Control of women was the bedrock of Inca power. When the Inca conquered a new territory, they built a temple and dedicated it to the Sun, the divine emblem of the victorious empire, and immediately selected *acllas* from the village girls. If a village rebelled against Inca rule, the punishment was the loss of its women. In other words, women had a symbolic meaning men did not possess. Removing women or girls from a community demonstrated its impotence and the meaning of capitulation more economically than killing the men – the usual response of victors in war.

Inca women held limited power. The queen *(Coya)* presided over religious rites dedicated to goddesses, ruled when the king was absent, and made final decisions when the privy council could not agree. Some among them were remembered as prudent advisers. During the month-long festival of the Moon every year, the queen was celebrated. She made gifts, gave feasts, received tribute, kept entourages, and lived sumptuously. All noblewomen possessed use-rights to considerable property, which gave them some independence, but they held station above only the commoner women.

Similar processes may have occurred during early state formation in Egypt and Sumer. Our information derives mainly from written materials, and, thus, from later years of statehood.

Egypt

The land called Egypt was settled early and developed horticulture long before any other part of the world, perhaps because of its unique environment. Before the latest Aswan Dam was built in the 1960s, ending the annual inundation of the Nile, most Egyptians lived crowded into the 34,000 square kilometres bordering the river. Every year, at the same time, the Nile flooded; as it receded, it left behind a layer of silt that renewed the topsoil, so two or three crops a year could be grown without effort. The region was extremely fertile and also secure: it was hard to reach because it was surrounded by deserts. The source of the Nile lies below the equator, so the river runs north. The northern part of the country is called Lower Egypt, and the southern part, Upper Egypt.

People lived in small, culturally diverse, autonomous horticultural groups. Archaeological remains from 4000 to 3100 BCE in Lower Egypt – houses, storerooms, graves – show little difference in wealth, suggesting an egalitarian society. In Upper Egypt, however, some people's graves held more and better objects than others. This distinction suggests differences in status, but the society did not amass surpluses, so status in early Upper Egyptian villages was probably of the "big man" variety. In big man societies a prominent household tries to produce more than others and gives gifts in hope of drawing followers and becoming important in the village. In extant big man societies (such as the Tlingit mentioned above), men have more prestige than women, but women are deeply involved not just in production but in acquisition and distribution, and they have considerable autonomy and power.

Villages cooperated in irrigation projects and, for a long time, depictions of men show them cooperating at work. Suddenly, near the end of the fourth millennium, images show one man towering over the others as they dig a canal or kill adversaries. Soon the word for "king" appears (pharaoh, from *PROA*, meaning "Great House," a term applied to Egyptian kings just as Americans use "White House" to refer to the president). No one knows why the social structure changed, but scholars theorize that big men began to compete with each other and armed themselves for the fight.

Gods were central to Egyptian village life. Each village had a shrine devoted to its own deity, which was praised when things went well and vilified when they did not. Two goddesses, Nekhbet and Edjo, were honoured throughout Egyptian prehistory. Neith, Hathor, Isis, and the sky-goddess Nut were worshipped, even after a state arose, as early mother-goddesses, uncreated sources of all being. Nut, Isis, and Hathor were revered as the maternal ancestors of the divine kings, and Isis continued to grow in importance over time.

Around 3100 BCE, Egypt was unified into a state by a pharaoh and a temple administration ruling from his capital in Memphis. The pharaoh claimed to be appointed by the gods. His rule was the cornerstone of the state: the king was the state. He controlled religion as the chief priest in all cults, and his Great Royal Wife was the priestess in the most important ones. It seems that the right to the throne and the divinity inherent in it were conveyed by the female line, that pharaohs became divine by marrying royal women. Military chieftains who became rulers and had commoner chief wives later married their own daughters to guarantee their divinity. In time, priests at major temples tried to increase their power by assimilating the gods of local communities and bringing local priests to the capital city. Then they demoted local deities and endowed a supreme god, Amon-Re, with their traits. But the people continued to worship goddesses and the priestesses who served them. Class stratification appeared at the beginning of the Old Kingdom, but women and men of the same class were buried equally, so the sexes were probably still equal. Unlike other male-dominant societies, ancient Egyptians believed that both women and men could achieve immortality.

At the beginning of the Old Kingdom (from 2770 to 2182 BCE), church and state were still one: the king was the chief priest, indeed a god, advised by lower-ranking priests and his married sisters. Protected by ocean and desert barriers, Egypt could maintain a policy of peace and non-aggression and it kept no standing army; community officials responsible for public works mustered men for a militia only at times of threat. Egyptians developed a system of writing. Zoser, the first king of the Old Kingdom, who ruled more absolutely than his predecessors, commissioned the first pyramid. These structures, astonishing even today, rise in the desert as tomb-memorials to one man's glory. But they also silently testify to the labour of poor men and women who were forced into corvée for the years required to finish the pyramids: they transported huge stones over great distances and raised them into position under the burning Egyptian sun.

During the Old Kingdom, stratification grew rigid. The elite was made up of the pharaoh and his kin, high government officials, and nobles and their attendants – priests, scribes, lawyers, and doctors. Beneath them were nomarchs (*arch* means "ruler"; local provinces were *nomes*), responsible for extracting grain and labour from the kin-groups. They co-opted families with gifts of land they could bequeath. Some nomarchs grew powerful and periodically rose in war against the central government.

Below them was a growing middle class (merchants, scribes, and artisans) and the majority, who were peasant farmers. Villages had considerable autonomy. Society was male dominant, but women were respected: they could testify in village tribunals that settled local disputes, were elected local representatives as liaisons to state agents, and were named executors of estates. Like royalty, commoners practised bilateral descent: women could inherit property, and a wife kept her own property in marriage, bequeathing it as she chose. A husband had to sign a marriage contract promising specific support for his wife and compensation if he divorced her. Mothers seem to have named children. In certain cases, daughters could take up a father's trade. Families were monogamous and nuclear – polygyny occurred mainly among royalty.

Most kings were male, but women were not barred from public life. Divinity, and succession, lay in the female line: the heir to the throne was the child of the Great Royal Wife and the highest state god, so kings married their sisters or daughters. Great Royal Wives acted as chief priestesses in important cults and managed the finances of cult centres, properties, and personnel. They possessed huge wealth in estates and palaces. A Great Royal Wife lived apart from her husband and his harem, served by a staff of advisers, tutors, stewards, and servants, including the most prominent men in the kingdom. To see his Royal Wife, a pharaoh had to travel to her palace.[6]

The earliest king lists record the names of kings and their mothers. Some kings were female: Nitokerty, pharaoh at the end of the Old Kingdom, was described in later chronicles as the most beautiful and the bravest woman of her age. Other records show that a woman (whose name was expunged from the king lists) ruled at the end of the Fifth Dynasty and built a pyramid. Five or six queens whose names and records were eradicated ruled in ancient dynasties. Powerful women without public power manoeuvred behind the scenes and were involved in several palace upheavals.

Women who worked outside the home were paid the same as men. In the third millennium BCE a noblewoman supervised female physicians. Women traded throughout the ancient period: in tomb murals they are depicted selling produce and goods in the marketplace, trapping birds, harvesting, and carrying baskets heavy with fruit. They winnowed wheat, ground it into flour, brewed beer, and picked and spun flax into thread they then wove into linen.

Old Kingdom rulers initiated grandiose government projects that required heavy taxes. This burden, coupled with a series of crop failures, led provincial nomarchs to rebel around 2200 BCE. Internecine warfare among nobles, desert tribes, and gangs of the dispossessed followed. The governor of Thebes prevailed and established "the Middle Kingdom," whose pharaohs devised a system to keep nomarchs from gaining enough wealth and power to rebel: instead of rewarding nomarchs with land that could be passed on, they made them provincial governors.

These governors lived in luxury, built elaborate tombs, and commissioned life-size statues of themselves and their wives. Imitating royalty, they began to trace their ancestry through the women of their lineage. Everyone was devoted to felicity and well-being: middle-class people and labourers were extremely concerned with bodily beauty, and both sexes used ointments, deodorants, and cosmetics. The lower classes grew rich enough to buy religious books and burials in coffins with copies of royal mortuary texts, which allowed them to participate in the afterlife.

Men seem to have appropriated the tasks and powers of major priestesses at the end of the Old Kingdom, but women still held such managerial positions as major-domo or treasurer on large private estates and could still own, sell, lease, and administer property (land, money, servants, slaves, or goods), make wills and marriage contracts in their own names, adopt heirs, free slaves, act as witnesses, and sue in court. Divorce required only payment of a penalty by the partner desiring it. Women lent money at interest to their husbands and cut children out of their wills: a woman of this period sued her own father. Letters and formal documents refer to women not as a man's wife or daughter, but by the title *Nb.t Pr*, "mistress of the house," or ` *nh n niwt*, "female citizen," or by a professional or a religious title. A woman, Sobekneferu, reigned as pharaoh in the Thirteenth Dynasty.

When the Middle Kingdom fell, a period of upheaval and invasion followed. For a time Egypt was ruled by foreigners, Hyksos from Western Asia, who introduced horses and war chariots to the territory. Unifying against the Hyksos military dominance, the Egyptians threw them out in 1560 BCE. The founder of the Eighteenth Dynasty, King Ahmose, honoured his mother in an inscription: "Queen Ahhotep rallied Egyptian soldiers against the Hyksos after they killed her older son in battle and helped to forge a united Egypt able to repel the invaders." Her daughter-in-law, also a strong queen, was honoured for centuries afterwards.

The Eighteenth Dynasty marked the beginning of the New Kingdom, a period of outstanding queens. Hatshepsut had a stronger claim to the throne than her husband through her lineage, and when he died she became regent for their young son. With the support of her ministers and the powerful men of the kingdom, she assumed kingship and adopted male clothes, a beard, and a wig. Hatshepsut led Egyptian armies south to secure Egypt's border and strengthened defences against Asian invasion. She improved the economy by making trade expeditions to foreign lands and brought back new plants for cultivation. She repaired old temples and erected buildings, including a splendid mortuary temple, Deir el Bahri, the only major ancient monument to a woman still extant. She wanted her only child to succeed her, but the girl died. Hatshepsut made her stepson

Thutmose III commander of the army and, in the latter part of her twenty-year reign, had him drawn with her on monument walls. But when he acceded, he returned the favour by eradicating her image from the reliefs on her temples.

About a century later, Tiy, a brilliant commoner who had married Amenhotep III, the most powerful and richest monarch in the world at the time, negotiated with foreign rulers and influenced politics for generations after her death. Her son, Akhenaten, created his own religion and worshipped a solar disk, Aton. Married to the beautiful Nefertiti, he went further than any other pharaoh in making public the loving relationship in his family.[7] He seems to have reigned with his wife, whose image appears in locations that would normally show only the king. When he died, Nefertiti may have ruled as Pharaoh Smenkhkare.

But the time when women could rule was ending. Nefertiti's daughter, widowed by the famous Pharaoh Tutankhamun, tried to succeed him and, to strengthen herself, she allied with the king of the Hittites, Egypt's chief rival. Her plan was discovered and stopped, and her behaviour fuelled a literary campaign of satire against women in high office.

In challenging Hyksos rule, the Egyptian male elite had become militaristic lovers of war chariots, costly machines paid for, like everything else, by the labour of peasants. The military establishment built to repel the Hyksos remained in place after their defeat and it changed Egypt into an aggressive imperialistic state. It raided Syria, Palestine, and beyond, until it controlled the territory from the Euphrates in Asia to Libya in Africa. For a time, domination paid for itself: captured gold mines, treasure, and food supported the army in the field. But Egypt had increasing trouble maintaining control over its spreading territories. Constant uprisings required more forts or command posts, more soldiers and weapons to put them down. Soldiers and weapons had to be paid for, and everything was supported by the labour of peasants, who had increasing difficulty paying such taxes.

By this time, the only free workers in Egypt were professional civil servants and the artists who decorated tombs. The state had enslaved huge numbers of prisoners of war. Male slaves could become free by enlisting in the army or the personal service of the pharaoh. Female slaves and refugees had no option but to work in the fields, in textile mills, and as domestic servants in palaces and temples, baking bread and singing and dancing in the homes of the nobility. Conscripted workers built temples, cities, and tombs and made weapons. Slaves worked in the quarries, cutting stone for the tombs of the pharaohs and their wives. Coerced to work by physical abuse, they ran away when they could.

Aware of the shakiness of Egyptian control, conquered territories stopped paying tribute. Egypt needed a strong leader and, eventually, Ramses I, a soldier, emerged to start his own dynasty. The soldier-kings of militaristic Egypt ruled through bureaucracies staffed by male commoners or slaves, not kin: government was "professionalized." As we will see, professionalization always means excluding women. All public offices in Egypt – civil service, governing bureaucracy, army, and priesthood – were professionalized. Priestesses now merely danced and sang in temple choirs, retaining only honorific titles. Kin connections became less important. In societies where a man names his family as administrators (hoping for loyalty), female kin have a chance to function politically. Without that entrée, women are shut out of the public realm.

In this period women were excluded from power, except for a queen, Tausert, who became regent for her son, then pharaoh in her own name, at the end of the Nineteenth Dynasty. Statues of queens, once equal in size and significance to those of the pharaohs, shrank. By the time of Ramses II, queens' statues stand no higher than the pharaoh's knee; the statue of the wife of Ramses I, in the temple to Amun at Karnak, stands in front of him, her head the size and at the level of his penis. The tiny statue of Ramses II's daughter at the temple now at Abu Simbel stands between his legs. Statues of his sons are also tiny beside their father. But his daughter Meryt-Amon, who became Ramses' second Chief Wife after her mother's death, erected a statue 10 metres high to herself. She seems to have inherited her father's ego.

Evidence was found recently that two women sat on a tribunal in the year 289 of the reign of Ramses III. This is the only evidence of women in this important capacity, but they probably sat on tribunals quite commonly.[8] Women were involved in two remarkable events during this reign. In the course of the first labour strike recorded in history, women may have incited a protest at a necropolis now called Deir el-Medina. The artisans working there were civil servants, paid by a food ration from the royal storehouses. The allowance had been erratic for seven months, but one month it was not sent at all and they went eighteen days without food. Artisans, wives, and children sat down and refused to work. The pharaoh's vizier immediately produced food and the government tried to mollify them. The second event was a rebellion plotted by Queen Tiy, a secondary wife of Ramses III, who wanted to kill him and crown her son. She won over the harem women, major palace officials, and a captain in the Nubian archers, but the conspiracy was discovered.

New Kingdom literature suggests that women were relatively free sexually. Laws punished adultery by both sexes by death, but records show that it more often led to divorce. Virginity was unimportant and, judging from the love poetry of the time, happily relinquished in romantic trysts. Some of this poetry took a female perspective and may have been composed by women. Extant contracts contain several marital arrangements, all of which granted women economic and political independence. One form, the *s` nh*, obligated the husband to maintain his wife in every way, with a cash allowance to be paid monthly or yearly. A man who signed such a contract had to pledge all his property as security. He could not dispose of any of it without his wife's consent or after divorce, even if the wife initiated it, unless she agreed to nullify the contract. These contracts date to Ptolemaic times, but similar agreements existed a thousand years earlier. Egyptian women could inherit property from their families or earn income to use as they pleased. Elsewhere in this period, women did not have such rights.

In 323 BCE Egypt was conquered by Alexander (called the Great), the Greek son of Philip II of Macedon. Following his father's path of aggression, Alexander dominated "the world." He spent his short life fighting and conquered vast territories. When he died at the age of thirty-two, his generals squabbled to determine who would control what. Ptolemy, a Greek general from Macedonia, won Egypt, Palestine, Cyrenaica (now part of Libya), and Cyprus. The Ptolemies ruled Egypt from 305 BCE to 30 BCE, a period called Hellenistic (Greek) throughout the Mediterranean.

The Greeks we know most about are the Athenians, who kept women invisible and mute. Macedonians seem to have had similar customs, but, during the reign of Philip II, they developed a different view of women, mainly because of Philip's lively wives. His biographer wrote that every time Philip made war, he made a marriage: several of his wives were non-Greeks from states whose women were active and who rode and used weapons (women seem to have had power in societies we know nothing about). Philip's first wife, Audata, an Illyrian, educated her daughter Cynane and her granddaughter Adea (Eurydice). Cynane fought with her father in her mother's native land and killed an Illyrian queen in combat. During the struggle for power following Alexander's death, she hired a mercenary army with her own money, entered the contest, and was killed. Adea, defeated in battle by a warrior queen, Olympias, who imprisoned her, killed herself. She was nineteen. One of Philip's wives was buried not with the usual accoutrements of royal women – earrings, bracelets, mirrors – but with arrowheads, bronze greaves (armour for the lower half of the leg) etched with depictions of horsemen, and a silver quiver. Other royal women of the period were buried similarly.

The Ptolemies did not impose Greek law on Egypt because Greek cities were self-governing: the Ptolemies did not want their power limited. They ruled directly, controlling and taxing everything – transportation, trade, manufacturing, banking, even abandoned babies, which they collected and sold. They determined what crops could be planted, where produce would be sold, and for how much. They became hugely rich.

Aristocratic rule is family rule, in which women often have a voice in policy and public power. Many women held power in Hellenistic Egypt. The first Ptolemy married his sixteen-year-old daughter, Arsinoe, to rich sixty-year-old Lysimachus, king of Thrace, who gave Arsinoe several cities as wedding gifts. Outliving him, she returned to Egypt, married her brother, and became Pharaoh. Berenice II, "the female pharaoh," ruled jointly with her husband until she was assassinated by her son, Ptolemy IV.

The Cleopatras were very rich. Cleopatra II owned the ships that transported grain owned by the royal house. Cleopatra III overthrew her mother, married her uncle, and ruled with both her sons successively. The brilliant Cleopatra VII, the first Ptolemaic ruler to learn Egyptian, first ruled alone, next with her brothers, each of whom she married and eliminated, and then ruled alone once again. Rome, which aimed to dominate the world, threatened Egypt for many years. Cleopatra made pacts with successive Roman rulers – Pompey, Caesar, and Antony – in a struggle to save Egypt for her children. The Cleopatra immortalized by Shakespeare was created by a hostile source, the Roman historian Plutarch, who made her a sexual serpent and seducer. A less biased British historian wrote, "Rome, who never condescended to fear any nation or people, did in her time fear two human beings: one was Hannibal, and the other was a woman."[9] A brilliant diplomat, soldier queen, and magnificent rider and hunter, Cleopatra led troops and commanded her own navy in battle. She left the battle at Actium strategically, not from cowardice. Defeated finally by the puritanical Octavius, she chose to commit a dignified suicide to avoid the fate of other leaders vanquished by Rome, who were paraded through its streets in chains.

By retaining Egyptian law, the Ptolemies' unintentionally benefited Egyptian women. Greek women living in Egypt were ruled by Greek law. Greeks regularly killed female infants, as demonstrated by a law requiring days of purification for abortion, childbirth, or child exposure. Among

Greeks in Hellenistic Egypt, sons outnumbered daughters four to one and were suckled longer than daughters.[10] Greek women living in Egypt under Greek law were not citizens: they could not travel beyond a day's round-trip without their husbands' permission or sign contracts for their own marriage; rather, fathers or father and groom signed them. A male guardian, *kyrios*, acted for them on all other legal actions. Still, in this era, the penalty for adultery (a crime only for women) was the prohibition of ornaments and jewellry.

Egyptian women were in a better situation, as were Jewish women living in Egypt, who were allowed to live by Jewish law. Egyptians and Jews forbade female infanticide. Egyptian women married by contract and had the right to leave their husbands without permission, to retain their dowries, and to make other property claims. Clauses in marriage contracts forbade husbands from taking second wives, keeping mistresses, living in another house, or begetting children outside marriage. Egyptian women owned property, rented it, and cultivated vineyards, gardens, and orchards (although they were forbidden to raise certain crops, such as wheat). Egyptian women did the same agricultural labour as men, even to clearing tree stumps, and paid the same taxes.

Status is treacherous for women: in patriarchies, it is always a tradeoff for freedom. Egyptian women who emulated the ruling class adopted Greek customs and took guardians, surrendering their independence. Why women trade freedom for status is a running question in this history. Men who rise in status win greater autonomy or power, but women who rise in status must cede control of their reproductive and personal life or their work.

Poor Egyptian women sold linen or other goods, wove, manufactured clothing, prepared food, and wet-nursed. In the Hellenistic period, Egyptian employers happily discarded the Egyptian tradition of equal pay for women and men, adopting Greek inequality. They paid women lower wages than men and gave women slaves fewer rations than men. The influence of Greek attitudes led to a gradual degradation of women in Egypt: many were enslaved and children took their mother's status. Children were prostituted; men captured young girls and sold them into prostitution.

The formation of a state in Egypt had only minor unhappy consequences for women; they were denied rights only gradually. But men defaced pyramids and monuments honouring female rulers, officially eradicated Nefertiti from history, and blamed all women when Nefertiti's daughter made a treacherous pact. Over thousands of years, men succeeded in excluding women from public life – until the Hellenistic period, when women again took part in the public realm because Egypt was governed by an aristocracy. And Egyptian women retained rights for millennia. They were not fully subdued until Islam overtook Egypt in 642.[11]

Mesopotamia

Sumer

Mesopotamia lay in the alluvial plain between the Tigris and the Euphrates rivers that, today, flow through Iraq. Wanderers called Sumerians, whose language, unrelated to any other, resembles Ural-Altaic, settled in the horticultural villages of the inhabitants of this area, people who knew weaving, pottery, and metallurgy. By 4000 BCE they had organized into large land-holding patrilineages ranked by age. They cooperated to build temples dedicated to a form of the goddess Nammu (or Inanna), the main deity. Men and women fished, caught birds, and farmed. Some historians think women controlled food processing as well as the distribution of crops stored in temples under Nammu's care. Water, the most precious resource in this arid region, was protected by goddesses like Bilulu, a rain and thunder deity.

Life was precarious: like the Nile, the Euphrates floods and drains, leaving land fertile, but it also floods unpredictably and sometimes disastrously. The myth of the great flood originated here. Kin-groups cooperated in irrigation projects, but periodically had to move. Around 3300 BCE, in a massive disaster, the Euphrates altered its course and one branch dried up. People left for towns such as Ur, Uruk, Lagash, and Kish, which grew rapidly; land conflicts erupted, escalating into wars. Clans seized other clans' land, killing their men and enslaving their women and children. Some clans were strong enough to keep their land, but had to pay tribute to a conqueror.

War requires leaders because it violates human nature: people have to be made to fight. At first appointed for the duration of a crisis (perhaps by the heads of patrilineages), leaders became permanent as war intensified. In time these leaders claimed superiority and used their clans to dominate a city and its surroundings. Each Sumerian town was a city-state. The Sumerian king list (compiled long after the rulers lived) avers that, after the flood, kingship came down from the heavens and fell to the lot of the city of Kish. The idea of kingship may have begun in Kish, but other cities soon had kings willing to fight for domination.

At the centre of a city was a temple complex, a prominent staged tower called a *ziggurat,* containing palaces, shrines, workshops, storerooms, kitchens, and gardens. State and church were probably one at first, as in Egypt: the temple/storehouse was the property of a city ruler and his wife. What had been a communal resource became an economic institution controlled by one man.[12] The temple complex, a massive household, stored, distributed, and manufactured almost everything necessary to sustain the royal family, which maintained its power by controlling the distribution of goods. Temples were still central to society, but no longer a communal resource guarded by the goddess. If women had controlled food distribution, they lost power in this shift. The goddess Nammu also lost primacy as Sumerian temples promoted gods over goddesses, although some people still worshipped the goddesses. Society hardened into ranked classes.

At first the elite left the kin-group structures intact and made their heads responsible for collecting taxes (paid in produce, animals, or goods) and providing people for corvée (just as the later Inca co-opted liaisons from the *ayllus*). The most despised and poorest groups – peasants, slaves, and bound workers – did the work that supported the whole society. Free workers may have had houses and garden plots inadequate to maintain them, so they needed to supplement them by working for the state. Free workers earned wages; bound workers and slaves were kept.

Corvée labour built and serviced the palaces and temples and cultivated temple lands. The extensive textile mills were run almost completely by female slaves, who also did a large proportion of the work in fields, gardens, orchards, herding, and canal maintenance. Women slaves worked in flour mills and in leather processing and were also domestic servants in palace and temple, musicians and dancers for the court, and concubines. The first mention of prostitution comes from Sumer, where priests prostituted female captives and slaves to draw men and money to the temples. From the first, prostitution was designed to profit men.

Elite women had considerable social power. The city ruler's wife supervised her household and helped administer the city and the temple. High-ranking women ran businesses and bought and sold property – houses and commodities like wool, flour, and metals. They were also high-ranking temple officials: the sisters and daughters of Sumerian rulers acted as high priestesses long after most goddesses were deposed. Priestesses, responsible for managing sacrifice, could be very powerful: the animals brought to the temple in their thousands had to be maintained and records kept. A monumental vase from Uruk of 2900–2500 BCE shows a line of men bearing tribute to an exalted female figure, probably Inanna: nothing comparable honouring a male figure exists in Sumerian art.

Worship of Inanna may have involved human sacrifice. Graves from 2700 to 2500 BCE contain inscriptions to queens (after one of whom, Pu-abi, or Shub-ad, an age was named) as well as human skeletons. One scholar believes that these were priestesses' tombs. Sixteen of the 755 uncovered graves contain human sacrifices, mostly women. Pu-abi was buried with sixty-four women and ten men, both sexes dressed elaborately: the women in headdress and jewellery; the men in the full regalia of guards, grooms, or charioteers. They were probably buried alive or voluntarily took poison.

Like the Inca and the Egyptians, the Sumerians used religion to assimilate the kin-groups. When Inanna was the primary goddess, kings made decrees in her name, capitalizing on people's devotion to her. But they gradually altered religious ideology. In early Sumerian myths, goddesses created everything, and Siduri, one of the most prominent, reigned in paradise. Later, a sun god usurped her realms, goddesses were demoted, and, by the later epic of the legendary king Gilgamesh, Siduri was a barmaid.

In the first myths about her, Inanna encompassed everything, controlling birth, death, and rebirth as mother, protector, and goddess of the vegetation and the weather, of the morning and the evening star. A later myth-poem named Bilulu, a male, as her consort and equal. In the even later "Enki and the World Order," the male Enki is the primary god. This ideological shift is not just a change of name and sex: Enki's nature differs from that of the goddess. With power over human states, goddesses were primarily beneficent and accessible; worshippers approached them directly. But Enki is a bureaucrat, presiding over a hierarchy of lesser gods. He assigns offices to them and to only two minor goddesses, not Inanna. She protests that he is discriminating against women, so he names two goddesses over birth and heaven and gives Inanna a new role, though it is unknown because the tablet is damaged and illlegible. Inanna later becomes goddess of love and war, then a healer, then a compassionate interceder with dominant male gods. After the Amorite conquest of Mesopotamia, Inanna became the goddess of prostitutes.

The shifts in these myths imply actual social changes. From a position of centrality and respect, women are demoted; Enki's ascension to chief god suggests that democracy had been superseded by a hierarchy, with the power held by men. Men demote women further, limiting them to the domestic (birth) and moral (heaven) realms. The notion of love appears along with the notion of war (perhaps neither existed earlier), and women are identified with both.

This linkage suggests that women, still men's objects of desire, were at war over their exclusion from the public realm. The naming of Innana goddess of war is the first occurrence of an identification that becomes common – women as the source of contention and disruption. As war became more widespread, women were associated with healing and with compassionate intercession. By this time, the male was fully dominant. As the world grew more masculine, females held power only through sex, and Inanna became the patron goddess of those who sell it.

A Theory of the Origin of the Stratification of the Sexes

Before state formation, women played the dominant role in what anthropologists call the "reproduction of life" – the continuation of the group through children and the continuation of the community through its daily survival. Men wrested control over this process by uniting to impose patrilineal succession, patrilocal marriage, and exogamy, leaving only remnants of the old matrilineality and matrilocality. But women were still respected and had some control over their own lives. When widescale war broke out, women rarely fought. Male thinkers today claim that women did not fight because they were physically weak or were always tending children, but women were soldiers in Germanic, Anglo-Saxon, and other cultures. Queens led troops into battle and commanded navies. Women are as fierce as men and can wield weapons and kill. Yet women did not customarily become soldiers.

Human thought is primarily symbolic: people often cannot see something happening in front of them if it refutes their symbolic vision of a situation. So, for instance, a nation accepts its rulers' reason for initiating wars even if the false-hood of the claim is apparent, because people want or need to believe in their rulers' goodness. The division between giving and taking life is profoundly symbolic. Many cultures polarize motherhood and killing, feeling that those who give life may not take it. The Hopi believe that women give and maintain life and that men germinate and guard life, but that men must be the killers. Some societies in which women regularly hunt exclude mothers from big game hunting; the crack corps of woman soldiers in Dahomey were required to be virgins. Mythic female hunters or soldiers, like Artemis or the Valkyries, are invariably virgins. This exclusion is not universal or necessary; it is symbolic.[13]

Perhaps, then, men were the soldiers. In the early stages of state formation, soldiers – often bound workers a step above slaves – had low status. But war is unpleasant; most men disliked fighting and had to be coerced. Still, coercion alone was insufficient: leaders might shame, punish, or execute reluctant men, but the soldiers regularly ran away. Leaders therefore began to reward men who fought well. The first rewards were probably status, community admiration, and wealth. Leaders of Germanic tribes were expected to share loot with their men; in the Hellenistic world, Greek soldiers were rewarded well for staying in an army that kept them away from home for a lifetime. Some rulers gave exemplary soldiers grants of land. As senior soldiers acquired status and wealth, the old kin-groups lost it, and women along with them. Since soldiers were men, the new rank was associated with males. A class arose in which women had no place at all: men did not need wives because of the invention of prostitution.

Elite women still enjoyed privileges and powers. But

constant war requires standing armies and military leaders, and soldiers made up the elite. They overthrew old decayed nobilities, becoming soldier kings. Like soldiers everywhere, they felt they had earned their status, not inherited it by descent from a goddess through their mothers. When men's mothers' ancestry became irrelevant, women's importance shrank even further: they could provide legitimacy – military chiefs married the daughters of the old aristocracy to bolster their claim to rule – but no longer conveyed the power to rule.

An early legal code from Lagash, the "reforms of Urukagina" (or Uruinimagina), provides the first written evidence of the degradation of women. The tablet records the election of King Urukagina and his wish to transfer his land to the goddess Ba'u, and it offers the first written gender-specific laws – laws governing only women. It names a new crime only women could commit – adultery – the first written mention of the concept. It states that, in the past, women had two men, but have now been made to give up this "crime." Scholars question whether this means that widows could no longer remarry, kings no longer had the right to brides' virginity, or married women could no longer take lovers. They insist it does not mean that women formerly had two husbands simultaneously, although that seems most likely. It also states that if a woman speaks in a certain way to a man (the word is illegible on the tablet), her mouth shall be crushed with a fired brick. Clearly, a male-dominant society made the new laws.

The Sargonic Period

Around 2350 BCE Sargon, a Semite from Akkad, unified

Sumer with Akkad to create the first real empire on Mesopotamian soil. He waged war over wider areas, for greater gains, with more soldiers than had ever been known. A Babylonian epic compared the undulating battlelines of his wars to two women giving birth, gushing blood in agony. He made his sons rulers over formerly independent city-states, and his daughters high priestesses of major temples. Probably the "illicit" son of a "celibate" priestess, Sargon, who rose to power with women's help, respected women and considered himself a protegée of the goddess Ishtar. His daughters must have been highly educated, for, as high priestesses, they generated a flowering of literary, artistic, and political activity unprecedented in the region. His daughter Enheduanna, high priestess of the moon god at Ur and perhaps of An, the supreme god of heaven at Uruk, has been called "the first systematic theologian." She spoke Sumerian and was a brilliant poet, whose works include two cycles of hymns to Inanna/Ishtar. Her work implicitly celebrated Sargon's uniting of Sumer and Akkad by considering it as done under the aegis of the goddess.

Sargon's demand for silver rather than goods in tribute payments strained the peasants. Men, held responsible for a lineage's taxes, sometimes fell into debt. Permitted to sell their families into debt bondage or to donate themselves to their creditors or temples, they sold daughters rather than the sons, who bore their lineage name. Temple officials acquired this female labour force as private citizens, in the first known example of private property. Private ownership slowly superseded collective or institutional ownership; state structures grew stronger and temples became more inaccessible. Gods and goddesses were no longer visible from the temple doors. Eventually, temples were walled off from the city and entry was forbidden to all who were not state connected.

War was constant and, whoever won, the common people lost. Defeated men were usually killed, castrated, or blinded, and the women were enslaved: the first slaves were women. Thus, prostitution, private property, and slavery all originated with men treating women as commodities. A large part of the population, male and female, was unfree. Called *geme* in Sumerian ration lists, they received only their keep for working the land – winnowing, removing grain, cutting thorns, and removing clods from furrows. Women slaves drove oxen and farmed, dug canals, and built reservoirs on irrigation projects, worked on construction projects, towed boats, laboured as porters, and pressed oil. Free woman workers were singers, scribes, barbers, midwives, doctors, wet nurses, governesses, and hairdressers. Thousands laboured in workshops attached to temples or estates, spinning and weaving, or as servants or shepherds.

One sign of women's lower status were the lesser rations they received compared with men. In ration lists from Gasur and Susa in the Sargonic period, bondsmen averaged 60 *sila* (quarts) of barley a month, bondswomen 30. Boys received 20 to 30 *sila*, girls 20, and infants 10. Some men got 30 or 40, but one received 120 *sila*. On one record, men got 30, 40, 50, 60, 75, and 125 *sila*; women received 30. Bound people also got a yearly ration of oil and wool and, on special occasions such as festivals, meat or milk, cheese, butter, onions, legumes, cucumbers, vegetables, dates, figs, apples, condiments, and beer or wine.

Much of what we know about women's status in Sumer comes from laws codified between approximately 2100 and 2000 BCE. In the city of Isin, an unmarried daughter could inherit equally with her brothers and stay in her father's house as long as she was single; women could leave their dowries to their children and could not be divorced for childlessness. The city of Eshnunna punished men who divorced wives by whom they had children, but executed women for adultery and men for homosexuality or for raping betrothed or married (male-owned) women. Eshnunna allowed marriage by purchase (making a wife a virtual slave) or by contract, though elite women could retain rights. Women could be witnesses and plaintiffs, and they could also be charged with crimes. This "right" may not seem a benefit, but societies that do not charge women with crimes do not grant them legal existence.

What mattered in rape cases was men's rights of ownership. Rape of unmarried, unbetrothed girls was not a serious matter. Rape of another man's virgin slave drew a fine of 5 shekels of silver, but rape of a betrothed virgin still living with her family was punished by death – betrothal equalled marriage, and a husband's rights had been usurped. If a couple eloped without parental consent or formal contract, the woman was not considered a wife. In one case, a man eloped with a woman, then made a marriage contract with her parents, and then claimed she was not a virgin. She was killed. If a woman committed adultery and left her husband for another man, he could kill her, but not the man.

Such standards of justice could arise only in a society where women had no voice and they were seen as a different species from men. Women of property retained some rights over it, but women's bodies were the property of their male kin. When women's bodies are not their own, they lose any scope for their minds. As these codes emerged, women almost disappeared from public life.

Female Infanticide

A Sumerian household, the estate of Me-sag, held 172 people, four men to each woman. About 69 percent of the children and 96 percent of Me-sag's 151 non-household workers were male. Even if wives were unlisted, the number of men is disproportionate. Scholars speculate that the Sumerians of this period committed female infanticide.

People in simple societies may have killed infants they could not feed in times of scarcity. Female infanticide is an entirely different matter. It occurs in societies with private property in which only males can own property, and it is justified by the need for male heirs. In such societies, men alone can perform religious rituals. Female infanticide is obviously a manifestation of low esteem for females. Since women's status was traditionally associated with their reproductive capacities, female infanticide also implies a low value for reproduction. It occurred in most ancient states.

One major concern of property owners, when property consists mainly of land, was that it not be divided into units too small to support a family. Some states passed laws of primogeniture, granting first-born sons the entire estate and disinheriting younger sons. Mesopotamia did not have primogeniture laws, but laws barred the sale of inherited land. Sons were expected to keep family estates intact. However, men got around these laws by adopting unrelated men as sons and willing them their land in exchange for money. Daughters were excluded from inheritance, but were given a dowry at marriage that was supposed to equal their share of the paternal estate. Dowry is customary in societies that consider land private property. Societies that hold land communally use bride-service or bride-wealth. Some societies have both customs.

Dowry, expected of propertied families, requires an outlay of goods or money and can be a hardship. To avoid it, men had baby daughters killed or exposed. Only fathers had the right to doom infants to death. Daughters are less likely to be killed, even by poor fathers, if they can become economic assets, earn wages, or be sold in marriage or in slavery.

Such economic-religious arrangements are logical and reasonable only if women are not really human beings but non-human animals. Laws in many societies explicitly state that those who cannot be held for taxes cannot own property, or those who cannot serve as soldiers cannot be citizens. Men may have had some guilt about these practices: despite widespread stories of fathers ordering baby girls killed, it is hard to find any record of infanticide. Scholars deduce it from demographic records: when numbers show far more men than women, they say, females are being killed by infanticide or by starvation.

Babylonia

Mesopotamia was torn by unremitting war before, during, and after Sargon's reign. During this period, class became permanent and the notion of private property emerged. Women were degraded into property and judged by a different legal and moral standard from men. By the time Sumer died, the old egalitarian, life-worshipping world of the mothers had been forgotten except for a remnant in language: in a world where most people were bound in one way or another, "freedom" was *amargi*, "return to the mother."

Around 1900 BCE the Amorites, who had gained influence in Mesopotamia, became dominant. A western Semitic warrior tribe, they took their historical name, Babylonians, from their capital, Babylon. They established an autocratic state and expanded it through war. Women did not have as much visibility and power in Old Babylonia as in early Sumer, but upper-class Amorite women acted in the political and economic realms. Records from Nuzi and from Mari, a great northern city, show that, in the eighteenth century BCE, they owned and managed property, made contracts, sued and served as witnesses (but not judges) in court, made loans, and adopted heirs. Some women paid tribute, or taxes, indicating that they had an independent legal existence. As prophets, consulted before a leader went to war or made an important decision, they advised kings.

A glimpse of the lives of privileged Amorite women emerges from a set of letters sent to the palace of Zimri Lim, a king of Mari. Most are from women, often his daughters, who had been given in diplomatic marriage or appointed as priestesses in foreign cities to guarantee the loyalty of their husbands' cities, offer the king diplomatic counsel, or spy for him. Some of these letters offer poignant pictures of these women's lives.

Princess Ibbatum wrote to her father to defend her husband, Himdiya, an official loyal to Zimri-Lim. Himdiya had intercepted a letter revealing a plot by an enemy of the king to reconquer the city of Amas. When he exposed the plot, the king appointed him governor of Amas and gave him Ibbatum as his wife. But rumours arose that he intended to betray Zimri-Lim. Ibbatum wrote to her father to describe the current political situation and to reassure him of Himdiya's loyalty.

Her sister, Inib-sarri, was given to Ibal-Addu, the king of Aslakka, which was under Zimri-Lim's control. Ibal-Addu swore loyalty to the king but was, in fact, planning a rebellion against him. Inib-sarri wrote to warn her father, urging him to keep Ibal-Addu's daughters hostage. Her husband apparently knew where her loyalty lay and kept her under guard, denying her "gifts" (perhaps food). Her letters to her father were pathetic: she said she had written to him often but that he told her only to stop crying; she begged to be allowed to return to Mari. Finally, Zimri-Lim gave her permission to leave Aslakka, but Ibal-Addu imprisoned her in a palace without heat. Wretched but resourceful, Inib-sarri continued to politic, spy, and struggle. In the last letter we have, she was still pleading to be brought home.

Princess Narantum, who was also imprisoned in a hostile environment and mistreated by palace officials, uses a psychological strategy. She tells her father that her abusers know she has not heard from him and say that if he does not care about her, why should they. Princess Kirum, who was overseeing the construction of a building, writes to offer Zimri-Lim political advice, reminding him of an occasion when he disregarded her advice to his own detriment.

Between 2000 and 1600 BCE some Amorite cities devised a new institution, the *naditu* – a priestess forbidden to bear children (*naditu* means fallow). Naditus first appeared when private property was emerging in Babylonia. Several sons could own land jointly, but if a daughter inherited, her husband would own part of the family estate. To avoid this division, wealthy men sent their daughters to a cloister, where they would live in comfort but not have legitimate children or husbands (though they were not necessarily celibate). When a *naditu*'s father died, her brothers were obliged to contribute to her upkeep from "her" land; she controlled its use and owned the income from it but could never take possession of it. Many *naditus* were active businesswomen who purchased houses on temple grounds, lent money, and bought and sold land, oil, grain, and other resources. They were scribes, and they directed the farmers who managed their animals or fields. They bought slaves or adopted young *naditus* to care for them in their old age, manumitting the slaves in return for the promise of care or leaving houses to their adoptive daughters. It is not known if they had freedom of movement or how much.

Extant temple records, including their correspondence, show that early *naditus* held administrative positions in cloisters. Later, men took these jobs, and when the First Dynasty of Babylon fell, *naditus* disappeared.[14]

Around 1800 BCE Hammurabi, the most famous Babylonian king, produced a famous code of laws based on the *lex talionis*, "an eye for an eye." Two-thirds of the 282 laws in Hammurabi's code deal with women, decreeing special treatment for them. It granted women certain rights. In 1931 the anthropologist George Dorsey asserted that Hammurabi's code offered woman "such recognition of her rights as a human being as are hardly equalled on earth today."[15]

Women had the right to testify in court, inherit, witness contracts, and work as scribes. Fathers or husbands could not take their property. Elite and merchant-class women were entrepreneurs and handled international trade. A woman controlled her own earnings; her dowry went to her children. In marriages by contract, the bride received a dowry from her father and gifts from the groom, and she kept both if he divorced her. But many wives were manumitted slaves or adoptees, with no fathers or *naditu* mothers. Some husbands freed slave-wives on condition that they continue to serve them, but many did not. The law obliged slave-wives to respect their mistresses, who were prohibited from troubling their husbands about slave-wives. Poor women had few rights: they or their children could be sold into slavery for three years to pay a husband's debts. A man could "pawn" a daughter as collateral; if he failed to redeem her before he died, her brothers had a month to buy her back or she would be sold into marriage or slavery.

Men could divorce their wives for childlessness, extravagance, conducting business, or embarrassing them; they could enslave wives for doing business on their own and kill them if they denied them conjugal "rights." Few women could sue for divorce. Poor housekeepers could undergo the "ordeal by water": they were thrown into a body of water and they lived only if they floated; otherwise they drowned. Men could declare a first wife "worthless," enslave her, and take a second wife.

Men found guilty of crimes were fined in cash or in kind; female wrongdoers were not only fined but their livelihood was ruined. An offending male might be fined some fruit; a woman was fined the fruit and her trees were also destroyed. Merchants found guilty of cheating were fined; a woman wine-seller found guilty of cheating had to undergo the ordeal by water. A husband who could prove his wife adulterous could kill her; if a woman was accused of adultery by someone other than her husband, she had to throw herself into the river even if she was innocent.[16] The most serious crime was husband-murder: a wife who caused her husband's death to marry another man was impaled or crucified. Punishments also varied by class.

The number of gender-specific laws suggests that women had been severely degraded. Their demotion is reflected in Babylonian religion myth. At first goddesses rule alone, then with a male consort, and finally they are subordinate wives of ruling male gods. Around the second millennium BCE the Amorites produced a new myth. Its modern translator and editor, Alexander Heidel, claims it is not a creation myth but a rewriting of history intended to justify the promotion of Marduk to chief god of the Babylonian pantheon. The god Marduk wants to usurp the throne of Tiamat, the divine mother. Her powers enable her to repel his attacks until he uses armed force to overthrow her. The epic celebrates his supremacy. Heidel believes the epic was commissioned when Hammurabi was trying, by armed force and other means, to establish his, and Babylonia's, political supremacy.

Assyria

Babylon was sacked in the sixteenth century BCE by the Hittites, a people from Asia Minor. The power next dominant in Mesopotamia was the Assyrian, around 1300 BCE, a western Semitic Amorite people named for Assur, their capital in Syria. Historians call their period of dominance the "cult of frightfulness." Extremely militaristic and cruel, they were obsessed with women: over half of the 112 extant Middle Assyrian Laws deal with women.

The Assyrians took to an extreme the tendency of the previous 2000 years in Mesopotamia to treat women as property: men could buy, sell, torture, or kill women. Girls, sold into marriage, could not inherit from their parents. Virginity was an absolute requirement, and brides found not to be virgins could be returned to their fathers or killed. A man could repudiate a wife without compensating her family. One adultery law granted the husband of an unfaithful wife the right to kill both the woman and her lover;

another let a husband charge a man who had sex with his wife with adultery, and the courts then entrusted him with the punishment of both offending parties. The punishment, which was usually private, had one condition: if the lover was killed, the wife had to be killed too. A wife who took her husband's property when he was ill or after he died was also killed. Women did not own property, nor could they be witnesses or bring suit. There was a new status: secondary wives.

Women were treated not as sentient beings, but as animals owned by men. If an unbetrothed virgin was raped, the attacker was not killed but had to marry the girl, if he was not already married, and was forbidden by marriage contract from divorcing her. If the man was married, he had to pay the girl's father by giving him his wife to be kept as a slave or a concubine. A man who hit another man's pregnant wife, causing her to lose the child, was punished by handing over his wife for the same abuse if she became pregnant.

The severest punishment in the Middle Assyrian Laws was levelled against women who performed abortions on themselves or others: they were impaled and denied burial. Gerda Lerner points out in *The Creation of Patriarchy* that their crime was not "murder" of a child, for infanticide was legal and widespread. But it was a male prerogative: fathers decided which daughters could live and which would be killed. Abortion, like adultery, was a crime only for women. For a woman to act independently was considered as serious a crime against the state as high treason or assault on the king – the only other crimes punished by impalement. The punishment was so savage because self-abortion usurps the power of the patriarch-father, the surrogate for the patriarch-ruler. Only men may kill. The Assyrian father, the absolute head of the family, has the right to inflict private justice on his family, his servants, and his slaves. Husbands totally controlled their wives' assets.

A woman did not need to do much to get into trouble: just going outdoors was dangerous. Hammurabi decreed that a woman who went outdoors while earning money for herself, perhaps as a trader, might be divorced or enslaved. The rape laws distinguished between rape of a married woman "passing along the street" on legitimate business, such as an errand for her husband, and women who strolled or loitered, the implication being that the latter sought illicit sex. Middle Assyrian women had to be careful how they dressed when they went out. Married women had to be veiled, but veiled prostitutes were punished. When married women went out of doors with their husbands' concubine, the concubine could veil, showing she was respectable, the property of a man. Young girls could go out without veils, but if a girl in the street was raped, the first question was whether her parents knew she was going out. If they knew and the man claimed he thought she was a prostitute, he went free. If they did not know she went out and he swore she consented, he had to pay her father three times the value of a virgin.

Like animals, women had money value and were sold into marriage, slavery, concubinage, or prostitution; they had no alternatives. Hammurabi's code allows a woman to return to her father if her husband mistreated her, but if he had paid a bride-price for her it had to be refunded. Some fathers therefore turned away their daughters. Assyrian law permitted husbands to punish wives in the harshest ways. In private he might scourge her, pull out her hair, bruise her and destroy her ears. But if he wanted to flog her, tear out

her breasts, or cut off her nose or ears, the law required that
he do so in public. The primary concern of law was property. Women figure prominently in ancient law codes because
they had become property; the focus of the law was to distinguish between the use of property by owners and by other
men. A woman's use of property (herself) by herself was a
crime against the state and therefore treason.

An Overview of Ancient Mesopotamia

Surely women tried to rise above their degradation, to be
treated well, to have some autonomy and safety. Some
women won minor victories: when other bondswomen got
30 quarts of barley, one got 35; a few widows won lawsuits
against brothers-in-law trying to take away their homes.
Some women achieved influence. People loved each other:
Lu-Dingir-Ra wrote to his mother in Nippur a long poem
of praise; suits over inheritance show some fathers being
kind to daughters. In some eras, a woman could refuse to
make love with her husband without risking death, and men
wrote love poems to wives.

These 3000 years were hard for everyone. War was nearly constant. Alliances broke down, governors of cities
rebelled against kings, and some overthrew them. One
leader followed another, each in his moment of dominance
attempting to consolidate his power forever. War altered
borders and the elite language and killed many people, but
did not change the lives of ordinary people. The economy
remained based in land, although the burdens on workers
grew with the large military expenses. Women, locked into
the necessities of life, went on doing what they everywhere
do: raising food and children, maintaining households.

By the end of this period, war had spread across north Africa. Egypt had become militaristic, enslaving women and children war captives, forcing men into the army, and branding or castrating them. Rulers valued their eunuch aides, who, having no wives or lovers, were considered to be loyal and were entrusted with guarding women's bodies. Slaves, like Joseph in Egypt, rose to high positions. Loyalty was hard to find, and slaves gained by offering it. Many became kings' councillors.

Slavery in ancient times was not as degrading as in its later forms. Slaves were their owners' colour, could become their equals, and, though social inferiors, they were not considered an inferior species. In some societies slaves could earn money and buy their freedom. In Mesopotamia and elsewhere, destitute people sold themselves into slavery, offering a number of years' work in return for an amount of money. Of course, for women, who were most often enslaved, slavery meant probable sexual use and motherhood.

Both men and women suffered from the new ideology of domination, but they did not suffer equally. Men had several advantages over women. Since an ideology of domination is intended to demonstrate male superiority, and since men were the main dominators, they tended, when delegating responsibility or power to an underling, to delegate it to men, not women. This transfer allowed some men to rise, socially, economically, and politically. Men, too, may have been used sexually, but not commonly enough to characterize men as a caste. Nor did men have babies as a consequence, but remained unencumbered, able to flee or seek the main chance elsewhere. In keeping with the ideology, rulers rewarded men for obedience by granting them the right to dominate their own women.

Everything conspired to degrade women. "Woman" became synonymous with possession, with slave. But there is one odd twist to the new alignment of the sexes. As saw with Spanish men and Andean women, women could rise by binding their male masters, husbands, or owners with sexual affection. And having children, which burdens women in servitude, also strengthens them. A woman can be energized by having a child, keeping it alive and functioning even in oppression. Struggling to help a child survive gives mothers pride and self-esteem, whatever their circumstances.

Still, women suffered an incalculable loss of status. They lost the right to an independent existence, to economic autonomy and pride: they lost physical freedom, the simple right to walk around, to rights over their own bodies. They lost most property rights, the right to a voice in their children's fates, and, except for a privileged minority, any voice in the running of the society in which they lived. By the Middle Assyrian period, even that minority had been dispossessed.

Women lost the right to sexual freedom, which we have not fully regained to this day.[17] J.S. Cooper studied seals, plaques, and vases with pictures of sexual actions, which reflect changes in male attitudes towards women in this period.[18] The earliest seals, from Tepe Gawra and Ur in Sumer, show men and women facing each other, sitting or standing, with a snake, the symbol of the goddess and regeneration, between them. Later, they sit face to face, with a scorpion in the frame. The scorpion meant sex in ancient symbolism, but it has a lethal sting and came to connote flattery and beguilement. In the same period, representations show a man lying on a woman in bed, and two women lying together above a larger picture of a woman and a goat – another lustful image. In two images, men approach women from behind, penises erect; the women are bent over, while another woman holds their hair. Later, men lie on women, entering them from the rear; three of the images show scorpions under the bed.

The animal imagery reveals worship of the female principle (the snake) giving way to fear of it (scorpion) and then to domination. Almost all the later representations show men entering women from behind. In others, a figure separated from the "lovers" by a boar, lion-headed eagle, lion, or dog, stretches his hands out over the woman's head or stands behind the man, holding a weapon. In some, a man holds a weapon over a woman's neck. The same period contains blurred depictions of what may be a male entering another male from the rear, and a female in the superior position in intercourse with a man. The latest Sumerian seals show females squatting on supine males, knees bent upward and legs widespread; in both, clothed males stand behind, grasping the women's wrists with one hand, a knife in the other.

The next group, from the Babylonian period, contains seven depictions of people having intercourse standing face to face, but with a bed in the scene. All wear nothing but jewellery. Seven others show a man standing, a woman bent, sometimes drinking through a straw (one bent figure may be a man). Two Babylonian reliefs show nude women squatting, holding their legs apart with their hands, over a disembodied erect phallus with testicles.

The latest set comes from Assur, home of the Assyrians. Several show women wearing bracelets and anklets (shackles?) lying on an altar; in one, a male grips her wrist and thigh; in another, the woman reaches back between her legs for the man's penis; two may show male-male intercourse. Cooper comments that male homosexuality is clearly attested in Mesopotamian texts and female homosexuality must have existed, although not in texts. He also remarks that anal intercourse was common in Mesopotamia, especially with priestesses who were not permitted to have children. But protected priestesses were unlikely to be forced into sex. Many pictures of women presenting their buttocks contain suggestions of coercion or violence. They probably depicted legal rape – the sexual practices of men with wives, concubines, servants, slaves, and prostitutes. Greek images of heterosexual practice, most probably depicting men with prostitutes, were similar. This art attests to the degradation of an entire sex.[19]

CHAPTER 4

A SECULAR STATE: CHINA

H ALF-MILLION-YEAR-OLD SKELETONS have been found in China, which has been inhabited for at least that length of time. Signs of human life date to the Paleolithic age; signs of culture, to the Neolithic age, beginning about 6000 BCE.[1] Chinese scholars divide Neolithic culture into two stages, Yang-shao and Lung-shan, which move from egalitarian matricentry to male dominance.

Yang-shao people lived between 5000 and 3000 BCE in north-central China by gathering, hunting, and fishing. They raised millet and wheat by slash-and-burn horticulture; bred pigs, dogs, sheep, and perhaps goats and cattle; and made pottery and silk. They may have lived in communal matrilineal clans – their settlements held group dwellings, graves, workshops and storage pits. They buried food with the dead, so they may have believed in life after death.

Marriage was probably matrilocal. Women may have had higher status than men, for women's graves from this period contain more valuable objects than men's. At one site, of the graves for which sex or age can be determined, 34 percent were women's, and they held four of the six pottery vessels in the layer, all the tools (including an axe, two awls, a chisel), half the ornaments, and jade. The other ornaments were with children, who were buried with women. One female grave contains many objects: its occupant may have had special status. No signs of war appear, and the only suggestion of stratification is the fact that many graves contain no goods at all.

After Confucius, Chinese scholars altered or expunged early myths; Taoists, who were anti-Confucians, tried to preserve them. Taoist myths see women everywhere in the cosmology. In the classic *Tao-te-ching*, the mother is the source of all creatures and the root of all nature: "The Valley Spirit never dies. It is called the dark female. It is called the root of Heaven and Earth. It goes on and on, it is something that always exists. Use it, it never runs out." The goddess Nu-kua created a man by accident when she was in the yellow earth.[2] Nu-kua, who was associated with the origin of agriculture, repaired the earth after a male god flooded it. And, for a time thereafter, men knew their mothers but not their fathers.[3]

Other myths tell of all-powerful dragon-women associated with Nu-kua, water, women, and rain – all essential to agricultural societies. Legends suggest that rulers were held responsible for harvests, that only females had the power to bring rain, and that failed rain-makers may have been burned. Later, Tang emperors co-opted the dragon symbol and, in the yin-yang dichotomy, most qualities associated with Nu-kua were attributed to yin. Yin was supreme to Taoists; yang, to Confucianists.

Ancient texts report that at ancient spring festivals held in "Holy Places" in the countryside, people prayed together for births and for rain.[4] Young people made love freely and exuberantly. Rain was female, so only women invoked it; women were believed to be impregnated by immersion in sacred rivers. The only ancestors reincarnated were mothers. Land, houses, and villages belonged to women, whom men approached warily. Men lived apart from women until farming began, when they claimed dominance over the female earth.[5] Even after men declared themselves chieftains, they remained subordinate to women, whom they needed beside them to rule. Later, they took over women's rain dances, dancing for thunder, not rain.

Lung-shan culture developed later than Yang-shao, in the south and east coast of China. Lung-shan people cultivated rice and raised chickens and horses, but still gathered and hunted. Their villages were a little larger than Yang-shao hamlets and were inhabited for longer periods. They dug wells, made elaborate pottery (some for ceremonial use), and divined by oracle bones. Removing the shoulder blades from pigs, sheep, or cattle, they heated them until they cracked; then diviners read the cracks for advice on the future. People who rely on oracles and diviners believe in gods; the gods of the Lung-shan people were probably ancestors who, able to see the future, transcended nature, human life, and the present. Lung-shan culture was combative: its villages were walled, and the ruins contain signs of violent death.

The graves in Lung-shan cemeteries (c. 4000–3000 BCE) hold more burial goods and more goods per grave than Yang-shao graves, suggesting a prosperous culture. In early times the graves of women and children have more goods than men's; later, the reverse is true. At one site, men's graves hold half the pots and all the tools except for spindle whorls, though one even has such a spinning device. Two male graves are quite rich, suggesting primacy. Stone phalluses were found in some gravesites. Lung-shan culture was male dominant.

Both cultures spread: Yang-shao from west to east, Lung-shan on the coast from south to north. At their intersection in northern Honan province, the Bronze Age began, with full stratification and male dominance.[6] During this period of the Shang Dynasty, a man, probably a local military chieftain, forcibly took command, justifying his act by declaring himself descended from the ultimate god, Shang Ti. This abstract deity, separate from and superior to nature, provided "divine" ancestry to the first Shang king. His kin claimed prerogatives by virtue of their relation to him and became the elite. As in Egypt, Mesopotamia, and the Andes, the rise of the state entailed a state religion and militarism.

The king granted land and the people who lived on it (now called "peasants") to his kin (now "nobles") in a form of feudalism. Nobles collected tribute for the king (keeping some for themselves), ruled, and waged war. Elite women were also granted lands and people (*enfeoffed*) and collected tribute – tortoise shells, oxen, dogs, horses, ivory, archers, and captives. Women led armies into battle, advised the king, and conducted rituals in his name. Succession may still have been matrilineal: many active noblewomen were sisters of kings. Sinologist Anne Holmes speculates that the ideograph *Fu*, which meant "Lady" and, later, "wife," was made up of the sign for "woman" and the sign either for "tree branch" or "feather" – a symbol of authority. (Male historians have chosen to read the second sign as a "broom.")[7]

With power and authority derived from inheritance or marriage, *Fu* were important. Much of what we know about ancient times comes from old oracle bones inscribed with questions, some mentioning *Fu*, or elite women:

- "On the day *jia-yin*, the diviner Zhong divined, asking: Will Fu-jing receive a good harvest?" Since only the elite used diviners, the question is not about a farmer but a female landowner.

- "On the day *jia-xu*, the king divined, asking: Should I command Fu-Jiao to assist in our affairs?"

- "On the day . . . the diviner . . . divined, asking: "Should the king not command Fu-jing to attack Lung-fang?"

- "On the day *ji-mao*, the diviner Gu divined, asking: Should Fu-hao conduct the Yü ceremony in honour of Father Yi with the sacrifice of slaughtered sheep and pigs?"

- "On the day *xin-wei*, the diviner Zheng divined, asking: Should the king order Fu-hao to join forces with Zhi-ji in the invasion of Ba-feng, the king to attack from Dong-X, to meet Fu-hao in Ba-fang?"

There are many references to Fu-hao, who seems to have been a military leader of some consequence. The king asked if he should order her to join forces with Marquis Gao to attack the Yi-fang; she led attacks against the Yi and Tufang, raised 13,000 men to fight the Jiang, and received heavenly assistance in following Zhifa to attack the Bufang. The only major Shang tomb uncovered intact was of a woman named Fu-hao; it contained beautifully made objects of jade, ivory, bone, stone, and bronze as well as human and dog sacrifices. Two Fu-haos are mentioned in oracle-bone inscriptions of different periods.

Highly educated priests, astrologers, and diviners adjusted the lunar calendar, recorded eclipses, did mathematics, and probably invented a decimal system. Some were women – indeed, female diviners still work in China and Taiwan. Female shamans worked among the poor. Artisans and workers, as well as land, were bestowed upon favoured nobles; beneath them were farmers, who had to pay tribute, corvée, and military service. At the bottom of the social scale were slaves – the war captives.

Cities, built inside pressed earth walls, held political and ceremonial buildings and some residences. Artisans lived outside in separate settlements. Farmers lived in the countryside in roofed pits, raising wheat, millet, sorghum, and barley with water buffalo, as they do today. They probably did not own their land, yet their production and taxes, their forced labour on construction projects and in the army, sustained the entire state. Everywhere, the lowliest members of society supported the elite.

The little we know of marriage customs suggests that the king and the powerful noblemen could have more than one wife. Only the wealthy could afford concubines but they were common, indicating that female subordination coexisted with a powerful and privileged female elite. That females were not highly regarded is suggested by oracle-bone inscriptions in which the birth of a boy is called "lucky," and of a girl, "unlucky." Women lost status in the Shang.

The Shang state was overthrown around 1000 BCE by the Zhou, a western people with a slightly different culture. Outsiders, they had to justify themselves and their right to rule, so they denounced Shang culture as corrupted by incompetence and debauchery, especially drinking. Depravity had lost the Shang the Mandate of Heaven, they said, and it was now granted to the Zhou, who also had divine ancestors. The Zhou king was the "Son of Heaven."

Throughout history, Chinese rulers have claimed this mandate, and usurpers have insisted that their predecessors lost it through unworthiness. This claim is remarkable because it holds rulers accountable. All regimes allege that god is on their side; Chinese rhetoric demands that rulers be competent and just to be worthy of the Mandate of Heaven. While Chinese rulers may not have been more competent or just than others, this notion is unique in its period, and it became the foundation for later ideas of accountability.

The Zhou Dynasty

The Zhou expanded the rudimentary feudal structure. The king ruled the region around the capital, granting his relatives and allies almost complete jurisdiction in their fiefs in outlying areas. Nobles grew enormously powerful and started dynasties of their own, passing titles and powers to their children. Here, as in Egypt, the political structure guaranteed continual rebellion and war. There is no evidence of the degrading of women in this period beyond the appearance of the yin-yang dichotomy, which, touted as a theory of interdependence and complementarity, in fact justifies male dominance. It defines women (yin) as soft, dark, mysterious, cold, moist, receptive, passive, and associated with water, death, and decline; men (yang) are defined as warm, bright, dry, hard, creative, assertive, and associated with life, growth, and light. A balance of these qualities is considered

necessary to ensure cosmic harmony, but they are not equally valued and the theory was used to justify women's subordination to men and their confinement in the domestic
sphere. The only work allowed to women was their traditional raising of silkworms and making silk, a product they
probably invented. Because female sexuality was seen as the
great threat to male order, women were taught to be chaste,
to produce legitimate sons for their husbands.

Chinese history, written by Confucian men, is pervaded
by moral judgments and virulent attacks on women. Confucius was born in 551 BCE; the historians lived later. They
expurgated ancient documents, rewriting history from a
Confucian perspective. They saw women stereotypically:
mothers were cruel or wise; wives and daughters virtuously
sacrificed themselves for husbands and fathers or ruined
them with rampant sexuality. The philosopher Mencius
extolled his exemplary mother, who proved her excellence by
moving to a better neighbourhood to give her son a proper
environment and provide him with an education. People of
the Zhou believed that good mothers conceived miraculous-
ly by swallowing an egg, bathing in dragon spittle, or step-
ping in a god's footprint, and that they gave birth through
an armpit or some body part other than the vagina, thereby
avoiding the contaminated genitals. Virgins and widows
were honoured, and a woman who committed suicide to
avoid the dishonour of rape or remarriage could become the
object of a local cult. Virgins were honoured by being "married" to nature gods like Ho Bo, lord of the Yellow River.
When the river "embraced" (drowned) her, she was wed.[8]

The ferocity of historians' attacks suggests that women
did not easily accept constriction. Although men erased
records of elite women, inscriptions on huge, engraved

bronze vessels of the Zhou period show that women had the resources and the power to have prestigious works of art made for them and that they officiated at religious ceremonies where the vessels were used. Another sign of female power is that the fall of western Zhou was blamed on a woman, Bao Si, the beautiful concubine of King Yu. Obsessed with her, partly because she never smiled, he used all his kingdom's resources to entertain her. He summoned clowns, acrobats, and performing animals and he had artisans make her beautiful objects, but he could not make her smile. One day, by accident, a bonfire signal was lighted, summoning distant armies from outlying fiefs to help the king. They sped to the capital in full regalia and pulled up short: nothing was wrong.

But Bao Si smiled. She smiled and burst out laughing. The king was enchanted. Afterwards, whenever he was desperate for a smile from her, he had the bonfires lit. His vassals wearied of this game and stopped paying attention to the signal. When real invaders came, the bonfires were lit but no one responded. The historians explained that Bao Si was evil incarnate because the seven-year-old girl who became her mother conceived when dragon spittle touched her. (Dragon spittle for semen seems to create good men but bad women.) The king was driven from the capital, ending the Zhou Dynasty. The next year (770 BCE) one of his sons was proclaimed king of eastern Zhou.

We can only speculate about poor women's lives in this period. Instruction in female self-sacrifice probably did not reach illiterate peasants. Men farmed, built waterworks, and made tools and utensils. Women worked in kitchen gardens, tended pigs and chickens, spun, wove, sewed, made baskets, mats, and pottery, cooked, and tended the young and the sick. Women worked in the fields at harvest and at sowing. In the south, they probably worked in rice paddies, once they existed, and, on the mulberry bushes (where silkworms grow), and made silk.

The family, a patriarchal extended family, was the basic unit of society; sons brought their wives to their fathers' houses. The family head administered justice, but if a member committed a serious crime, the entire family, held responsible, could be killed. In early Zhou, young commoners still chose their mates during the Spring Festival. Nobles did not marry freely, but noblemen could divorce their wives for cause – even for talking too much.

The Chinese may once have sacrificed humans, but now offered animals, grain, vegetables, or liquor. Seventy-two horses harnessed to twelve chariots and eight dogs with bells around their necks were buried alive in one sacrificial pit. Chinese religion had no dogma or church – the father performed rites – but there was much debate of philososphical issues arising from the ideas of Confucius and, later, Mencius, Mo-tzu, Lao-tzu, and others.

Confucius (b. 551 BCE) lived under the eastern Zhou. His philosophy, drawn from earlier thinkers, became the cornerstone of Chinese morality after the Han Dynasty (206 BCE–220 CE), long after his death. Confucianism became state doctrine, but was not always drawn from his ideas. Confucius taught that humans were morally good by nature but had degenerated. To find virtue again, education was necessary, especially for the elite, who most influenced society. Confucius scorned manual labour, admiring learning and rank. He taught that the family was the foundation of the state, summing up human relationships in five fixed arrangements: ruler-subject, parent-child, elder brother

–younger brother, husband-wife, and friend-friend. Confucius influenced Mencius (c. 380–289 BCE), who taught that sovereigns must earn the right to rule. When the unjust lose the good will of the people, they also lose the Mandate of Heaven and should be overthrown.

The Qin Dynasty

For 500 years, eastern Zhou fiefs fought and killed each other, until only three were left. Then the Qin rode out of the same western valley that nurtured the Zhou and unified the small Chinese state: the first Qin emperor, Qin Shi Huang, enlarged it. In the Qin Dynasty's brief tenure, he ferociously reorganized the state, extirpating feudal elements, eradicating rivals, and centralizing control. He set up a bureaucracy and divided the country into provinces, appointing provincial officials and making districts the basic unit of government. The Zhou had established primogeniture, but Qin favoured "partible" inheritance – the equal division of family property among sons.

Qin abolished serfdom and gave peasants the right to own, sell, and buy land. But they paid heavy taxes and a poll tax, and were subject to conscription and corvée; many fell into debt. Qin launched enormous projects: a network of roads radiating from the capital for the army; a set of fortifications in the north which, joined together, initiated the Great Wall; and, for his mausoleum, he conscripted 700,000 labourers and sacrificed them when it was finished. He freed the serfs, but enslaved masses. He tried to control thought and burned books by Confucius, Mencius, and others, banning philosophical debate to purge the idea of holding rulers accountable. He was, perhaps, the first totalitarian dictator.

The Han and Later Dynasties[9]

When Qin died, provincial leaders erupted in civil war. A commoner won, establishing the Han Dynasty around 200 BCE. During the Han, the Confucian classics were literally inscribed in stone to provide the principles that guided Chinese society throughout the late imperial period. Important changes occurred after the Han – wars, foreign domination, experiments with new economic and political structures, and new religions. But Chinese culture, and its official stance towards women, remained much the same after the Han.

Classical Confucian texts, the scholarly comment on the philosopher's work, defined women in China from the Han to the Qing dynasties. Confucius was concerned only with men, but two of his statements about women were used as the bases for legal codes in every dynasty after the Tang. First, he advised mourning women that their funeral dress should follow their fathers' rank before marriage, their husbands' rank after marriage, and their sons' after widowhood. This advice was expanded by later scholars into the rule of "follow thrice," which held that women's place in society was determined by their men. Second, as humanity is divided into yin and yang, human affairs are divided into "inner" and "outer" realms, a private world of women and a public sphere of men. Women rule at home, men in the world: both should scrupulously observe the separation, women by not asking about public affairs, and men by not asking about the household.

Later generations of men used Confucius' statements as a base for demanding universal obedience to authority and requiring women to obey father, husband, and son. They ignored Confucius' rule barring widows from remarriage when it benefited men economically but followed it when it did not. Later generations tend to alter the teachings of revered mentors so as to strengthen the rules governing women, as occurred in Islam as well.

To teach women their place, Han scholars wrote biographies of exemplary women. Early stories of bold, independent daughters, "virtuous" women, ascetics, mystics, and evil (jealous or vindictive) women gave way to stories of self-effacing women committing suicide in the name of chastity or dedicating celibate widowhoods to serving their parents-in-law. In some regions, it became customary for young widows to "follow" their husbands in death by starving themselves, strangling themselves with their sashes, or leaping into wells. "Virtuous suicide" was honoured by the Ming, although the Qing considered it barbaric and cowardly. But scholars glorified it throughout Chinese history – for women, not men. From a female point of view, a woman whose life was intolerable could use the threat of suicide to intimidate her persecutors. Suicide greatly dishonoured a family – it was not treated lightly.[10] Girls (for they were only girls) so miserable in marriage that they drowned themselves in their red wedding gowns were believed to haunt the husbands' family houses, which were usually abandoned.

Women were barred from formal government; only one woman ruled in her own right, and a few ruled as regents. The Han ruled through a bureaucracy, appointing some officials and selecting others by a civil service examination. Passage qualified poor young men for government jobs that let them and their families rise socially. The exam became more important as time went on; it was abolished, reinstated, modernized, expanded, but never opened to women.

Confucius thought virtue required education, but women, expected to be virtuous, were not educated. In the words of a late Ming saying: "Only the virtuous man is talented; only the untalented woman is virtuous."

Still, some women managed to educate themselves and enter politics. The single most exemplary woman in Chinese records is Ban Zhao, a Han scholar who wrote the world's first known treatise on female education. From an educated and aristocratic family, she was married at fourteen, as was typical for the time, widowed early, and refused to remarry. She became a historian and taught the palace women, including the next empress-regent, who consulted Ban Zhao on state affairs. When Ban Zhao's brother died, she completed his history of the Han and a treatise on astronomy. Altogether, her narrative poetry, essays, and treatises filled sixteen volumes, but they all vanished, except a treatise on women and the history attributed to her brother. Until the late Qing, Ban Zhao was honoured for her long celibate widowhood and as a moralist for women; her memory was revived when reformers began urging that women be educated to become "good wives and wise mothers."

When the Han fell, civil war and disruption during the Period of the Six Dynasties brought chaos, hardship, and more female infanticide, not just among the poor. Periods of severe hardship often beget religions of withdrawal, and Buddhism and Taoism arose in this period. Both consider the material world illusory. Taoism (and Neo-Taoism) believed that ideas are relative and that things exist only as contrasts: there is no good without evil or life without death. Behind everything is the Tao (the Way), which later thinkers saw as a blessed nothingness attainable only in mystical states. Humans should seek naturalness, spontaneity, and disengagement. The highest Taoist goddess of the Tang Dynasty, Hsi Wang Mu, the Queen Mother of the West, controlled immortality, mediating between earth and heaven. The "ultimate yin," threatening and compassionate, she nurtures marginal people and women outside traditional families, like dancers or Taoist nuns.

Buddhism teaches that human life is bondage to an illusion that earthly things are real – matter. Enlightenment can break the chain of desire that recycles souls in earthly rebirths and escape from the cycle by disengagement, education, ethics, and meditation, thereby achieving Nirvana, or heavenly obliteration. Offering an alternative to Confucian warrants of the inflexible Heavenly Will, Buddhism generated hundreds of mystic, ascetic sects and a monastic movement. People denied selfhood in Confucian society were drawn by its openness; women entered its monasteries, often to get an education unobtainable elsewhere. Yet Buddhist texts contain the most woman hatred outside the Judaeo-Christian tradition. The "Tale of King Udayana of Vatsa," for example, calls women evil, more detestable than "the dead snake and dog." "Why should fools / Be addicted to these [women], / To a skeletal post / Covered by skin and flesh / Their stench is offensive / Like rotten food." Buddhists preferred women living outside the cloister as Buddhist mothers to nuns, with whom they were in competition.[11]

The Han, China's dominant ethnic group (not the dynasty), still claim superiority over non-Han people. In this period, tribal peoples intermarried with the Chinese elite in the north. Active aristocratic northern women, unlike "mild, compliant" southern women, horrified Chinese historians.[12] Han scholars considered northern "Sino-barbarian aristocratic" women inferior to Han women trained in Confucian virtue, but Han women made trouble too. A salon culture arose in southern Buddhist and Taoist territories: people aware of the new religions gathered in private homes and mountain retreats to make sprightly, witty conversation about the scriptures. Elite women visited freely, to the outrage of a scholar who found them flagrantly immoral: instead of making silk or cap tassels, spinning hemp, and overseeing the cooking, they "tripped and danced" through the marketplace, spent time with friends and relatives, stayed out at night with their attendants, caused hubbub in the roads, listened to indecent jokes, and spent the night at another house. They went to Buddhist temples, watched people fighting and hunting, travelled outside their own districts, pulled open the curtains of their carriages and looked out at the towns they passed. "They drink from wine cups along the road. They play music and sing as they go along."[13]

Scholars loathed female freedom. For centuries, women had supervised the home production of everything used in large prosperous households employing hundreds of slaves and "guests." In one noble family, every woman spun and wove, and 700 slaves did handicrafts. The new fashion urged that wealthy women be educated to make better mothers and more interesting wives: mothers taught children calligraphy, music, literature, composition, manners, and religion. Buddhist nuns lectured on the scriptures, drawing audiences of thousands, including royal and aristocratic women. Religious women were sainted after death. China had no formal religion or church; Confucianism was the state religion and scholars were its "priests." Like all priestly castes, they were the most ardent supporters and propagators of male dominance, highly conservative men who resented women's new freedoms.

By the end of the Tang Dynasty, Chinese society contained three main classes: an elite centred in the capital; scholar-officials (the "prefectural aristocracy"); and commoners, free and unfree. All were endogamous, required to marry in their own class. Law forbade marriage between free and unfree. Palace women, guarded by eunuchs, lived in seclusion that was lax at first, but grew stricter. Still, elite Tang women had some independence within their prison and could contact people outside.

Summoned to the harem as consorts were upper-class women of great beauty or high family status. Officials periodically searched the countryside for girls of twelve or thirteen, preferably literate and of good family. Later, the palace set regional and local quotas for girls to be consorts or servants. When recruiters were expected, some families with daughters arranged hasty marriages with any man available, but for others, palace service was an entrée: palace servants were paid, their wages could be sent to their families, and a girl could make contacts useful for a sibling's marriage or a father's advancement. Girls were trained in the skills needed to pass entrance examinations for service – poise, deportment, embroidery, cleaning, and housekeeping.

The palace was a hierarchically ranked bureaucracy. The harem held 2000–3000 women, some with children, all with visiting relatives; harem women had rank as regents (ruling for a minor heir), consorts (legal wives), courtesans, concubines, and staff administrators. Emperors sealed alliances with other states by marriage, choosing regents from the many consorts in the imperial harem. Women regents ruled for twenty-five years of the 155-year Song period, so ably that even scholars did not condemn them.

The only way a lower-class woman could rise socially

was to become a courtesan. Xue Tao, a poet forced into slavery by her father's death, since women could not survive alone, became a concubine and published more than 500 poems. She was acclaimed by poets of her time, yet fewer than one hundred of her poems survive. Courtesans often achieved renown in writing, painting, or calligraphy. We know little about early women artists and much of their work is lost, but after the Song, the work of many women painters was saved. The most famous early woman calligrapher and painter was Guan Daosheng (1279–1368), during the Yuan Dynasty.[14]

Few women in this period gained prominence or autonomy. A new Taoist deity appeared, the Queen Mother of the West (Hsi Wang Mu), an ambivalent new role model. Neither dutiful daughter nor obedient self-sacrificing wife and mother, Hsi Wang Mu was associated with the ancient goddesses of rain, water, wind, and rainbows; with water spirits – dragons, frogs, fish, serpents; and with images of yin that were powerful, gorgeous, fertile, and seductive to men. In poetry she resembles Western figures like Lamia or La Belle Dame Sans Merci. Abidingly youthful (depicted as about twenty), she attracted young men, seduced them by promising them the secret of immortality, and made love with them, after which they fell ill and died. Enormously popular, she was worshipped as the patron of female Taoist priests and adepts and of "singing girls" (the euphemistic name for courtesans and prostitutes), who were trained to sing and dance as well as offer sexual services.

Similar figures appear in nineteenth-century Europe. People seem to invent gods appropriate to their time. Women forced into subordination become hostile to the men they must please to survive. Men sense the anger beneath women's compliance and develop an image of woman as irresistibly beautiful and seductive, but also malicious, reflecting women's hatred of their condition and the men who enforce it and men's fear of the oppressed.

Little is known of women's property rights in China. The historical record suggests they lacked formal rights to inherit from the time of the first Chinese state, yet records show men leaving large legacies to daughters and, in some periods, giving them dowries (much smaller than their brothers' inheritance). Women were cut out of inheritance early on by being excluded from their lineage, the succession to hereditary titles and property. Families traced descent through men, as if females did not exist. In the Han, women managed households, the basic unit of production, but men headed the household, distributed income, and paid taxes. The state sanctioned male but not female juridical and punitive authority – a father, not a mother, could judge or punish a child. Still, some historians believe that women still inherited in the Song. During the Ming and the Qing dynasties they could inherit only if there were no other children. But this transfer occurred only rarely: men preferred to adopt male heirs (not necessarily a relation, just males willing to take their family name) than to leave property to daughters.

Similar uncertainty pervades our knowledge of marriage customs. The Chinese character for "surname," *xing*, contains a female radical (the ideograph contains the sign for *woman*). Some scholars believe this means that lineage was traced through mothers – marriage within a surname group had long been taboo by law and custom. But paternal cross-cousin marriage was the rule in some regions. It is hard to generalize about so huge a country with so many isolated communities: for example, Confucian moralists enjoined widow remarriage and condemned levirate marriage, but these prohibitions were not always enforced.

Between the Tang and the Song, laws relieved women of liability for acts committed by their natal families. Families were held responsible for the acts of members; freedom from this responsibility meant that women were no longer considered family members. Non-members of their natal families, women were also non-members of their marital family until they gave birth to a son.

The Chinese worshipped their ancestors, but only men conducted formal sacrificial rites honouring dead male and female ancestors in lineage ancestral halls. Women could worship only at home, where families kept a shelf of tablets memorializing their forebears. But because women were excluded from their natal families, a married woman could never honour her own ancestors. Nor had she a place on her own family's or her husband's family's shelf: nothing memorialized a female until she bore a son. If she died sonless, no one would ever honour her. Women became fiercely determined to have sons: for women as well as men, daughters were of no significance.

Female Footbinding: Women as Works of Art

Controls on women intensified after China was conquered by the Mongols, who created the Yuan Dynasty. Both Chinese and Mongols, intent on keeping their cultures separate, focused on guarding women (and the inheritance rights of sons) from rape and intermarriage by banning widow remarriage, emphasizing female chastity, and binding girls' feet. Tiny feet became a mark of elite Han culture; the feet of peasant women, who had to work, were more loosely bound. Whenever the custom began, it was common by the Yuan. Although urged for "aesthetic" reasons, it was really an effort to control women, as well-known verses show:

> Why must feet be bound?
> To prevent uncivilized running around![15]

Footbinding was torture lasting for years. When girls were five or six, their feet were tightly swathed. But the bones kept growing; swathing could only twist the foot backward so it grew under, rather than out, until the sole nearly touched the heel. This twisting was agonizing. Every night the bindings were taken off, the child's feet bathed and massaged to try to keep them from becoming gangrenous, and the bandages replaced. If the girl did not die of gangrene, the bindings were removed only when her bones stopped growing. She was crippled for life. For centuries Chinese girls grew up weeping from pain, knowing what it meant to be born female. Only peasants and some non-Han minorities, such as the Hakka and the Manchu, did not bind girls' feet. Sometimes families who expected a daughter to marry into a higher class would bind her feet but fail to find her the hoped-for husband. Then she would have to do the labour appropriate to her class — work in the fields or pull canal barges — on crippled stumps of feet.

How could mothers allow their little girls to be tortured? Think about it: you are a young Chinese woman of good family, dressed in gorgeous silks, your hair elaborately dressed, your face powdered and serene. You carry a parasol to keep your skin pale and totter about on your deformed feet, helped or carried everywhere you go — a pain but also a luxury. As you pass a browned Hakka woman at work in the fields on large calloused feet, she gazes at you enviously: she labours hard, long hours, and knows you don't have to do anything at all. You both know that women in "debased" professions – prostitutes, barbers, tanners, actors – are forbidden to bind their feet, forbidden to intermarry with even low-class people, and that their men are forbidden to sit for civil service examinations. You know that bound feet are a mark of Han culture, the superior culture. What do you feel? You are a work of art, not a woman. You are superior, not subject to the contempt your society feels for women.

Consider women in times closer to our own, corseted so tightly they cannot breathe. Or notice women today tottering on high heels that ruin their feet, in tight short skirts that restrict freedom of movement, with elaborate hairdos that must be protected from wind and rain, and flawless makeup needing continual attention. Long painted fingernails show that she does not work with her hands, though such nails are dangerous to anyone who uses her hands at all.

Today, no law or custom forces women to constrict themselves this way. They do it to gain status, to set themselves off from the common herd of a despised species. Elite women always adopt fashions that impede freedom of movement and action, and those who want to appear to be elite always imitate them. Men mock women as slaves to fashion, but women's concern with fashion has a subtext. All women know that females are seen as barely more than animals. People speak with scorn, contempt, and derision of fat women, old women, women in sacklike dresses, poor women, women sweeping streets, wrinkled women, toothless women, women with pendulous breasts or bellies or buttocks, skinny women, blue-haired women, little old ladies in tennis shoes, and women decked out in beehive hairdos and ornate jewellery walking in disdained Miami hotels.

To escape this general disparagement, women try to present themselves as above criticism or contempt. Such presentation is fostered by apparel that is clearly not designed for everyday life, apparel the big-footed Hakka woman could not wear. Women who adopt uncomfortable attire are desperate to distinguish themselves from the scorned common run. High fashion turns women into works of art, and women have always been willing to sacrifice freedom for the appearance of transcendence. What power is to a man, illusion is to a woman. You can count on this: in any society, in any period, whatever style emerges to distinguish the elite from ordinary women will physically constrict.

The Late Imperial Era

The rich grew richer in late Imperial China and cities expanded. Women ran restaurants, sold fish or vegetables in shops, or moved to the lively prostitutes' quarter. Wealthy families hired concubines, maids, cooks, dressmakers, and singing-dancing girls for parties. Once girls could earn money, female infanticide shrank and families began to educate daughters. Literacy grew; books on women (which had been limited to defining the Confucian ideal) began to treat practical matters and ways for women to better their lives. Fictions portrayed women sympathetically, as the moral equals of men.

Later, women's lives seemed to become grim. Confined to the home, unable to walk, barred from inheritance, married very young, giving birth to girls, which earned scorn and led to their babies being drowned, they were often widowed at twenty or thirty, condemned for trying to remarry, and lacked a place in family worship. Women were held responsible for rape: a 1646 law required them to defend chastity with their lives. They were honoured for committing suicide or being killed resisting rape, but not if they died after rape. And they were blamed for breakdowns in the Chinese family ideal of five generations under one roof. The system, set up so parents could control sons and their wives, set woman against woman.

Slavery was banned by imperial edict in the Qing era because the government wanted a strong landowning peasant class to pay taxes and provide a buffer against the power of great landowners. Some hereditary serf and "debased" groups survived, but China never had a "slave culture" or depended on slaves for manual labour. But women were sold and bought as slaves, as sexual and labouring servants, and as adoptees raised in servitude for eventual marriage to a son in the family.

Women's lack of self-esteem may be plumbed by the single hope held out to them by the new female deity who emerged during the Song, Bodhisattva Guanyin: if women purified themselves by celibacy and vegetarianism, they could transmigrate and return to life as men, and thereby enter Nirvana. Guanyin originated in India in the thirteenth century as the male deity, Avalokitesvara. She is an anomaly: most goddesses were swallowed up by gods. Princess Guanyin defied her parents' wishes that she marry and sacrificed herself for her father, to return as a Bodhisattva (enlightened being). Her cult of the White Lotus drew thousands of women to lay communities. Communities of nuns and single women are still devoted to it, expecting the

Maitreya, Buddha of Light, to return to earth and initiate an era of Great Peace presided over by the Eternal Mother (Wusheng laomu).[16]

CHAPTER 5

A RELIGIOUS STATE: INDIA

COMPLEX SOCIETIES DEVELOPED EARLY IN INDIA, in cities like Harappa and Mohenjo-Daro. Indian tradition holds that as early as 3000 BCE, villages ruled by clan councils were linked to central cities. Evidence of script and agriculture (farming with ploughs, associated with male dominance) dates to around 2500 BCE in the Indus Valley.[1] Our knowledge of early Indus societies comes mainly from oral material, written down later. For example, an ancient marriage hymn expresses hope that a bride will speak with composure and success in public assemblies in her old age. This desire suggests male superiority, since the role is reserved for the bride's old age. Many patrilineal societies deny women a public voice until after menopause.[2] Indian women were later barred from all public assemblies, and historian Veena Oldenburg believes that gender and age hierarchies may have existed in ancient days.[3]

Most histories of India begin with the Aryan invasion. Sometime after 1700 BCE, Aryans entered north India through the Hindu Kush Mountains. "Aryan" (noble ones) refers to some Indo-European languages spoken by the "people from the sea" who invaded Greece, Crete, and Iran. Blond, blue eyed, warlike, with male gods, and a sense of racial superiority, they were patrilineal, patrilocal, and stratified (priests, warriors, commoners), but not completely male dominated. Their term *vispatni* means "female head of clan."

Aryan herders moved east and south for a short distance, fighting and assimilating with the local farmers. They never reached the south, where to this day different languages are spoken. Both groups supported the priests who produced the Vedas, four hymn collections that gave Vedic culture its name. The earliest, the RgVeda (c. 1000–800 BCE), was composed in Vedic Sanskrit, an archaic form of Sanskrit – perhaps Aryan merged with the local language. Almost all our knowledge of Vedic society comes from Vedic narratives, but most RgVeda hymns were composed by male priests, and the RgVeda is "a book by men about male concerns in a world dominated by men."[4] Their concern with women was mainly to regulate, control, and disparage them.[5] But women, too, composed hymns and may have been priests able to perform sacrifice.

The Early Vedic Period (1200 BCE to 900 BCE)

Early Vedic people farmed and herded, raising vegetables, barley, sheep, goats, and oxen. Women wove woollen cloth, though they probably did not yet have cotton. Loving milk, cream, and ghee (clarified butter), Vedic people valued cattle, a medium of exchange. Men stole cattle in raids and distributed them in assemblies of the *vis* (clan). Women tended the animals – the word *duhitr* (daughter) derives from *duh*, "to milk" – but earned nothing. The clan or tribe owned the cattle; men performed the rituals of cattle exchange; and male priests sacrificed them. Women could attend clan meetings but had no voice in distribution. Chiefs *(rajanyas)* received more booty than other members of the *vis*; only rajanyas and priests performed major ritual exchanges. Class stratification is not reflected in graves, which show minimal differences in wealth. Difference showed only in status.

A few women in the Vedas successfully challenged their restrictions. Vispala, "seeking booty," fights a battle. She loses a leg but gets an iron leg from the Asvins, the divine physicians. Mudgalani, Indra's mythical charioteer, "won a car-load [of cattle] worth a thousand." Goddesses invoked as "Mother of the herds of cattle," guardians of the herd that provided their food, underwent ordeals, perhaps indicating lessened female power.[6]

Clans raided each other, often under "kings" chosen to lead them in battle. Some clans had hereditary leadership; others elected leaders. Raiders probably killed conquered men and enslaved the women: in one record a priest received fifty female slaves for performing a sacrifice. Slavewomen probably did domestic and sexual service and pastoral work – feeding animals, mucking out stalls, milking them. Indian women still do these jobs.

Vedic religion had no temples or images; its most important rite was sacrifice of animals, grain, or *soma*, an alcoholic or psychedelic liquor (the highest gift), to the priests. The earliest passages in the RgVeda bar women from inheriting and sacrificing, yet hymns record women offering sacrifice. Its major gods were male – Indra, the storm god, and Agni, the god of sacrificial fire – but goddesses were entreated for riches or booty from a raid. The invocation of goddesses probably reflects an ongoing conflict between adherents of patriliny and matriliny.[7] Patriliny was not yet universal: there is only one term for father, whether the father's or the mother's, whereas fully patrilineal cultures distinguish between paternal and maternal grandfathers. Some individuals took their mother's names.

In fully male-dominant societies, marriage rules establish male control, but the Vedas include many forms of marriage, even polyandry (having more than one husband).[8] Brother-sister and mother-son incest may have been accepted and are not condemned in Indian literature until the Yama-Yami myth.[9] Yami, the twin sister of Yama, god of death and the fathers, approaches him sexually and is rebuffed. She appeals to Tzastar, a crafts god, who supports her; Yama appeals to Mitra and Varuna, high-ranking patriarchal gods, and wins, suggesting a conflict between priests and artisans. But the high gods of the RgVeda, Agni and Indra, have typical patriarchal marriages: Agni, "the most manly one," has "many a youthful consort" – wives, seduced maidens, and his sister. One attribute of Indra, who is compared to a king dwelling among his wives, is to provide single men with wives.

Textual images depict marriage as emotionally equal. One prayer begs, "May we once firmly cling to thy fair favours even as husbands to their wives" and beg "as unmarried men who long for wives." Men long for Indra like "yearning wives clinging to yearning husbands"; the relation of god and worshipper is like marital affection: "Close to her husband clings the wife, and in embrace intertwined, both give and take the bliss of love." Several hymns acknowledge and describe female sexuality and desire.

Yet many signs point to male dominance and contempt for women. Supplications request sons, never daughters, and men alone pray for children – women do so only for an exceptional reason, like an impotent husband. (One wonders how they thought the wife of an impotent man could get children.) There are lists of qualities that endear a wife to a husband, not the reverse. Transvestites learning their new role are ordered to adopt the comportment imposed on Vedic girls: "Cast down thine eyes and look not up. More closely set thy feet. Let none see what thy garment veils, for thou, a *Brahmana*, hast become a dame."

A few invocations to goddesses focus on their strength: the Maruts on horseback "stretch their thighs apart like women when the babe is born"; Sarasvati is "a fort of iron" and "a foe-slayer" who can "burst with her strong waves the ridges of the hills . . . whose limitless unbroken flood, swift moving with a rapid rush / Comes onward with tempestuous roar." Sarasvati (literally "she who is possessed of the essence") is a river who later becomes the goddess of learning. The goddess Aditi is heaven, air, mother, father, son, all gods, all humans, all that has been and shall be born; all-encompassing, she has the capacity to remove sin. Vak calls herself first of the gods, who provides food for all, gives breath, and holds together all that exists.

But Indra, the primary god, despises women, saying "the mind of woman brooks not discipline. Her intellect hath little weight." Indra has trouble asserting dominance and struggles endlessly with females, but has the power to refuse to be born through the birth canal, issuing instead from his mother's side. His mother Aditi, shamed by her strange child, hides him, but he springs up, assumes his "vesture" (connoting the investiture of priests), and fills heaven and earth. Indra fights powerful Dawn and finally crushes her, forcing her to flee from her chariot in fear. The goddesses Heaven and Earth also flee from him in fear. Indra crushes the heads of "sorceresses" and kills his enemy's mother, Danu, and the hostile female spirit, Druh.

Despite the RgVeda's intention to abolish women's rights, it inadvertently suggests their importance by preserving some poetry by women. Internal evidence supports the orthodox tradition that twenty woman seers contributed to it. The early RgVeda contains no injunctions against women owning cattle or widows remarrying. Most scholars believe that women in the early period could work and own property and that girls were educated at home. An early Upanishad (a prose treatise, a coda to the Vedas) offers a ritual to insure the birth of a scholarly daughter. Women owned property, both movables (jewels, coin, clothing) and immovables (land, houses); they farmed, wove and dyed cloth, embroidered, taught, and made bows and arrows. Lower-class women traded.

Archaeological remains from the later Vedic period (1000/900 BCE to 600 BCE) show a marked increase in the number of settlements, which usually means that people are farming. In some regions, kings *(rajas)* become permanent fixtures. Patrilineality and patrilocality are more common, rank is more important, and political institutions arise. Writing appears, mainly for business purposes, along with the first evidence of caste distinctions.

Varna (caste), a Portuguese word, means colour. Aryans were white, and the indigenous peoples probably were dark, some very dark. Caste arose from skin colour: the lightest was highest. There were four *varnas*, based on occupation (which must already have been colour-stratified) and a purity/pollution hierarchy. The *Brahmins*, priest-teachers who probably devised the system, decreed themselves the highest. Beneath them were *Kshatriya*, warriors (often rulers); *Vaisyas*, merchants and professionals; and *Sudras*, artisans, menials, and farmers. Some scholars think *Sudras* were the indigenes the Aryans conquered.

In time, the system became extraordinarily complex and, today, there are thousands of castes.[10] At first no class was considered *achhooth*, "untouchable"; slaves, *Dasas*, were forced to do work that was considered defiling – midwifery or laundering, in which one might touch blood – cleaning up excrement, scavenging, and working with carrion (as leather tanners do) or with dead bodies in cremation and burial grounds. Slaves and tribal groups were outside the caste system.

The sacred literature of this period (*Pancavimsa [PVB]*, *Aitareya [AB]*, and *Satapatha Brahmanas [SB]*) traces the gradual exclusion of women from sacrifice. The *PVB* recounts that two women offered a thousand cattle to two male sages, who wanted to take them but were reluctant to accept, publicly, a gift from women. Women's offerings were devalued, then disappeared, yet one text stipulates that a wife must accompany a man when he sacrifices, or he is incomplete.[11] That women's presence was necessary suggests that they once performed the rituals. As gods increasingly absorb the traits of goddesses, depicted as hostile enemies of religion, male hostility to and fear of the female grows. Those traits are especially marked in rituals for large-scale sacrifices to establish or legitimate a hierarchical order that explicitly denies goddesses *virya* – valour or virility – and commands men not to bring their wives when they are offering the sacrifice accompanied by a drink, as sharing drink means sharing strength. In reciting the words of the *soma* sacrifice, priests utter the verses meant for women so softly that women do not retort or protest.

The literature of this period suggests a long time of conflict between men intent on degrading women and women's insistence on performing their traditional roles. The priests exploit men's fear of women's bodies and sexuality as they attempt to nullify female power. They order men to avoid women before many ritual occasions; they create rituals to shame women who have sexual relations with men other than their husbands, but not men in similar situations. They invent a new ritual, the *ashvamedha*, the "greatest" Vedic ritual, celebrated by the ruler of a territory.

The *ashvamedha*, "horse sacrifice," took a year. A cavalcade of priests and their retinue toured the entire domain of the king with a horse designated as sacred. At the end of a year, they sacrificed the horse and required the raja's chief wife to copulate with the dead beast while other wives and priests made bawdy conversation. Supposed to insure the fertility of the realm by symbolic magic, the ritual was used to impress the populace with the raja's authority and power. If local groups protested or rebelled, they were hit with religio-political propaganda; if necessary, the entourage used force. Copulation of the highest ranking woman in the realm with a beast, in a ritual presided over by male priests, was a strong statement about sexual power.

Another new development in this period was worship of paternal male ancestors. Priests began to teach that men could be made immortal by their sons' worship, excluding women from the sacrificial rituals. In religious documents, women are more and more compared in status to Sudras, the lowest caste. Priests become concerned with establishing the "right" kind of marriage. Both egalitarian and male-dominant marriage existed, but increasingly the latter was the norm. Yet goddesses still possessed great power and, despite the books, customs varied from region to region (as they still do). Not everyone in the vast subcontinent accepted the religion from which the books emerged, and many continued to practise ancient customs.

The Rise of Buddhism and Jainism, 600 to 200 BCE

After 600 BCE agriculture and iron tools became more common; settlements grew into cities with craft specialization, private property, and an affluent class. Long-distance trade brought Indians into contact with other patriarchal societies, strengthening the patriarchism of Vedic society. Ambitious rajas made war widely, massacring kin-groups and annihilating autonomous minorities. War eroded old traditions and customs; the rural kin-groups in which women held rights by custom and tradition were dissolved. Amid this social and political disruption, two religions of withdrawal emerged – Buddhism and Jainism. Founded by Gautama (the Buddha) and Mahavira, both born about 550 BCE, these religions taught denial and transcendence of earthly life.

The last segment of the Vedas, the Upanishads, also reflects the withdrawal that often attends disruptions in society. It replaced the Vedic rituals and sacrifices that had been intended to increase well-being and prosperity with a vision of earthly existence as pain and bondage. The priests who composed the Upanishads questioned the world's reality, deciding that what is real is the individual soul *(atman)*, an essence originating in a transcendent principle *(Brahman)*. Incarnated in flesh, the soul is trapped in endless cycles of birth, suffering, death, and rebirth in forms dictated by its acts in its last life – behaviour, even thoughts, are judged and rewarded or punished.

This law of retributive justice is *karma*. Good karma frees the *atman* from this cycle. The path to release is the practice of yoga, a complicated system of mental and physical discipline offering relief from desire (which keeps one locked in earthly cycles) and attainment of eternal transcendence, or ecstasy. But salvation was open only to elite men, mainly priests, who used the karma theory to exalt themselves and to teach others lowliness, claiming that obedience to caste laws was a prerequisite to rebirth in a higher status. Women could be saved only if they were reborn as high-caste males.

Gautama and Mahavira offered a more democratic message. Both accepted the basic assumptions of the Upanishads, but opposed caste distinctions, insisting that behaviour, not birth, defined a person. They urged a yoga (discipline) more accessible to ordinary people: Gautama emphasized intellectual enlightenment and meditation; Mahavira, asceticism. Their teachings mitigated inequality but did not condemn it, so, like Jesus later, they did not challenge the political structure. Both religions considered monasticism the ideal, but promised rewards to lay people who concentrated on duty, ethics, and virtue. Far from threatening the authorities, the new religions pleased them: concentration on the self, ethics, and virtue distracted people from politics and laid the ground for social solidarity.

For Indian women, monasticism was an escape, as it was later for Chinese and for Christian women. Forced into marriage, childbearing, and domestic servitude too young to fight back, women had really no options. Vedic religion denied women and low-caste men any possibility of salvation: they were not candidates for *moksha*. Buddhism offered Nibbana (Nirvana) to everyone, regardless of sex or caste. Yet Gautama did not want women monastics: he wanted women to remain hardworking inferiors maintaining husbands and families. But his foster mother, Maha Prajapati Gotami, pressured him until he reluctantly agreed to allow women to renounce the world. Gloomily predicting that the monastic order would be ruined by the innate weaknesses of women, he barred them from the priesthood and structured the orders so that nuns would perpetually have to defer to the authority of their equal counterparts, the monks, and to priests.

Still women entered monasteries with vigour and will. Their experiences are recorded in the *Therigatha* ("Psalms of the Sisters"), orally transmitted songs that may date to the time of the Buddha but were not written down until 80 BCE.[12] Some went into monasteries along with a husband, father, or brother, or as widows. One was forced into it by her father; one followed a woman friend from love. But of the seventy-three nuns whose songs have survived, fifty joined after hearing the Buddha or a renowned woman Buddhist speak. Class differences and prior marital status fell away in the monastery: whatever their background, the nuns sang of freedom.[13] Sangha, who was wealthy, celebrates her freedom from worldly desire; Bhadda sings that she has wandered from place to place, living on alms for fifty years. Mutta, daughter of a poor priest and wife of a poor husband, sings:

O free, indeed! O gloriously free
Am I in freedom from three crooked things:
From quern, from mortar, from my crookbacked lord,
Ay, but I'm free from rebirth and from death,
And all that dragged me back is hurled away.

Some women became distinguished preachers. Dhammadinna joined the order soon after her husband and attained enlightenment quickly; he did not and, displeased by her progress, interrogated her. She "answered every question as one might cut out a lotus-stalk with a knife," and the Buddha appointed her a preacher. A tradition of women teachers arose. Sukka was converted by hearing Dhammadinna, who "taught the doctrine in such wise that she seemed to be giving [her audience] sweet mead to drink and sprinkling them with ambrosia and they all listened to her rapt, motionless, intent."

Women's sermons were not preserved, but their songs show a common-sense, non-extremist approach to religion. Punna (or Punnika) mocked a *brahmana* who masochistically purifies himself in an icy river, arguing that if water can free people from evil karma, "fishes and . . . tortoises . . . frogs and water-snakes, crocodiles" will go straight to heaven. Women celebrated the support and affection of other women after everyone else, even their children, had forsaken them. Many sisters sang of overcoming sexual desire and attaining an asexual state. Yet the priests wrote that the greatest impediment to women's reaching Nibbana was sexuality (men's sexuality somehow did not hinder them) and the temptation they offered male ascetics, for which women were responsible.

While some withdrew from the world, others conquered

it. In the sixth century BCE a Persian king, Darius I, overran the Indus valley and made it a province of his empire, extracting an annual tribute of gold and men, as mercenary fighters in his armies. Two hundred years later Alexander the Great invaded the same valley and fought local rajas in the Punjab for two years. Repelling invaders usually mobilizes local men and trains them in power-seeking. After Alexander died, his empire collapsed, but Indians went on fighting for dominance. Chandragupta Maurya, a prince from north India, eventually established the Mauryan Empire, the first real Indian state, a dynasty that lasted over two hundred years.

Brahminism Dominant, 200 BCE to 540 CE

As the Mauryan Empire collapsed, foreigners invaded the Northwest and the Deccan (south India), battling for dominance. Cities grew, nourishing a mercantile community increasing in size and power. Active outgoing Vaisyas, the merchant caste, upset the traditional balance of power between Brahmins and Kshatriyas, who had long shared political control and prestige in an agricultural society. Change confused people, and they needed a new codification of law. About 200 BCE a Brahmin called Manu produced a code that was followed by all the new rulers. Brahminism rested on the Vedas; the Laws of Manu became the core of Hinduism.

The Laws of Manu *(Manusmriti)* name four goals in life: *dharma* (duty), *artha* (wealth and power), *kama* (sex and pleasure), and *moksha* (final salvation). Man's primary duty is to learn and to uphold the law. All men need and want money, power, sex, and sensual pleasure, but they must pursue them with moderation and in balance with *dharma.*

Later, the Mahabharata and Bhagavad-Gita taught that man's primary duty is to perform the duties of his caste and his place in the world with excellence.

The *Manusmriti* names the Brahmin caste supreme over all others, even the Kshatriyas (who were often reckoned equal to Brahmins, especially in the Punjab). The three top castes – Brahmins, Kshatriyas, and Vaisyas – are the "clean" castes, "twice born," because men were initiated into religion at puberty in a "second birth" that made them self-aware members of an occupational group *(jati)*. When the Vedas were first taught, only men of these varnas were allowed to learn to read them. Members of a *jati* must be born into it, have their food cooked only by members of their own or a higher group, remain loyal to their hereditary occupations, and be endogamous, marrying only within the *jati*, though outside their lineage *(gotra)*. Caste distinctions generate hundreds of subrules – an untouchable, for instance, may not draw water from a well owned by higher-caste people. So in times of drought, low-caste women may have to walk miles to find a wet well they can use.

Brahmins wanted their women dependent and subordinate: their status "followed" men's, like that of Chinese women. Manu decreed that women were members of their fathers' *gotra, jati,* and *varna* until marriage, and of their husbands' afterward. Although intermarriage among castes was forbidden, women did marry "up" (the reality was flexible). To encourage marriage into a higher group or class ("hypergamy"), the dowry system arose, as families with daughters, scrambling for upper-caste grooms, added a dowry as temptation.

According to Manu, a woman:

should do nothing independently
even in her own house.
In childhood subject to her father,
in youth to her husband,
and when her husband is dead to her sons,
she should never enjoy independence . . .
    She should always be cheerful,
and skillful in her domestic duties,
with her household vessels well cleansed,
and her hand tight on the purse strings . . .
    In season and out of season
her lord, who wed her with sacred rites,
ever gives happiness to his wife,
both here and in the other world.
    Though he be uncouth and prone to pleasure,
though he have no good points at all,
the virtuous wife should ever
worship her lord as a god.

A daughter may inherit her father's property if she has no brothers. Unlike the Chinese, some Indian fathers named their daughters "sons," making them their heirs in the hope that grandsons would fulfil the ritual obligations. Manu, preoccupied with chastity, ruled that girls should be married young to older men, forbidden to remarry, and punished for adultery according to caste. A woman who had sex with a higher-caste man was humiliated – given filthy garments and food only to keep her alive until she menstruated and was returned to her husband's bed. One who had sex with a lower-caste man was thrown to the dogs – literally.

Since women could not attain *moksha*, they were forbidden to learn Sanskrit or to read the Vedas. Husbands could beat their wives in accordance with a sixteenth-century text: "a woman, a drum, a dog, and a slave can be beaten."[14] But elsewhere Manu warned men that the gods would reject their offerings if they abused women, and he taught reverence for wives:

> Where women are honoured, Gods reside fain.
> Where they are not honoured,
> all religious ceremonies go in vain.
>   The teacher is ten times more venerable
> than a sub-teacher,
> the father a hundred times more than the teacher,
> but a mother a thousand times more than the father.

Around the first century CE the two great epics of Indian culture, the *Mahabharata* and the *Ramayana* of Valmiki, received final form, completing the literary base of Brahminism. The importance of these books to Indian life cannot be overestimated; they are as essential to Hindu culture as the Torah to Judaism or the Bible to Christianity. Like the Vedas, they record earlier events and myths, but in classical Sanskrit (derived from archaic Sanskrit), the elite language of India. Both string religious rules, commentary, myths, and legends on a narrative: the *Mahabharata* (of which the *Bhagavad-Gita* is part) treats war; the *Ramayana*, gender. Both guide religious and social life. The *Mahabharata* teaches:

> The wife is half the man,
> the best of friends,
> the root of the three ends of life,
> and of all that will help him in the other world.
> With a wife a man does mighty deeds . . .

With a wife man finds courage . . .
A wife is the safest refuge . . .
A man aflame with sorrow in his soul,
or sick with disease,
finds comfort in his wife,
as a man parched with heat
finds relief in water.
Even a man in the grip of rage
will not be harsh to a woman,
remembering that on her depend
the joys of love, happiness, and virtue.
For woman is the everlasting field,
in which the Self is born.

While this teaching does not see women as being Selves, it is at least respectful.

In the same period a great Sanskrit poet, Kalidasa, wrote a play, *Shakuntala,* which fixed the image of the Good Hindu Woman for future generations.[15] We have no record of the actual lives of women in these periods, only these stories, which are still vivid and instructive to Indian women. We may take them as describing actual women, who modelled their behaviour on them. *Shakuntala* depicts a woman who remains loyal to an abusive husband, as in the medieval European tale of Patient Griselde.

Out deer-hunting, King Dusyanta spies Shakuntala, the foster daughter of a sage. They fall instantly in love, discuss it for two acts, then consummate their passion. The king gives Shakuntala a ring as a pledge of *gandharva,* marriage, then returns to court. Shakuntala has adventures, including a bath in a river, where she loses the ring, and an encounter with a hermit, who dooms her to be forgotten until her lover sees the ring he gave her. When her foster father realizes she is pregnant, he sends her to the king, who does not recognize her. Shakuntala, in tears, is carried to a "golden peak" where penitents atone for sins. A fisherman discovers the ring inside a fish and takes it to the king, who immediately recovers his memory. He grieves, but he's busy. Later, he goes to the peak and sees a little boy wrestling with a lion cub. Told the child is Shakuntala's, he is overcome by joy. The reunited family lives happily ever after.[16]

Brahmin ambivalence about women pervades the play. Shakuntala's girlhood friend laments that their bodily maturing turns them into sexual objects; her father grieves that maturity turns the most precious being in his life into a social burden and a threat. Commenting that girls must be married young to avoid the unspeakable stigma attached to an unmarried mother, he describes the obedience and humility expected of wives in all circumstances. Shakuntala embodies culturally ideal female virtue: she is beautiful, fragile, clinging, sensual but faithful, innocent, a virgin, protected, and pious. Sexual experience transforms her into a grief-stricken sufferer, enduring but never reproachful, raising a beautiful son despite her circumstances. Physically frail (watering flowers tires her!), she is morally powerful. When her husband falls at her feet in remorse, she replies that the fault is not his (he is faultless), but hers in a former life.

Shakuntala and the epic *Ramayana*, which offers a similar role model for women, are primarily concerned with constructing female gender – teaching women how to act.[17] The *Mahabharata* focuses on constructing male gender. One exemplary story tells of a wife who sits with her sleeping husband's head in her lap, watching over him and her baby, who is playing in front of the fire. The baby wanders near the fire, but the woman does not move lest she disturb her sleeping lord. When the child actually enters the flames, she prays to Agni to keep the baby from harm. And Agni rewards her wifely devotion by keeping the child, sitting amid the flames, unscathed.

Indian culture did grant women sexuality.[18] Sexuality was the highest approved pleasure, and a man was duty bound to satisfy his wife/wives as well as himself. Yet Indian writers often call women's sexuality unbridled, ever-present, all-demanding, and insatiable, suggesting that men feared what they desired. Indian culture produced the most important erotic work ever written, Vatsayana's *Kamasutra*, a sex manual and social history aware of how gender is constructed and of ways to satisfy women's bodies erotically.

Marriage was the main fact of life for Indian women.[19] Indissoluble even if unconsummated, it was also monogamous. Rich, powerful men could have more than one wife; ordinary men could not, unless the first bore no children or at least no sons. Some Himalayan hill people were polyandrous. In some periods, widows could remarry, but they lost rights to property inherited from husbands.

The only free Indian women in this period were prostitutes. They were not bound by rules of caste, class, or modesty. In literature, prostitutes are beautiful, cultivated, accomplished, wealthy, of high rank, the envy of wives and the inevitable victors in rivalries between them. Real prostitutes were often poor and lower class. Wifehood was the only path to respectability, but courtesans were the only women likely to be educated. Their rigorous training in the mastery of sixty-four arts, creative talents, and intellectual skills, including facility in Sanskrit, led the *Kamasutra* to urge kings and learned men to honour and praise courtesans, seek their favour, and treat them well. State or court (depending on the period) protected and supervised them and their houses; treatises recommended them as spies and secret agents.

In 320 CE the Guptas took control of an empire half the size of the Mauryan and set out to expand it. Their reign was the classical age of Indian culture, producing great poetry, plays, sculptures, and cave temples like those at Ajanta and Ellora. But women's rights were increasingly curtailed as Brahminism and the Laws of Manu became ever more dominant. Buddhism and Jainism faded after the seventh century, and women's only path to single life vanished. No record of female infanticide exists in India, but most scholars believe it was common in this period and after. No one wanted daughters, who were discouraged from asceticism and from studying religion, music, or art, now the mark of courtesans. Women and poor men did not learn Sanskrit. Women were to be procreators and servants. What women felt in response to such extreme stifling may have been reflected in two new religions – Tantrism and the Bhakti cult.

Through the wars, whatever dynasties came and went over the centuries, people in back streets of cities and in the countryside still worshipped goddesses. Shrines to goddesses of fertility or healing are scattered over India, drawing thousands of devotees. The word goddess *(devi)* is still the highest accolade given the good woman, the good mother. Modern Hindu films still feature men falling to their knees before their *devis*.

In classical Hindu tradition, the female principle animates the universe and provides its creative energy. Called Shakti, it is embodied in the consorts of the three main Hindu gods, Brahma the creator, Vishnu the preserver, and

Shiva the destroyer. Energy needs direction, which requires knowledge, so the female principle is also consciousness or knowledge. In Devi worship, Shiva and Shakti form the eternal couple, their emblems the lingam (penis, signified by a raised finger) and the yoni (vulva, signified by a circle of thumb and finger). Shakti has many avatars: Saraswati, the goddess of wisdom and learning; Lakshmi, of domestic happiness and wealth; Radha, of success and destiny; Lalita, of playfulness; and Kameshvari, of lust. Her most powerful and well-known manifestations are Parvati, who is nurturing, peaceful, and domesticated; Menaka, the intellect and consciousness of the universe; and Durga, the invincible, who rides a tiger (Indian soldiers still cry "Jai Durga Ki" – victory to Durga – as they enter combat).

One aspect of Shakti bred another: Kali, the destroyer and liberator. Depicted as black, withered, hideous, her bloody tongue hanging out, and wearing a garland of skulls, she embodies lust, bloody sacrifices, and intoxicants. She castrates and punishes, kills her consort, and dances over his corpse in fiendish glee. Kali reflects men's fear of the women they dispossessed and subjugated, and women's rage at the fact. Her followers founded Tantrism, worship of a cruel, lustful, orgiastic, psychedelic female principle. It affected both Hinduism and Buddhism.

The Bhakti movement was democratic, inspired by the idea of a compassionate Buddha, a teacher and saviour, and by a passage in the *Bhagavad-Gita* in which Krishna (an incarnation of Vishnu) declared his immanence in every believer, whom he will rescue, out of mutual love, from the eternal cycle of rebirth without the priestly intervention. Bhaktism promised salvation to untouchables and to women lacking knowledge of Sanskritic or ritual. The compassionate god could be worshipped directly at home, so women could be the family religous guide. Before, they could only fast; now they prayed and ritually bathed, fed, and worshipped the household gods.

Bhakti literature, written in the vernacular, inspired great devotional poetry in Tamil, Hindi, and other languages. Teachers led sects that sang and discussed together. Women drawn to the religion became teachers and poets; the devotional songs of Mira Bai, the most notable female devotee of Krishna, are sung in Indian homes today. The movement swept the subcontinent and, from the eleventh century on, was the strongest barrier to the proselytizing zeal of Muslims, who were appearing in increasing numbers in India. Islam, an egalitarian religion (for males), appealed to low-caste Indians. Bhaktism kept many Hindu.

Another sect that arose at this time was Devadasi, or "Slave of the Gods." Devadasis, found all over India but mainly in the south, saw the god in his temple as an earthly king with wives, courtiers, statesmen, ministers, and attendant prostitutes. The last were hereditary professionals (except for eldest daughters sometimes given by Brahmins) who kept the god happy with dance, song, and devotion. They also pleasured the god's "courtiers," male worshippers who paid the temple a fee. Despite (or because of) tales of orgiastic behaviour, they were popular with worshippers, who often gave large gifts directly to the Devadasis. The profession was outlawed by the British in 1947 on moral grounds. Prostitution was the only occupation in patriarchal society that allowed women, who were used sexually in any case, to support themselves and to be educated and autonomous. That women can maintain independence only by prostitution tells us little about them but much about men.[20]

CHAPTER 6

A MILITARISTIC STATE: MEXICO

THE FIRST SETTLERS IN THE AMERICAS trekked all the way from Asia across the Bering Strait or sailed from Polynesia to North America about 30,000 years ago. The journey probably took thousands of years: some groups settled along the way; others pushed farther south. The Olmec, the first southern settlers we know of, lived on the Gulf Coast and Guatemala, had pictorial script, a calendar based on solar and lunar cycles, and, long before Europe, a number system including zero. Olmec culture lasted from around 1500 to 400 BCE and influenced the Maya. Another people built the great city of Teotihuacan in central Mexico, which flourished from 100 to 750 CE. Pyramids line its great avenues, built perhaps for their first deity, the goddess Coatlicue, and, later, the plumed-serpent Quetzalcoatl, a peaceful god to whom they sacrificed butterflies and snakes. Teotihuacan was wrecked by invaders about the time two other Mexican societies collapsed from drought, erosion, and war.

Maya followed the Olmec on the Gulf Coast, in Guatemala, and on the Yucatan peninsula. They too built pyramids, developed a writing system, created art, and advanced mathematics and astronomy. About the eleventh century CE the Toltec, a warlike people from central Mexico, gradually penetrated the Yucatan and assimilated with them. Like other Central Americans, they worshipped Quetzalcoatl and a god, Tezcalipoca, "smoking mirror," who required human sacrifice. The fierce Toltec invented a game, *tlachtli*, played on a court with a rubber ball, in which losers were sacrificed. Toltec women were as tough as the men, active political leaders and soldiers until the eleventh century. In a 1008 battle, Toltec women fought alongside men until they were all killed, even the elderly and the children. A Codex (a painted scroll recording history in pictures resembling modern comic strips) shows a Toltec princess being insulted by men in a town in 1038. Returning with a party of warriors, she imprisons the men and has their hearts torn from their chests in sacrifice. Throughout these events, the princess is egged on by priests.

The Aztec, kin to the Toltec, were the last Asian arrivals in the valley of Mexico. They too recorded their history in Codices, four of which remain from ancient times (with some new ones). Symbols carved on buildings, temples, and graves preserve Aztec myths and beliefs. The Aztec kept extensive economic records. The Spanish later wrote uncomprehending reports on this civilization.

The Aztec left Aztlan in north Mexico around 820 CE to migrate south, led by four chiefs and a priestess in charge of the emblems of their god, Huitzilopochtli, the hum-mingbird. Living in matrilineal kin-groups (their word for "great-grandmother" means "founder of the lineage"), they farmed communally held land allocated by elders, raising corn, beans, squash, and chilis. They hunted and ate guinea pigs, dogs, and wild and domesticated ducks. They had no domesticated draft animals. Early Aztec society was some-what egalitarian, with a governing council of chiefs, two of whom were named by each lineage – one for war, the other for religion and social matters. Titles, such as "father and mother of the people" and "snake woman," suggest that women were chiefs. Like Andeans, the Aztec world was divided by sex, and the sexes were equal and complementary.

Women were chiefs, priestesses, healers, farmers, and vendors, with the same rights and use of land as men. Linguistic evidence from Nahuatl, the Aztec language, shows that, at this time, the highest Aztec god was androgy-nous. Their myths and religion involved gender parallelism based in the belief that, for fertility and prosperity, both sexes must work together. Female figurines from Mexico's central plateau often emphasize the head, not the body. Male figurines do not appear until later. Even after rank emerges, women had rich grave goods.

The Aztec kept moving and entered the valley of Mexico, then dotted with lakes, in 1253. On the shore of the largest lake, Texcoco, several small states of Toltec descent – Azcapotzalco, Culhuacan, and Texcoco – waged constant war. A Codex records that the Aztec halted outside Tula, the Toltec capital, where women ruled, because of a conflict between Malinalxoch and Huitzilopochtli, a sister and brother, both probably chiefs. Huitzilopochtli wanted to invade Tula, but Malinalxoch wanted to settle where they were. Huitzilopochtli urged his followers to abandon Malinalxoch, calling her a sorceress who used supernatural powers over animals to control the clan. He wanted his men to show "the valour of arms and their courage" by conquering Tula. What happened next is open to question. Either Huitzilopochtli and his men invaded Tula, and Malinalxoch remained behind with her followers and founded a community on the site. Or (a version suppressed because of the conquerors' shame) Malinalxoch was killed by Huitzilopochtli's men. Her son Copil remained with the settlers. Later, Copil went to Chapultepec to avenge his mother and was also killed; his heart was buried on the site of the new Aztec capital, Tenochtitlan. It seems that males were challenging the sexual equality of earlier days by force of arms.

The Aztec arrived in Chapultepec in 1248 and settled there. They were not yet primarily warriors, a necessary skill in this territory, and signed on as mercenaries for the city-states to learn soldiering. They asked Coxcox, the chief of Culhuacan, to marry his daughter to their chief; he agreed. The Aztec record that the god Huitzilopochtli (Aztec priests) ordered the girl sacrificed. When her father arrived for the wedding, he found the priest dressed in his daughter's skin. He attacked them, defeating and enslaving the Aztec. The Codex explains that the Aztec killed the girl because the god wanted to create a goddess of discord or war; dominating the women they married from neighbouring peoples, they believed, would guarantee dominance over the entire population.[1] Later, in 1376, the Culhuacans let another princess marry an Aztec; her son, Acamapichtli, became the first Aztec king.

In 1325 the Aztec settled on a swampy island in Lake Texcoco and built it up into fertile farmland and a majestic capital city, Tenochtitlan.[2] They transformed themselves from what one scholar calls "belligerent agriculturalists" to an "organization of priest-warriors."[3] The clans in the central plateau were constantly at war, which perhaps contributed to their shift to patrilineality, recorded in a Codex describing the father as "the source of the lineage" and defining the ideal father as one who rears and teaches others, stores up for others, cares for his assets, and lives a model life. The mother "has children and suckles them . . . is sincere, diligent, vigilant, agile, energetic in work, watchful, solicitous, and full of anxiety." Apprehensive, careful, thrifty, and constantly at work, she serves others.

Tenochtitlan was the centre for twenty federated tribes, ruled by a council of elders, four of whom had executive authority to judge, execute, and mediate between commoners and the military. Its first chief speaker, named in 1376, was called "the father and mother of the people," and his second-in-command, "Snake Woman," but all the officials were male. Lineages paid tribute to a priest-warrior elite: gender parallelism was now only symbolic. The small elite ramified in time as elite men, with many wives, produced many children, and a noble class emerged, often ranked by the mothers' status. Elite succession passed through women, though children inherited from both parents. Virginity was a primary concern in elite brides – a mark of patriarchy.

Under King Itzcoatl (1429–40), the Aztec became militaristic, allying with, then overrunning, neighbours, seizing their land and giving it to men in the royal lineage. Military leaders promised titles to all valorous fighters, but only the king's kin got them. After an important victory over the Tepanec, the Aztec altered their political structure: succession would now pass in the male line of the royal family and be determined by four lords of the royal lineage. Claiming ownership of all land, the king stepped up production to provide for military needs.

The new state had three classes: an elite (royals, priests, priestesses, and military leaders), a middle class of merchants and traders, and a lower class of craftworkers and peasants (the producers). Off the social ladder were prisoners of war, criminals who broke Aztec law, and an urban underclass of gamblers, prostitutes, sleazy merchants, and marginals. Government-imposed regional crop specialization kept localities from being independent. In areas where Aztec control was strong, they set up a strict tax system, giving taxpaying men, the only ones who owned land, the cacao beans needed to patronize the markets. Men who lacked the beans were easily detected; the punishment was sacrifice by having their hearts cut out of their bodies.

Itzcoatl changed the ideology of the Aztec state and rewrote Aztec history, destroying most of the earlier Codices. Historians think he also commissioned a new mythology justifying his wars of conquest and his new political structure. He and his priests placed a single god at the apex of a hierarchy of male gods.[4] The Aztec claimed that Huitzilopochtli chose them for a special mission – to unify all states in service to the sun, which was kept in its rounds by feeding on the blood of captives of "flowery wars" (a euphemism similar to the one calling nuclear missiles "peace-keepers").

When the state took over all the land, kin-groups were dispossessed and dissolved. Farming-herding women had to find other ways to live. Older women became matchmakers, healers, midwives, and embroiderers, who were highly valued (only high-status people were permitted to wear

embroidery). Married embroiderers were paid independently of their husbands. Widows paid no taxes if they remained
single. But the main job open to such women was prostitution. Aztec women were eventually denied participation in
religious rites, unable any longer to serve the gods or to enter
an afterlife which, like the Norse Valhalla, was a privileged
realm for warriors alone. The only women who could enter
it were those who died in childbirth. In the early Aztec state,
childbearing was seen as heroism as great as soldiery.

After shifting to patrilineality, the Aztec barred women
from inheritance. The only way a woman could improve her
fortunes was to become a wife or concubine to a higher-
ranking man; children of elite fathers were nobles despite
low-class mothers. Division of labour by sex had long been
a feature of Aztec life: codices show men teaching boys to
fish, cultivate, and work metal, and women teaching girls to
weave, tend babies, and cook. Women were also physicians,
priestesses, and local merchants; lower-class women farmed
and hunted. Children were taught gender roles from birth:
newborn boys were shown a shield with four arrows, presented four times to the sun, and told: "You are a quechol
bird; your home, when you have seen the light of the world,
is only a nest . . . you are predestined to delight the sun with
the blood of your enemies." Girl babies, shown spindles and
shuttles, were told: "You must be like the heart in the body.
You must not leave the home . . . You must be like embers
in the hearth." Similar conceptions figured at death: warriors were burned on a pyre with slaves; women were buried
with spinning and weaving tools.

To fulfil their mission of domination, the Aztec
arranged wars with kings of subject tribes, who sent warriors
out to meet them but did not really try to win. Their

unsupported soldiers were easily captured and taken to the temple for sacrifice. Their kings sat hidden from view by banks of flowers, watching them mount the temple steps, waiting to enjoy the privilege of banqueting on their flesh afterwards.

Another means the Aztec used to attain dominance over neighbouring states was diplomatic marriages between their elite women and the chiefs of other groups. Aztec princesses married to cement alliances and guarantee payment of tribute were their husbands' principal wives, and they passed their lands and status on to their children. Nothing sufficed, though: the Aztec had to keep on making war to reap human hearts for sacrifice. The preferred victims were war captives brought to the capital and forced to climb the pyramid, where priests waited to cut out their hearts. Aztec religion did not just condone this act; it demanded it. The priests taught that god clamoured for human hearts. Blood sacrifice was "the central concern of the Aztec state," and the flint knife used to cut out hearts the ultimate principle of their universe.[5]

Elite privileges included eating from sacrificed bodies and keeping huge game parks for hunting wild game. As in Europe, the nobles punished commoners for "poaching" on these preserves. Elite children of both sexes were educated as priests and bureaucrats, but only boys attended military school, which held a long male initiation and stressed physical work for the community. After school, boys visited a "house of singing and revelry" for sex, then were graduated to youth houses, where they took their place in a ranked hierarchy. Once a boy took a prisoner in war, he was given a share of tribute and accepted as a commander in war councils. They played *tlachtli*, the Toltec game, and sacrificed the losers.

Aztec soldiers lived the sexual politics they were taught.

Wherever they went, they raped local women and forced them into a barracks brothel. Men captured in war were sacrificed; captured women were enslaved. Men who reached Aztec standards of manhood were granted the right to abuse and degrade women, but those who did not were abused. Boys were pressured to become soldiers: fathers killed sons who were insufficiently warlike, and women mocked boys who had not taken a captive. Many boys committed suicide.

Some women protested Aztec values by publicly mourning during festivities for men about to go to war and by crying publicly – all they dared to do – for sacrificial victims. Women of an Aztec ally whose men had to fight beside them "flaunted their backsides" at Aztec emissaries and so enraged them that the Aztec broke the alliance. But there was little freedom for anyone in this society. Elite girls were guarded, forbidden to walk outdoors by themselves lest they lose their virginity, and removed from school at sixteen, once they had learned to cook and weave. Marriages were arranged; after the marriage feast, the couple went to the groom's family home, where the girl's skirt was tied to the boy's blanket. In her husband's house, she was subject to her mother-in-law until she produced four children. Men could divorce barren wives, and women could divorce husbands for physical abuse, desertion, or non-support.

Young widows were encouraged to remarry and produce more children; some became their brothers-in-law's concubines. Women were executed for adultery, murder, rebellion, or cross-dressing. As usual, commoner women had harder but freer lives. Commoners were burdened by overwhelming taxes and field work, and women also had to support their families. One job was processing maize – arduously shelling, stone-grinding, and washing it, then making and cooking tortillas. Women wove, and they prepared foods for sale at market. They had less range than men: a Spaniard listed thirty-five male trades, but only fifteen female trades.

While elites pursued their "holy" mission, a strong mercantile class developed its own religious and judicial organization. It traced descent matrilineally, and women were prominent within it. They produced feather goods and textiles, wich were important in long-distance trade. Women of subjugated groups made cotton cloth, the main part of tribute payments to the Aztec; the Chief Speaker honoured guests and rewarded inferiors with cloth made by Aztec women. Rich merchants threatened the state, which limited their activities and barred them from public office, but it was too dependent on them to oppress them further. Only merchant-class women could get rich, buy land, and take up their fathers' trade.

The hegemony of the priest-warriors reached its height during the reign of Moctezuma I, around 1440. Kin-groups had lost any voice in state affairs, and nobles were swallowing the lands of common folk, who were increasingly enslaved for debt or publicly executed for drunkenness or theft. Commoner women could no longer rise through sexuality – only children with two noble parents could now be part of the nobility. At the end, nobles began to eat the common people themselves: Moctezuma fattened young boys to be served with squash to his lords and priests.

By the time the Spanish arrived in the early sixteenth century, the Aztec elite was completely estranged. Neighbouring people resented the Aztec primarily for abusing their women, but also for their obsession with human sacrifice. Historians marvel at the ease and rapidity with which a small band of Spanish adventurers conquered civilizations as sophisticated as Inca Peru and Mexico – Peru in six years, Mexico in three. Cortez had only 600 men, seventeen horses, and ten cannon; Tenochtitlan held 200,000 people. The *conquistadors* did have stronger armour, a fleet, cannon, and horses, they were ruthless, and they received reinforcements from Spain. But Spain sent little aid to the tiny force facing native armies on their own terrain. Typically, historians saw the Spanish victory as proof of the superiority of European culture and the white race.

But the victory was due to Mexican hatred for the Aztec. "The army that conquered Tenochtitlan was really an Indian army captained by a few Spaniards."[6] The poor Indians did not suspect that their new conquerors would be equally cruel and would eradicate their way of life. The Spaniards brought greed, notions of private property, and a religion – Roman Catholicism – that justified conquest and domination by a new elite. These conquerors took the land and used women much as the old elite did, turning indigenous men into peasants.[7]

CONCLUSION

AN ANALYSIS OF
THE STATE

W HEN LOUIS XIV OF FRANCE DECLARED "L'état, c'est
moi," he said what many heads of state assume – that
they personally incarnate the state. Because people revere the
countries where they live, they are often willing to sacrifice
their lives for them. They may also revere their head of state;
certainly, they are encouraged to do so by state propaganda.
But heads of state are almost never primarily concerned with
the well-being of the people; their main interest is maintaining or extending their power, and that of their family, clique,
party, or class.

The state is the physical embodiment of an idea, patriarchy, an ideology based on the lie that some people are superior to others according to divine will. They are not superi-
or in a given attribute, but altogether better, humanly superior, and therefore entitled to more status, resources, and

power than others. Only inherent superiority can give one person or group the right to dictate to others, execute people, make war, and suppress dissent.

Democracy developed in an attempt to curb the worst characteristics of states. It is vaunted to hold that all people are equal (and thus to be non-patriarchal), but no democracy ever existed that in fact did so. The first democracy (Athens) held a handful of citizen men to be superior to women, slaves, and men who did not own property. The United States, founded explicitly on the ground that all men were created equal, not only omitted women from the human race but operated as a slave-owning state.

Democracies claim that they do not subscribe to the lie of patriarchy but hold everyone equal. A society of equals votes for one man to be held a limited superior for a limited time, in order to govern not as a divine appointee, but as the people's choice. But patriarchal thinking, with its idolization of power and belief in transcendence, permeates all societies and cannot simply be ignored. Power cliques develop in patriarchies, and soon enough become supreme, even over the elected governor. In our time, these cliques are multinational corporations. Politics cannot change unless patriarchy ceases to be the primary structure of our thought.

Patriarchy insists that some people are better than others because its primary reason for existing is to assert that men are superior to women. But because this claim is a falsehood, it is regularly challenged. States built on lies are insecure and are easily threatened; leaders must endlessly propagandize, insisting their lies are truths.

Early rulers based their claim to superiority in relation with a god. In every early state we examined, a high god was placed above other gods before a man or a family or a clique asserted its supremacy. At that time, the matricentric tradition still existed, and most people believed that the divine was located in women. Men co-opted the female by asserting a relationship with a goddess (Sargon) or a divine female (Egyptian rulers even married a woman or their own daughters to gain legitimacy). After patrilineality was well established, men could claim direct descent from a god, as the early Chinese rulers did. Early Hebrew priests claimed a direct relationship with god to legitimate the male lineage of their class, a ruling class.

Once the principle of male superiority was generally accepted, men no longer required the aegis of a female. At this point, soldier-kings became the rulers, drawing men to support them by asserting male solidarity. Patriarchy was conceived as a revolution against female domination; men pulled together against a sex described as inferior in order to usurp women's powers. But they did not really want women's powers: they did not want the responsibility for producing and raising children and the daily work of sustaining men. They wanted symbolic powers – ownership of children and women.

The assertion of female inferiority prepares the ground for men's subjection, because the principle of superiority ramifies endlessly. If one man can be superior to another, the second man may also be superior to a third, and so on. If men can be superior to women, some men can be superior to other men. Male solidarity attempts to blur that fact, to assert that "down deep" all men are brothers. But this ideal is far from realization in this world – men are united only when they are opposed to women. Male superiority is the psychological core of patriarchy, but its political and economic purpose is the subjection of other men. Men have regularly rebelled against one ruler or another, but have never rebelled against the principle of superiority – the only rebellion that can end the injustice and misery that arises from invidious distinctions – or generic discrimination.

Patriarchy makes men unhappy, but degrades women.[1] Every early state passed laws regulating women alone; the laws of these states resemble each other despite their separation in time and space, and such laws grow harsher as time moves on. Perhaps it is a matter of *quos laeserunt et odorunt,* "those we hurt, we hate," as Seneca wrote. The most striking fact about the laws regarding women is that they all prescribe similar roles for women. This commonality teaches us nothing about women, but much about men.

Early states required that people submit to a new bondage. Given the relative freedom of life in early kin-groups, one may wonder why people did so. But bondage itself was not new. Clan life was tightly bound. Everyone lived the same way, by the same means – farming, gathering, herding, crafts. Although they lived communally and in relative equality, some people were surely more talented or wiser than others, or were natural leaders whose voices carried further than others'. These people were *ad hoc* leaders (*ad hoc* leadership remains a characteristic of Amerindian societies: the one who is best at a given thing leads the activity; someone else leads the next activity). It is a small step from that to permanent leadership. And people free within a community were not free of it: they probably saw themselves as clan members more than as individuals. Everyone was absolutely bound by clan rules and shared in its rewards; there was no way to live outside the clan or to evade its rules.

The first chiefs – female and male – governed by consensus, which is still a common form in simpler societies. The first steps into dominance were slow and hesitant, and were probably resisted. What caused those steps is questionable: crowding, perhaps, or farming, which involves a kind of ownership of land. Perhaps the priests in a society decided they should dictate to others how they should live. Perhaps a prosperous segment of a clan was inspired by dreams of power. Something propelled men to raise their hands against each other – against their mothers and sisters and lovers.

Once war emerged, every ugliness happened. The frequency and viciousness of war in the period historians call "the cult of frightfulness" spread the new doctrine wherever it occurred. To be bound in such a situation might feel secure, just as Africans often bound themselves to others during the hideous years when slave traders were kidnapping wildly on the continent. War subdued most clans. Sumerian scholars, judging by the ration lists, believe that almost everyone outside the elite in Sumerian society was a bound worker, not free to leave or to choose any but the assigned tasks. That this bondage was harsher than the old bondedness is shown by the frequency with which men (mainly) ran away. (Men could find ways to live alone, or join other clans, or, most likely, sign up as soldiers in the service of another lord; women, who often have children, could not, and had nowhere to go that would not make them prey to some man.) Bondage is tyranny, but it was reached by gradual steps, and people probably thought, as most of us do today, that the way things are is the way they always were.

The first laws we know about that make females inferior are those of Uruk (Sumer). These laws list a new crime – adultery – that only women could commit. And in Sumer, a new occupation – prostitution – is devised by the temple priests. The coincidence (in the same culture, if not at the same moment) of an assertion of female inferiority, the criminalization of free sexuality in women, and the use of female sexuality in commercial transactions benefiting men demonstrates the new male vision of women: as sexual objects to be possessed and used by men.

Of course female sexuality is important to men; it is their main link to adult women, their reason for dependency on women. But it is not the only reason. Statistics show that, worldwide, women today work far harder than men, essentially maintaining them. With the exception of a tiny elite class, women have always worked. Their work supported Athenian and Hebrew men, for example. And early laws governed working women, limiting the amount of money a woman might handle or the kind of work she might do. No laws I know of require women to work, yet it was clearly mandatory that they do so in many societies: consider the Chinese scholars' rage at women taking leisure for study and play, or the belief of Athenian men that it was women's duty to run the home factory, or the insistence of Hebrew men that women do all the work while they sit in the city gate. Later societies had laws stating that women's earnings belonged to their husbands. The other area of women's existence that men most regulated was their sexuality, which was also appropriated. If women's work was owed to men, so were their bodies.

All the societies we have examined create a legal double standard, invented to bring women under men's control in all areas of life and to forbid any independent action on women's part. There are differences among states: in Egypt and Babylonia, women for a long time retained the right to do business in the world and the right to inherit and function as priestesses. But almost all female rights vanished in

Assyria, where law treated women strictly as property. And only in Yang-shao culture and that of the early oracle-bone inscriptions is there any sign of Chinese women ever being equal with men; whatever the reality was, no record exists of Chinese women with rights in business or inheritance.

Every state made it dangerous for a woman to go out of the house alone, either by law or by custom. Assyrian law implied that women alone on the street were seeking sexual business – as if that were the only motivation for a woman to go out – and were treated accordingly. As far as I know, the Chinese had no law forbidding women from going out, but the custom of constricting women to the domestic compound was utterly binding (and later, their feet were bound). So it was also in Athens (where women were reproached for merely looking out their doors), among the Hebrews, and, later, in Islam. In India I have met women who are forbidden to leave their domestic compound. In other societies, the threat of rape hung over any woman who ventured out alone; women were blamed for their own rape in every society we have examined and they could be killed for it. Freedom of movement was either specifically forbidden or freighted with peril for women.

It was even more dangerous for women to take charge of their own reproduction by using abortifacients: this initiative was treason in Babylon and Assyria. The importance of abortion and birth control cannot be overstated. Because of female physiognomy and men's generally greater physical strength (and in patriarchies, moral authority), men can rape women. Where men can rape, women cannot control their own bodies without access to birth control and abortion. Wise women in most societies probably had some knowledge of birth control and how to cause abortions. To deny women the right to use it is to deny them the right to a will of their own.

Once the female body was firmly in control, laws could offer refinements. In religious states, women, once the main avenues to goddesses, were deemed incapable of the highest spirituality and excluded from participating in religious rites. In societies that worshipped ancestors, like China, women were denied a place in the family pantheon until they had borne a son. Only males could memorialize ancestors in religious rituals in Athens and other states. When private property became common, women's lack of power to maintain the ancestors was invoked in denying them property rights. In time, control over property was denied even to elite women. Women lacked so many rights that they came to seem inherently weak, their failures caused not by law but by identity: a woman was inadequate *by nature*. So it made sense, then, to deny women the right to learn Sanskrit – they are incapable of *moksha* in any case – or Latin, or to exclude them from schools. It probably seemed natural for Athens to deny women citizenship. Since women could not sit for civil service exams in China, it made no sense to educate them. Confucius wrote that virtue arose from education, but that applied only to men.

The states we have discussed were distant from each other in time and space; when they arose, they often had no contact with or knowledge of each other, and their origins ranged from the mid-fourth millennium BCE to the first millennium CE. Yet in all these states, men passed similar laws regarding women: all these laws enforced women's dependency, inability to act independently, obedience to men, sexual slavery, and fidelity.

The clichés still current about male attitudes towards

women are visible in the laws regulating female behaviour in early states. Above all, men wanted to control women's sexual and reproductive capacities. They even denied the female contribution to the fetus (e.g., Aristotle and European thinkers) and taught that female sexual pleasure depended on the penis (e.g., Western thinking at least from Freud on).[2] These assumptions almost reverse the facts: the female contribution to the fetus is far greater than the male's, and most females do not require a penile organ for sexual pleasure. We must question the reasons for men's insistent concern with female reproduction.

The kinds of laws passed in the earliest states are enacted over and over again in later societies. An important motivation behind new forms of scientific or political thought is to subjugate or exclude women. New religions, in contrast, welcome women, who join in throngs; but once the religion is established, it subjugates or excludes women. Given the degree of male will and power exercised against women throughout history, it is amazing that women remain a force to contend with.

Historians often debate whether women have more rights and capacities in religious or secular, Catholic or Protestant, capitalist or communist, or militaristic or humanitarian states. Such debates assume that the oppression of women is incidental to another aspect of culture. It is not: it is primary, whatever the agenda of a culture. All early states deprived women of their status as human beings and of the rights men possessed. Religious states like India used religion to justify this constriction; China's guiding secular philosophy, Confucianism, constricted women as much as India's religious laws. Militarism tends to diminish women's rights whenever it arises: military men take power by virtue of their accomplishments, not their birth, and do not need women to legitimate them. Moreover, soldiering is a brutal occupation which, like some male initiations, involves suppressing the emotions associated with women. Yet among the militaristic Aztec, citizen women had more rights than citizen women in India or China. The women of militaristic Sparta had more rights than the women of humanistic Athens. "Democratic" states use reason to accomplish the same end.

Whatever leaders claim (then and now), their first (and often, only) concern is maintaining their power. But no elite or leader – not even a twentieth-century dictator with huge complexes of technology at his command – has monolithic power. Alliances and enmities continually shift; new bases of power arise within and outside the state. States are ripped by constant struggle. Maintaining power is a full-time job. The existence of an elite guarantees perpetual conflict. Resentment of elite privileges leads to discontent, subversion, and rebellion. Elitehood also creates paranoia: the superiority claimed by elites is a falsehood that must continually be reasserted and that others resent. Possession of privileges also inculcates fear in those who possess them. The superstitious belief that more control can be enough and can make one transcendent (impregnable) leads worried chiefs to try to increase their territories and control. Awareness of these facts inspired socialist thought, but socialism failed because it could not break with the idea of male superiority.

No people is subdued once and forever; subordination must be reinforced continually by propaganda, bribery, and force. To awe people into submission, leaders of states and institutions invent ceremonies celebrating their gods and their origins which explain and vindicate elite dominance.

Those who believe these myths and ideologies attribute a group's success in war to its god's powers. Leaders subvert kin-groups by massacre, dispersal, or co-option, appointing members to collect tribute or govern at a low level, and tacitly allowing them to enrich themselves out of their kin's labour.

Both men and women collude in their oppression when they accept their society's myths, but many believe the myths and propaganda teaching male superiority. Laws forcing women into marriage by denying them any other avenue of support, or allowing them access to power only through sons, co-opt their loyalty. Women may even accept constriction if it puts them in the superior group, makes them "ladies" in worlds that despise women.

Unlike men, women have not, until the feminist movement, had sex-based solidarity. This isolation is not accidental; solidarity is what men have most feared in women. To prevent its formation, every state we know about separated women from each other, imprisoning them in the home, where they were under the direct surveillance of husbands or kin. When women began to ally with each other and to politic during the French Revolution, men barred female assembly. In India today, men suspiciously eye women who gather at wells or pumps. Women are afraid to speak to each other, although no law forbids it. Simply making men central, by making them necessary to survival, is enough to set women against each other.

By the end of the process of state formation, women were first and foremost not members of families, lineages, or classes but a caste, a group one was born into and could not change, a fate that determined their role in life. State formation forced new living arrangements and initiated ideas that pervaded political, economic, and social life, as well as religion, morality, and art. Egalitarian clans were supplanted by classes with unequal shares of the national production. Their rulers occupied a new realm, the public realm or political world, which was concerned above all with power and wealth and had the power to determine right. To challenge them was treason. The elite story of its past was called *history*. It changed when a new elite overthrew the old.

After state formation, no one was autonomous: rulers depended on their subjects' loyalty; members of the hierarchy depended on the tolerance of those above them and the obedience of those beneath them. Although men defined women and peasants as dependants and taught that their duty was to support their betters, men, in truth, were highly dependent on women, and elites have always lived on the work of peasants. After state formation, only people of rank had rights; the lower classes had mainly obligations. They were bound to their superiors, but not the reverse. State formation created new words – king, noble, royal, peasant, slave, serf, prostitute, concubine, treason, adultery – and a new world.

PART THREE

GOD, GLORY, AND DELUSIONS OF GRANDEUR

BELIEF IN HUMAN SUPERIORITY requires a belief in transcendence, the notion that some human beings can rise above their own humanity. Such intimations of immortality are consistently accompanied by belief in transcendent deities (always male), who are superior to and in control of people and events on earth. Invention of these gods always preceded the rise of states; they gradually superseded the more ancient goddesses, who had some control of earthly events but were not omnipotent. The goddesses gave or withheld corn, oil, crops, and fecundity, in women and in the earth. The potent but not omnipotent goddesses were worshipped only as long as they delivered, and they could be vilified if they failed. The new gods, in contrast, brooked no impiety.

CHAPTER 7

JUDAISM

THE BIBLICAL TALES OF THE PATRIARCHS – Abraham, Isaac, Jacob, and Joseph – are not historical: they interweave fictional romance, history, and the myths of neighbouring peoples (Abraham from Ugarit, the flood from the Babylonian epic of Gilgamesh). In the fifth century BCE a group of Jewish priests compiled and edited them from a new ideological perspective. Just as Confucianists rewrote Chinese history, and Muslim sages Arab history, so these priests gave the books from Genesis to Kings – the Torah – their present form, defining the terms of Judaism. The editors' agenda was to teach patriarchy, asserting an ancient bond between their god and certain chosen men who were said to have established the Hebrew people. Like the claims to divine connection made by state-forming leaders in Egypt, Mesopotamia, China, Peru, and Mexico, these narratives state that, for thousands of years, the Hebrews were a coherent people worshipping Yahweh, who guided their establishment of the divine order on earth.

But there was no ancient ethnic group called Hebrews with physical, cultural, or linguistic differences from other Semitic Near Eastern peoples. The biblical texts amalgamate words and roots from different languages: the Transjordanian "shibboleth" dialect is proto-Aramaic, Jacob (Deuteronomy 26) is called "a fugitive Aramean," and the Song of Deborah, the earliest passage in the Bible, contains several Aramaisms. Scholars now believe that stories were drawn from widely known Near Eastern legends to provide the Hebrews with a past and with religious legitimacy.

Who, then, are the Hebrews? George Mendenhall, a distinguished Hebrew scholar, offers a widely accepted theory about Hebrew origins. In the early Bronze Age (c. 2300–2000 BCE), the clannish Amorites (kin to Babylonians and Assyrians) left northeast Syria in a major migration. Some may have gone to Egypt, from which, generations later, about seventy families of Semitic slave captives escaped, led by a family – Moses, Miriam, and Aaron – who unified the group by propounding a god who promised deliverance in return for absolute obedience and loyalty. The Bible attributes to miracle the fact that people without military training or survival skills in desert terrain managed, within Moses' lifetime, to overthrow the governments of two rich, fertile areas of Transjordan and settle this land. Within another generation they had occupied Palestine from Beersheba to northern Galilee, and by the middle of the next century they numbered a quarter of a million people. Mendenhall finds this account impossible without some further explanation, and he has one.

When the emigrants left Egypt, Canaan was a province

of Egypt. Its people were deeply dissatisfied. A poor country with little trade, small farms, infertile land, and thin yields made thinner by incessant war, Canaan was governed by Pharaoh's appointees, a new class of professional military men drawn from the militaristic Egyptian state. They expected peasants in the subjugated provinces to support the rulers, the military establishment, large construction projects, and luxurious royal lifestyles. The cities and grand palaces of Egypt now needed walls to protect them from their own poor peasants.

Taxes thrust many people into poverty, but rulers did not abate their demands. Small farmers and artisans who could not pay their taxes could be enslaved for debt. They could also flee, but tax collectors held communities, not individuals, liable. They pressured the guilds, which were responsible for crimes, taxes, and providing recruits for the army in each community. There was also a third alternative: from the time of Hammurabi's Code, the law held that a man who uttered the phrase "I hate my king and my city" could renounce his bond to a city, its protection, and his obligations (taxes and corvée). In a world where individuals could not survive alone, this course was risky. But groups were protected by numbers, and the Egyptian state was too weak to retaliate. People who renounced the state were called "Hap/piru" or "Abiru" (Habiru), later Hebrew. These groups sold themselves as slaves to citizens of other states, hired out as mercenaries to a foreign king, or joined outlaw gangs. Such alternatives were open only to men willing to desert their families. Mendenhall thinks that a fourth alternative was joining the exiles in the desert, and that the number of the Egyptian émigrés was swelled by defectors from Canaan whose kin remained. Thus, he suggests, Israel was founded on radical rejection of established political authority and traditional religion.

The Amorites, the émigrés, and the Habiru had tribal religions – each clan had its own household gods. But for diverse groups to unite into a coherent nation able to defend and maintain itself, tribal divisions had to melt. To this end, Mendenhall believes, Moses transformed Yahweh into a single universal god. (The émigrés did not always worship a single god: "the Gods of the Habiru" are named as witnesses in Hittite treaties of the period.) Newcomers empathized with a tale of escape from Egyptian bondage and a god who made it possible. The escape is celebrated in the Passover ritual, still the centrepiece of Jewish education. Leaders unified the new "tribe" by stressing rejection of earthly kings and positing the higher law of Yahweh – which explicitly granted the land to the people who work it, not to some king or Pharaoh. It is, after all, the promised holy land. Moses invented a new deity, Yahweh, to fuse strangers into the Twelve Tribes of Israel.

Mendenhall believes that the Hebrews made a conscious effort not to reconstruct the stratified, power-centred society they had left. They rejected Canaanite mores, insisting that one code should govern them all and that poor people, slaves, and non-citizens should matter. Power, they said, is the prerogative only of god. Religious leaders were careful not to prohibit acts that might be important in a local religion so long as they were compatible with Yahwist laws. They emphasized the Exodus and the Sinai covenant, major metaphors for divine help in escape from oppression. These events remained powerful even after people forgot the past and demanded a king.[1]

The myths and legends in Genesis reflect the traditions of

Near Eastern peoples generally. Some scholars believe that before David established a kingdom, the people of Israel were matrilineal and that there were no patriarchs, but four matriarchs – Sarah, Rebecca, Rachel, and Leah.[2] Biblical scholar David Bakan believes there were five – Leah, Rachel, Rebekah, Hagar, and Keturah; that the tribe of Levi, the priests, were Leah's descendants; and that Israel *(SR)* was named for Sarah *(SR)*, Jacob's name-change being added later to make a male the founder.

Many early tales suggest matricentric arrangements: Abraham and Sarah are brother and sister, but not by the same mother; since descent is traced through the mother alone, they may marry. Samson and Jacob live with their wives' families after marriage; Joseph's children by his Egyptian wife belong to her lineage. The sequence of Jacob stories reflects contested customs: Rebekah believes she has the right to confer the blessing – mother-right. Jacob marries matrilocally, does bride-service for his wives, is cheated by Laban (his wives' uncle, not father) but can do nothing about it, and must ask Laban's permission to leave. Leah and Rachel name their children. Word-roots point to matricentric origins even after a distinct Hebrew language had evolved: kin-group is *rahem*, "womb"; a tribal subdivision is *batn*, "belly"; and the word for clan or tribe is the same as for *"mother."* Jewishness still passes in the female line; the prayer to recover from illness mentions only patient and mother.

Some biblical scholars believe Yahweh was originally conceived as asexual or androgynous, since he is characterized by "compassion" – a word rooted on the Hebrew "womb" – and described as "giving birth" to Israel, "suckling" and watching over his child.[3] But the Yahweh of Exodus is not just male but patriarchal. Consider Numbers

12: 1–15: Moses marries an Ethiopian woman, directly violating his god's laws. Miriam and Aaron, Moses' siblings, reprimand him, asking whether Moses is the only prophet or if god also speaks through them. Overhearing them, god punishes not Moses or Aaron but Miriam, striking her with leprosy. Even Moses cries out at this injustice. God says, "If her father had but spit in her face, should she not be ashamed seven days? Let her be shut out from the camp seven days, and after that let her be received in again." God does not punish Moses for breaking his rule. Whatever the social reality of Moses' time, the story teaches that women may not challenge men.

In the thirteenth century BCE, Canaan hill country was nearly uninhabited: twenty-three occupied sites dotted 10,400 square kilometres of rocky arid soil. It was not yet patriarchal. The only rulers were "judges." Miriam led the émigrés from Egypt. In the mountains of Ephraim, "a prophetess . . . was judging Israel": Deborah mediated disputes and led armies. At Barak's request, she accompanies him into battle against Sisera, predicting his delivery to a woman. The defeated Sisera escapes and begs help from Jael, who gives him haven and food, then hammers a nail into his temple while he sleeps. Deborah composes a victory song, probably the oldest bit of the Bible. Around this time a woman, Rahab, saves Moses' spies in Jericho.

By 1200 BCE there were 114 sites in the hills, almost all new, probably settled by Canaanite and Egyptian émigrés. Their lives were harsh. Canaanites knew how to smelt iron (which eased ploughing hard land), but it was not widely available for another two hundred years. Only three crops could grow in the Palestine hills without irrigation – olive trees, grapevines, and, with some rain and much labour, wheat.[4] The Hebrews terraced the land – perhaps the first humans to do so. In their frontier communities they lived austerely, with simple pottery and crude basic tools – grinders, querns, flint blades, mortars and pestles – all used in cereal production. They dug pits to store the surplus in their houses or amid their dwellings. They did not seem to have surplus food to trade for wheat or manufactured goods.

Constant war added to the burden of life. Raiding parties crossed the Jordan, tribe warred with tribe. Archaeological records show widespread destruction of fortifications and cities, and the art of this period is obsessed with military themes. War was perhaps most intense at the onset of the Hebrew occupation of the hills and when the Philistines began invading Canaan.

Canaanite cities were defended by warriors who rode in chariots and used cross-bows. The Hebrews had no such things – and no government, public buildings, projects, fortifications, or temples. Their unwalled cities lacked even public space: to make a contract, people went to where the old men sat in the city gate and declared their agreement to buy or sell. The largest political unit was the tribe, unified by geography, not lineage. Each tribe included about fifty clans, or "phratries," of varied size. A village might hold one or more clans or part of a clan: clans were based on kinship. The family was the basic unit of society. Lacking a military class and a central government, tribes responded to military threats by, essentially, calling out the militia. No village had enough people to fight off a raiding party, so villages had to help each other, even if a given attack did not threaten them. Men also cooperated on major projects like building cisterns, which were essential in a region where rainfall is seasonal.

Women did most of the production and maintenance

work.[5] Life was unquestionably hard: women lived to a little over thirty, men to about forty, and half the children died before they were five. Later, the rabbis stipulated that girls be twelve and boys, thirteen, before they married. Josiah and Amon were crowned at fourteen. Carol Meyers believes that the "curse" laid on humans in Genesis reflects this early period when men had to till unyielding soil in unremitting labour and women had to reproduce prolifically and work hard. She reads it as an acknowledgement of reality: "I will greatly increase your work and your pregnancies. Along with toil you shall give birth to children."

In later times, women still managed Israel's domestic sphere. As in Athens, home was the site of production, a factory. The good wife of Proverbs 31 does all the work, supporting the family while her husband sits in the city gate all day, gossiping:

> She seeks wool and flax
> And willingly works with her hands.
> She is like the merchant ships
> She brings her food from afar.
> She also rises while it is yet night,
> And provides food for her household,
> And a portion for her maidservants.
> She considers a field and buys it;
> From her profits she plants a vineyard.
> She girds herself with strength,
> And strengthens her arms.
> She perceives that her merchandise is good,
> And her lamp does not go out by night.
> She stretches out her hands to the distaff,
> And her hand holds the spindle.

She extends her hand to the poor,
Yes, she reaches out her hands to the needy.
She is not afraid of snow for her household,
For all her household is clothed with scarlet.
She makes tapestry for herself;
Her clothing is fine linen and purple . . .
She makes linen garments and sells them,
And supplies sashes for the merchants . . .
She watches over the ways of her household,
And does not eat the bread of idleness.

Palestine had a tradition of goddess or fertility worship: its Iron Age sites yield many terracotta figurines showing the female upper body nude or semi-nude. Yahwism may have been the official religion, but many people went on worshipping goddesses. Reproach of goddess-worshipping "backsliders" recurs throughout the Old Testament.

When the family is the basic unit of production, especially when men are frequently absent, women often have high status. This standing was not the case in Athens, and may not have been in Israel. Women may have been respected, but the Bible is rife with tales of the sexual abuse of women. The story of the Levite's concubine recapitulates that of Lot and the strangers: in both, village men come to a host's door, demanding a stranger to bugger; both hosts offer female replacements – Lot, his daughters; the Levite, his concubine. After the Levite's concubine is raped and murdered, the tribes attack the tribe of Benjamin, who shelters the rapists. They kill most of the men but all the women, children, and animals, and vow to deny their daughters to the remaining Benjamite men. In the world of these stories, women are not human beings, not even subhuman. Most slaves are women, and all well-to-do men have maidservant-concubines. Women are expected to be chaste before marriage and faithful after it.

In 1000 BCE the Philistines were defeated by an army led by David, an outlaw, a true Habiru of the desert, who united Israel, declared himself king, and founded a capital in Jerusalem. We can deduce something about women's political and social reality at this time from David's relations with them. To forge a relation with Saul, the king, David marries Michal, his daughter, for whom he pays a hundred Philistine foreskins. Michal loves David and saves him from her mad father, but he abandons her. (Later, she scorns him.) After Abigail saves her household from David's outlaw gang, he marries her, then Ahinoam of Jezreel. After spying on the naked Bathsheba, David summons her. She conceives Solomon, and David murders her loyal husband to avoid scandal. David's son Absalom rapes his father's ten concubines to challenge him and Abishag is made to keep the dying old man warm in bed. The story of Tamar and Amnon indicates that marriage between children of the same father but different mothers was still permitted. Some women have authority: a wise woman from Tekoa acts as a diplomat to persuade David to see the estranged Absalom; another in Abel Beth Ma'achah averts war by persuading the town council to turn in a traitor.

The "wise" Solomon bankrupted the kingdom by building the temple in Jerusalem, large palaces, and stables for his 4000 horses and by maintaining 700 wives and 300 concubines. When imported building materials exceeded revenues, Solomon instituted corvée: every three months 30,000 Hebrews went to work for King Hiram of Tyre to pay off the debt. On Solomon's death, the state split: the ten northern tribes became the Kingdom of Israel; the two southern tribes, the Kingdom of Judah. In 722 BCE Assyria conquered Israel, dispersing its people, the "ten lost tribes." Judah (whence "Jews") was invaded by Egypt, Phoenicia, Moab, Philistia, Assyria, and, in 586, Nebuchadnezzar's Chaldeans, who resettled the elite in Babylon. In 539 the Persian Cyrus took Babylon and let the Jews leave.

Over these centuries, despite their conflicts, Hebrews, Canaanites, and later, Philistines, lived together. The Canaanites who joined the Hebrews retained their own customs and their parallel male and female gods, El and Asherah and their children Baal and Anat (who are married). The first recorded repression of worship of gods other than Yahweh occurs during the reign of Asa (913–873? BCE). In the mid-ninth century BCE Elijah and Elisha led a monotheistic movement. The prophet Amos stormed Jerusalem about 800 BCE, demanding social justice. Hosea, Micah, and Isaiah (mid/end eighth century BCE) exhorted Jews to abandon other gods and goddesses. In the seventh century a Jerusalem lawyer wrote a set of laws that was accepted by the king and that constitutes most of Deuteronomy 12–26 and 28, the core of the Deuteronomic movement. These laws stipulate that sacrifice to Yahweh could be made only in Jerusalem. During the exile in Babylon, Jews developed a non-sacrificial form of worship requiring only a meeting place (Gr: *synagogue*). This simplicity eventually characterized Judaism.

The exiles returned to Jerusalem after 539 BCE and gradually rebuilt the temple and recodified laws drawn largely from modified Hammurabic and Canaanite law. Hebrew law enjoined generosity to the poor and to strangers and limited the term of slavery for Hebrew males, though females enslaved for their fathers' or their husbands' debt could escape only into marriage, concubinage, or prostitution. Women were defined as sexual servants.

Both in overall perspective and in law, Israelite society denied women a voice. The perspective of the Bible places god within history and time, giving certain men significance as enactors of god's will and purpose on earth. Man is a creature with free will whose task is to fulfil god's will, with the enlightenment of scripture as interpreted by male priests. As Gerda Lerner writes, "Men . . . live and move through history."[6] Women are merely their adjuncts, sexually defined and regulated; only their degree of bondage differs with class.

The central chapters of Leviticus treat men's bodies as being at risk when they come into contact with women and with food prepared by women. Chapter 11 deals with what may not pass the lips of the mouth; chapter 12 with purification after childbirth (passage through other lips). An infant's sex determines a woman's degree of pollution: with a boy she is "unclean" for seven days and requires thirty-three days of purification; with a girl she is "unclean" for two weeks and needs sixty-six days of purification. Chapters 13 and 14 treat skin disease and bodily issues – leprosy and sexual and ulcerative discharges. Copulation is unclean, but the pollution lasts only a day and is purified by bathing. But menstrual discharge is contagious pollution, poisoning everything a woman touches. She must sacrifice to the priests during her period and for seven days beyond, contaminated for almost half of every month. These chapters conflate diseases like leprosy or running sores with ordinary conditions of womanhood – menstruation and childbirth. Sexual intercourse with menstruating women, men, or animals is punished by exile from the community. Married women could not own property, sign contracts, act at law, testify, or inherit.

Leviticus contains many laws that were ignored, as is obvious from the rest of the Bible. Hebrew women probably took pride in themselves and their daily work despite their "pollution," but in the Bible the large vibrant female figures of the early periods give way by the fifth century to docile Ruth, who followed her mother-in-law to her land and eventually provided her with issue, and to Esther, conscripted into the king's harem, using her sexual powers to persuade the king to help her people. Hebrew history shows the same progression we have seen elsewhere: powerful women give way to sexual women, who overcome their pollution by using their sexual powers for male-sanctioned ends.

War continued. Palestine was a Persian vassal for two hundred years; Alexander conquered it in 332 and, on his death, it became a vassal of the Ptolemies' Egypt. In 63 BCE Rome conquered it, but the Jews rebelled in 70 CE. The dominator of so much territory could not permit even one example of courage to stand: Rome destroyed Jerusalem, scattered Jews throughout its empire, and hounded the last survivors. Over a three-year period it sent hundreds of soldiers and masses of equipment over desert trails to raze the natural fortress at Masada. Rome finally won: a rock in a desert and a thousand dead bodies. The Jewish state was destroyed, but Jewish culture was not. Jews have maintained their traditions throughout the Diaspora; beyond that, Hebrew law and literature, particularly the Old Testament, helped form Western culture. In every culture Jews inhabit they vitally demand social justice and protest political oppression. Alas, they also maintain old Jewish attitudes towards women.[7]

CHAPTER 8

GREECE

T HE FIRST KNOWN INHABITANTS of the Greek peninsula
and islands were Indo-Europeans who settled there in
1900 BCE and spoke an early form of Greek. Farmers and
herders, they lived in relatively egalitarian clans or tribes. Ad
hoc leaders led religious functions; justice was handled pri-
vately. Mycenae, important in literature as the city of
Agamemnon, Klytemnestra, Elektra, and Orestes, became
dominant. The king and the bureaucrats counted and
recorded all peoples' material possessions: acreage, animals,
even pots. It was a slave society, and most, if not all, slaves
were women. Mycenaean rulers built themselves grandiose
tombs. In 1130 BCE Greek Dorians with iron weapons
wiped out Mycenae. Whatever the Dorians saw, they burned
to the ground.

The most ancient Greek religion we know about, the

cult of Demeter, was centred at Eleusis. Demeter is Mother Earth, the goddess of agriculture (Ceres in Latin, from which comes "cereal"). Hades, the god of the underworld, kidnaps and rapes her daughter, Persephone. Demeter roams the Earth seeking her, until she is told the truth by the Sun. Enraged, she wanders to Eleusis, where she is welcomed. Angry with Zeus for permitting the violation of her daughter, she makes the Earth barren and creates winter. Fearing the destruction of the Earth, Zeus promises Persephone's release if she has not eaten anything. But she has eaten some pomegranate seeds (the number varies), so she may spend only six months (or two-thirds) of the year with her mother and the rest in Hades. The cult of Demeter was open to Greeks of all sexes and classes. In the seventh century Athens pre-empted the sanctuary and tried vainly to replace Demeter with the god Iakchos Triptolemos.

Despite signs of ancient goddess worship, women are men's domestic and sexual servants in the earliest Greek records. In the Homeric epics (put in their present form in the 700s BCE but set in c. 1230 BCE), noblewomen make beds, do laundry, spin, weave, and prepare and serve food. Paintings of Heracles, a Dorian hero, show the goddess Athene pouring wine and serving meals for him.

Around 800 BCE cities arose, centred on a marketplace and surrounded by fortifications. Each was a state like the Sumerian city-states, a *polis* ruled by a king and council. Conflict often led councils to depose kings. Rule by a group of unrelated men – oligarchy – allows women less voice than any other form of government. Rule by a man – king, emperor, pharaoh – with a family frequently grants women influence and sometimes even public power, because women often have power within families. This is true in family-based feudal or aristocratic regimes. But group rule by unrelated men evokes male solidarity, because men are in constant rivalry. Since unrelated men are connected only by their difference from women, men in oligarchies must demonstrate independence of, even contempt for, women to prove they are "real" men. The term "oligarchy" usually denotes ancient states, but most modern governments are oligarchies: the United States, Russia, China, Australia, Canada are governed by groups of unrelated men.

Sparta

In the ninth century BCE Dorians invaded the Peloponnesus, conquered Laconia and the Messenian plain, and founded Sparta. About 640 BCE the Messenians rebelled, invaded Laconia, and nearly defeated their conquerors. The Greek historian Thucydides wrote that the rebellion lasted ten years; later historians estimate four or five. In any case, it terrified the Spartans, who determined that such an uprising would not happen again. They murdered or expelled all the Messenian leaders, confiscated their land, and impressed the Messenians into serfdom. The serfs *(helots)* were to farm and support the elite.

Sparta reorganized itself into an armed camp. The Spartiates (descendants of the Dorian conquerors) set up a puppet king, council, and assembly similar to those in democratic city-states, but they were really governed by the *ephorate*, a board of five men who presided over the council and the assembly, controlling most aspects of Spartan society. There were three classes: Spartiates, *perioeci* ("dwellers around"), and serfs. Spartiates, a twentieth of the population, had all the political rights. The perioeci – a free, mainly Laconian middle-class subject to Sparta – were permitted to trade and manufacture, but were obliged to serve in Spartan armies. Helots, 80 percent of the population, could keep what they produced beyond what was taken by the Spartiates. They could leave the Peloponnesus, but if they returned they would be totally enslaved. They were treated shamefully, but most remained.

Sparta regulated citizens as strictly as the serfs: barred from agriculture and business, they were trained as an exclusively military class (like Aztec males). Boys began military training at seven; at twelve, they were taken from home, never to return. They learned music (battle songs) and law, but they were frequently and brutally whipped to teach them obedience and to suppress individuality. Youths drafted into the secret police were sent to infiltrate the helots and to murder potential rebels or subversives. At maturity they entered the army and spent the rest of their lives in austere male institutions, in homosocial and homosexual activities, living in barracks and eating in mess halls. The talented were rewarded by being sent to the front lines of battle.

Sparta was sex segregated. Women often thrive in such societies. In simple societies like the Hopi, for instance, men have higher status, but women have considerable power in their own realm because it is their own realm. Accounts of life in harems often stress the relative freedom and scope available to women within them. Since a major drive of male supremacy is to prove control, it requires a caste or class to be controlled. Usually, this group is women. But Spartan men had to spend all their energies controlling the 80 percent of the population that was enslaved, so they did not have energy or interest left over for women.

So women had considerable freedom. Sparta had male

infanticide: all girls were reared to adulthood, but boys, examined at birth, were exposed if they showed signs of weakness or sickliness. In contrast with other Greek cities, Spartan girls were decently fed and trained in philosophy, rhetoric, racing, wrestling, and throwing the discus and javelin. Boys were trained to be soldiers; girls, strong mothers. Both performed athletics at public festivals naked or wearing a *chiton* (a short tunic that exposed one breast), a custom considered scandalous in other Greek cities.

The structure of society fostered homosexuality, and men shunned marriage. But the city needed warriors, so passed a law denying unmarried men citizenship. Marriage was prearranged rape – men kidnapped women at night. But men spent little time with their wives; Plutarch remarked that Spartans "had children before they ever saw their wives' faces in daylight."[1] Female homosexuality, although not mentioned, probably existed. Adultery was not a serious crime, nor was paternity an issue: Sparta wanted soldiers and did not much care how it got them. Like the Aztec, Spartans saw childbearing as a service to the state: the only tombs with names were those of men killed in battle and women killed in childbirth.

Spartiate women had more freedom and autonomy than women in other Greek city-states. Leaving household work to slaves, women managed the home and reared the children, knowing that their sons were destined to become state property. They spent much of their time working out in gymnasia and making music. After land (previously owned by the state) could be bought and sold, Spartiate women, who could manage property, grew rich. By the fourth century BCE they owned two-fifths of the land in the state and were so powerful that Aristotle blamed Sparta's decline on them.

Spartan society was much admired by other Greek city-states, who saw it as a model of virtue, discipline, hierarchical obedience, and asceticism. Lycurgus, who oversaw the codification of Spartan law in the seventh century, became the philosophers' ideal human being, but Sparta banned philosophers because they disagreed and there was no room for argument in Sparta. Other Greek cities did not imitate the Spartan model because they thought its perfect order was a result of freeing women – which they were unwilling to do.

Athens

In time, strongmen called "tyrants" overthrew many Greek oligarchies. One city-state, Athens, deposed the tyrants and initiated a new form of government, rule by the *demos* (the people) – democracy. We know more about Athens than any other Greek city-state because of its brilliant culture – drama, poetry, history, science, and philosophy. Its "golden age," the fifth century BCE, is held up as a pinnacle of human achievement; its thought and values still inform philosophy, politics, and literature. Yet this culture defined humanness by omitting most of the human race, just as Athenian "democracy" omitted most Athenians.

From the start, elite Athenian men's sense of themselves and their city was explicitly hostile to women. Greek scholar Eva Keuls shows that the earliest, most widespread myth of the founding of Athens was a battle between Greek heroes and the Amazons, a mythical society of warlike women who were as brave, strong, and skilled as men.[2] There is a possibility that Amazons existed: Herodotus wrote of a battle between them and Greek soldiers in the fifth century BCE. According to legend, these fierce women cut off their right breast so as to improve their skill at archery. Despite many ancient accounts of Amazons, modern historians have always denied that they existed, but recent excavations at Kazakhstan near the Russian border have unearthed evidence of women warriors buried with weapons. They were part of a community that contained men, but the grave goods of this community suggest that women had far higher status than had been assumed among Eurasian nomads.[3] Armed women appear on Thracian goblets from 6000 to 4000 BCE, and, after the ninth century, references and portrayals abound of a band of Greek men stabbing, attacking, and clubbing naked Amazons and carrying them off to rape them. Over eight hundred depictions survive in paintings, sculpture, pottery, in the western metopes of the Parthenon, in the Temple of Theseus, and in the Stoa Poikile (Painted Porch).

The ancient Greeks may, at one time, have been threatened by a group of women soldiers. Certainly, myths about the Parnassian gods abound in examples of violence against women, especially rapes. In a work noted for its woman hatred, the eighth-century Greek poet Hesiod recounted the origin myth of Gaia (Earth). Gaia generates a son, Ouranos (Heaven), who helps her produce the Titans – Prometheus, Kronos, and others, including monsters. Fearing his offspring, Ouranos locks Gaia's fetuses in her womb; she retaliates by giving her youngest son, Kronos, a sickle and positioning him to castrate his father. Kronos becomes king of the gods; with his sister Rhea he fathers another set of offspring, the Olympians, but he, too, fears his children and swallows them as soon as they are born. (Fathers' murder of children in Greek myth parallels Abraham's willingness in the Bible story to sacrifice Isaac.) After giving birth to her youngest son, Zeus, Rhea hands Kronos a rock wrapped in swaddling and hides her baby. When Zeus is grown, Gaia supplies him with a potion to give Kronos, which causes him to regurgitate the babies he has swallowed. Zeus becomes supreme by swallowing his wife, Metis (Intelligence), and defeating the Titans. Zeus now has androgynous powers and he produces Athena from his head. Athena, the patron of Athens, is a co-opted female: a virgin, she always supports males and a masculine point of view in the late myths. She represents male domination, war, and justice. Male assimilation of female powers recurs in Greek literature, in small details and in large.[4] Males violently usurp female powers: Zeus swallows Metis to get her powers; he impregnates Semele, kills her with a thunderbolt, removes her fetus, sews it into his thigh, and gives birth to Dionysus.

Myths asserting father-right arose along with a middle class that overthrew older aristocratic or feudal rulers.[5] In Greece a middle class developed after the discovery of iron, which made agriculture easier and yields greater, bringing prosperity. But "prosperity," a deceptive term, often intensifies stratification, enriching a few and impoverishing others. Many small farm families lost everything and were enslaved. Their rebellion led to political reorganization and the appointment of an aristocrat, Solon, to reform the legal code. Called a father of democracy, Solon prescribed reforms that, modified by later rulers, created a wholly new form of government. He limited the amount of land any man could own, prohibited enslavement for debt, established a governing council and court system, and gave all citizens suffrage and the right to serve in the assembly. He even offered Athenian citizenship to craftsmen from other cities.

Given other governments of the period, the Athenian

model is admirable. Yet only about 6 percent of the population were citizens: women and slaves could not be citizens, and women were rigidly constricted. The legal term for wife, *damar*, means "to subdue, or tame." Brides were welcomed with the same ritual as new slaves, *katachysmata*, good luck "downpourings" – a basket of nuts poured over the head. Women and slaves were unprotected in law, but fathers or husbands could not kill adult women as they could in Mesopotamia. Solon legally distinguished between "good women" and "whores" (who were put in state-owned brothels), regulating where "good women" could go, how far they could walk, what they could eat and drink, what they could serve at feasts or wear when mourning, and what could be included in their trousseaus. He even established secret police to spy on them.

Female infanticide was common: families might choose to raise more than one son but thought it unnecessary to raise more than one daughter. Some killed all their daughters; others raised their daughters as servants in their own homes. Killing babies was illegal, but abandoning them was not.[6] Disposal location determined a baby's fate: those left in conspicuous places were found and raised as brothel slaves; the hidden died. Girls were fed little, and almost no protein. The state was not concerned about the low proportion of females in the population because many men were homosexual and married late; females married successively. Girls of twelve or fourteen were married to men over thirty, who often died in Athens' frequent wars: many were dead by forty-five, leaving widows under thirty who were passed on to another husband to bear more children. Despite high war casualty rates, men lived longer than women, averaging forty-five years to women's thirty-six – probably because of their poor diet and early motherhood, before their bodies were fully grown.⁷ Like Spartiates, Athenian men married reluctantly. But only male descendants could maintain a family's legal existence; only males could memorialize ancestors in religious rituals, so the state appointed a magistrate to ensure that no family became extinct (lacked male descendants). Marriage was mandatory for men.

Wedding ritual defined the purpose of marriage to be the "ploughing of legitimate children." Sexual pleasure was not expected: it was considered obscene to combine marriage and desire. Women had to be virgins at marriage and faithful after it. "Respectable" women probably never undressed in front of their husbands: female nudity was associated with prostitutes and hetaerai (women trained in social and intellectual graces, like India's courtesans and Japanese geishas). Men hired them for dinner parties, to which they never took their wives. Marital sex was often rape: a passage in an Athenian work describes a "doorkeeper," perhaps a common attendant at weddings, whose job it was to guard the bedroom door to prevent the bride's women friends from rushing in when they heard her scream. A literary fragment recounts a dialogue between two women who wish to rid themselves of husbands who "do violence" to them.

Marriage was unhappy, by law. Athenian law held a man's acts invalid if he was sick, constrained, senile, or under the influence of drugs or a woman – and in marriage, mutuality means influence. Spouses were separated by age, experience, and education: boys were educated, girls not; girls were sequestered, boys not. Women were confined not just to the house but to a section of the house for life. A women's police monitored their activities. Female slaves, locked in the women's quarters at night, could not have children without their male owners' permission. Compared to luxurious foreign cities, Athens was poor, with small dark houses and narrow streets. Women spent their days in cramped sweatshops, working and supervising slaves, bombarded by commands not to be seen or heard. A Greek writer held that proper women were ashamed to be seen even by members of their household; a fourth-century orator rebuked the "respectable women" who hovered in their doorways asking for news after Athens was defeated in war, for letting themselves be seen, bringing "shame on themselves." Pericles said a woman who leaves her house should be of such an age that those who meet her would ask not whose wife, but whose mother, she is.[8]

Women were also nameless. Only male children were listed in *phratry* (tribe) records. To claim citizenship, boys had to be descended from two citizen parents, but what was recorded were the fathers' and the maternal grandfathers' names. Daughters must have been called something, but women's names rarely appear.[9]

Rape was an obsession in Athens. The number of rapes in Greek mythology is shocking even if one follows only the career of Zeus or Apollo. *The Love of the Gods in Attic Art of the Fifth Century B.C.* lists 395 cases of rape by major Olympic male gods. Several early myths connect rape with marriage, giving it social sanction (as in Sparta).

The Athenian world was arranged to provide nourishment, leisure, and well-being for male citizens. Men spent little time in their dark, squalid, unsanitary, smelly houses; rather, they passed their days gossiping and politicking in light-filled public squares and buildings. Taught the opposite ethic from women, men were idle and scorned those who worked; leisure was the prerequisite for citizenship, according to Aristotle. The only activities proper for men were games – philosophical debate, athletics, and war. Boys were taken from the women's quarter at six, after which they ate with the men of the house. They were educated professionally outside the home, trained in athletics at public palestrai and gymnasia, and given military training. Athenian men had to serve ten years in the military. Above all, men were trained to be competitive: a noted Greek scholar commented that they would contest *anything*: male beauty, riddle solving, singing, drinking, even the ability to stay awake.[10] Another wrote that nothing had meaning to the Greeks if it did not involve defeating someone else.[11] Indeed, even young girls competed in athletic contests at Olympia, where married women were barred from male events on pain of death.[12]

Men, permitted physical and intellectual pursuits, were graciously served food and drink and were sexually indulged by prostitutes in brothels, by hetaerai in conversation, and by male prostitutes, mainly boys (male prostitution was illegal but common). An underclass of slaves and the poor was available for "symposia," drinking parties held in private homes, during which older men drank, ate, competed, and had sex with male or female prostitutes or concubines (never wives). Boys were introduced to sex with prostitutes or older men. Pederasty (sex with a child) was a rite of passage: boys were forced to submit to anal sex with older "lovers." Receiving the penis was considered humiliating, and sodomizing was used to initiate boys into male supremacist behaviour. Mutual sex between adult men was not accepted, yet this form of hierarchical homosexuality was practised, suggesting that Athenians were wary of sex that did not involve power.

Sex with prostitutes and hetaerai also involved force. Eva Keuls shows photographs of paintings on vessels used in symposia, many depicting forced anal copulation with hetaerai or prostitutes. Male customers are shown with a raised hand, containing a money pouch, above a woman. Many paintings show men beating prostitutes with objects, and at least two show older hetaerai forced to perform fellatio, which was apparently considered more repugnant than intercourse. The women are always naked.[13]

Women had some rights. Fathers or husbands could not kill them freely. Able to make financial transactions under the value of one *medimnos* of barley (which could keep a family for a few days), women were small market dealers. The daughter of a propertied family had the right to a dowry. Her husband got it at marriage; she could not use it or approve its use, but if he divorced her, he had to return it with interest. Men "owned" everything and the law required them to support wives living with them, but, in fact, women supported men by their household labour and household production. By law subject to a *kyrios* ("lord") father, husband, or son forever, women could not be independent. A female could inherit if she was the only child, but she had to marry her father's nearest male relative to guarantee that the property remained in his family. If her father died after she was married, she had to leave her family to marry an uncle or cousin less than a generation older than the deceased. She never controlled the property of which she was the vehicle.

Adultery by a "citizen" woman (a woman whose father was a citizen) was punished by mandatory divorce and exclusion from festivals and religious ceremonies – the equivalent to being denied any freedom. A man who copulated with a married woman was killed. This punishment may seem a reversal of customs elsewhere, but the Athenians' major concern was guaranteeing the "integrity" of the "family" – the sons' legitimacy. For a man to betray this male code was a serious crime. Men who raped or seduced unmarried free women were fined, and the women were sold into slavery.

Poor women's lives were freer and more precarious. Free women were wet nurses, grape pickers, and wool workers; they ran inns and cafés and filled marketplaces, selling everything. They did textile work, water carrying, and, when older, could take on the work open to menopausal women – matchmaking, midwifery, and professional mourning. Few Athenian women worked in the fields, but other Greek women did (and do), carrying heavy loads like water jugs (*hydria* in Greece), which weigh 27 kilograms filled. Most poor Athenian women (most of them slaves) were prostitutes; free women became hetaerai. The only women in Athens who controlled substantial amounts of money were prostitutes.[14]

Athens was the cultural centre of Greece and, although it did not educate its own women, distinguished women emigrated there. Diotima taught Socrates; Axiothea dressed as a man to study with Plato, who, perhaps not aware she was female, called her "the mind bright enough to grasp" his ideas. Theano, a mathematician expert in medicine, physics, and psychology, articulated the theory of the "golden mean" credited to her husband, Pythagoras. Cresilas won third prize in a sculpture competition behind Polyclitus and Phidias. A tradition of female poetry reached its apex with Sappho of Lesbos, whose poems present a view of love strikingly different from male poets'. Sappho too loves women, but she celebrates mutuality and lovers' need for each other, not conquest.[15] Only fragments of her work remain. Among Sappho's students and followers, Erinna wrote poetry that male contemporaries called as great as Homer's; Myrtis, rated second only to Sappho, taught Pindar. Pindar's work endures, but the women are known only because their names are mentioned by male contemporaries.

Despite the laws, male homosexuality was common and accepted in Athens; female homosexuality is not mentioned except by Sappho. Women were very isolated inside their houses, released only during religious ceremonies and festivals. For one feast (Thesmophoria), they went out dressed as men and held a mock political assembly. Women joined the cult of Maenads, celebrated by ritual madness, and the Adonia, a festival mourning Adonis' death.[16]

Adonis was foreign, the child of a seduction or incest and associated with vegetation; he was beautiful, tender, shy, timid, and able to give women orgasms – a true alternative to Athenian men. Women celebrated Adonia by bewailing Adonis' death – he was gored in the groin by a boar, a symbol of aggressive masculinity. They spent a night on the roof of a house amid broken pots of herbs and vegetables, then carried his effigy through the city to bury it at sea – an emotional ceremony that let them break rules and find release. The Adonia influenced Aristophanes' anti-war play, *Lysistrata*. Amy Swerdlow, who studied vase paintings of women, believes that Athenian women had their own culture, where they found affection and pleasure working wool or bathing together.[17] Keuls thinks such paintings were symbolic because women had no leisure. Since women had no voice, we do not know the truth.

Oppressors fear those they oppress: Greek myth and literature depict women as uncontrollable and violent. Male killers were heroes or victims of fate beyond their control; female killers were monsters. Many myths focused on wives who killed their husbands (Clytemnestra, the Danaids, the Lemnian women) or children (Medea); many depict raving women dismembering men.

Men's fear of women paralleled an obsession with the penis, the major symbolic object in Athens. Many vase paintings show men or satyrs with huge erect penises. Phalluses dotted the city on "herms," rectangular columns representing Hermes with heads and erect penises. Phalluses capped altars – large numbers were found in the sanctuary of Aphrodite on the Acropolis. A huge phallus was carried around the city in a parade celebrating the yearly dramatic festival. Phallus worship symbolized the culture and pervaded political life as "democracy" grew more imperial.

In 415 CE a subversive act stunned Athens: in the darkness of night some avengers knocked the penises off almost all the Hermes steles in the city, hundreds of them. Men took this destruction as a sign of conspiracy, a plot to overthrow the government, for, among other things, Hermes was the god of travel. At the time, Athens was exhausted from a long series of wars that had killed a large number of its men, yet it was preparing to launch a purposeless invasion of Sicily. Alcibiades appealed to the city's macho self-image, and the fleet was made ready. A year earlier, Athens had sacked the island of Melos – killed its men and enslaved its women and children – for the crime of remaining neutral in Athens' war against Sparta. Eva Keuls theorizes that Athenian women, heartsick at the loss of men in that war and fearing for themselves the fate of the Melians, protested in the only way they could. They could not speak in public, but, during the festival of Adonia, they could walk in the streets at night in disguise. Keuls believes that women opposed the Peloponnesian War by castrating the herms. Athens lost the war. Sparta did not enslave the population or impose its culture on them, but Athens lost its dominant status.

Athenian culture was created by men for men, for the 6 percent of the population who lived parasitically on the labour of the rest. Moreover, writers' remarks about women and speeches placed in women's mouths by Greek dramatists and poets show that Athenian men were aware of women's wretchedness. The Athenian system exploited the labour of women and slaves to give a tiny leisure class space, drinking parties, and philosophy. Like Hebrew patriarchs sitting all day in the city gate, men talked and played while women worked from dawn until dark to provide their wants. This structure was not unusual. What makes the Greek system so insidious is that the privileged were not content only to set up the structure; they also rationalized it, justified it with all their intellectual and creative power. No literature in the world vilifies women more viciously or more often than the Greek, depicting them as violent, emotional, barbaric monsters, or, like Aristotle, as "deformed" men, an inferior species. Athenian men defined women as inferior despite the example of distinguished woman artists and thinkers among them.[18] And this female inferiority justified Athenian men in the economic and reproductive enslavement of women.

Biblical and Athenian thought together formed Western culture, and their false definitions of the sexes remain to this day. The Greek definition of women as subhuman was no less damaging than their definition of men as existing in the realm of volition. Men freely chose their lives and transcended necessity. They had control over others, whose task it was to support and serve them.

In 359 BCE Philip II, king of Macedon, a city-state in northern Greece, set out to conquer the world, starting with Greece. When he was assassinated in 336, his son Alexander took up his mantle and invaded the Balkans, Asia Minor, the Middle East, Egypt, and Persia before he died in 323 BCE. War continued throughout the ensuing Hellenistic period, as Alexander's generals vied to control his empire. The wars kept Greek men away from home, loosening male control in the city-states, and, after 350 BCE, Greek women won some rights. Girls in some states were educated, and marriage softened into more of a partnership. Women still needed a man's aegis, but, with it, they could make contracts, buy and sell property, inherit and bequeath. Women participated in elections in Pompeii; one woman was a high magistrate in Histria; another, a political appointee in Phrygia. In Asia Minor a woman, Phyle, occupied the highest state office and built a reservoir and aqueducts.

Life improved for women, but not in Athens. Aristotle's judgment that the deliberative part of woman's soul is impotent and needs supervision marked women in that city forever. Some thinkers murmured about emancipating women, and the New Comedy acknowledged women's sexuality and showed dignified women with some freedom and authority in the household. But laws governing women became even more repressive. Demetrius, the last major Athenian lawmaker, reinstated the women's police and enlisted cooks, caterers, and entertainers to report women who lived in "luxury."

Women taught in the academies of Alexandria. In the first century CE Mary/Miriam the Prophetess, a Jewish scientist living in Alexandria, wrote an alchemy (chemistry) text, the *Maria Practica.* She invented a water bath for maintaining a constant temperature in scientific experiments (a *bain-marie*, which is still used), a reflux device for sublimation of metals, a still (the first distillation mechanism), and she synthesized a metal alloy with black sulfide, Mary's black. Hypatia (c. 370–415 CE) was a great mathematician and astronomer. Renowned for her learning, eloquence, and beauty, she taught at Alexandria, heading the Neo-Platonist school there, and drew Christian and pagan students from all over the Greek world. None of her many mathematical and astronomical theses has survived. She invented the hydroscope (the first laboratory tool for measuring the specific gravity of liquid), a hydrometer, a distillation system, and a plane astrolabe to measure the position of the sun and stars; once she perfected it, she could solve problems in spherical astronomy. The archbishop of Alexandria, Cyril, resented her influence and incited fanatical monks to persecute her and other Neo-Platonists. She was courageous in the face of this mob, but was killed horribly in 415.

In other Greek cities women struggled for freedom over several hundred years. They won a diminished thing – by the time they were allowed to own property, property ownership no longer conveyed citizenship; by the time they became officials of the polis, it was no longer the seat of governmental power. And Rome, the empire that would soon hold Greek women in its grasp, took Athens, not Hellenistic Greece, as its model.[19]

CHAPTER 9

ROME

ROME SWALLOWED ATHENIAN CULTURE: it stole the gods of the Greek Pantheon and renamed them; it took Greek art, especially sculpture; and it adopted Athenian attitudes towards masculinity and women – which it may already have shared. It too had a misogynistic origin myth. Yet Roman women were able to wrest some measure of freedom from their culture. Indeed, there are two Roman origin myths. One ascribes the founding of the city to brothers, Romulus and Remus, but the real hero of the story is their mother, Ilia. Another, resembling the Greek psychomachia, bases Rome's founding in a rape: a gang of male marauders from Alba attacks the neighbouring Sabines and kidnaps their women. They marry them under the rule of *confarreatio*, a word derived from *far*, a grain (e.g., *farina*), meaning "sharing the grain." Later this word means "marriage."

In reality, the Italian peninsula was inhabited from at least the Paleolithic Age and settled over eons by European, Mediterranean, and North African peoples. Archaeologists in Paestum, an old city south of Naples, recently found large numbers of artifacts associated with goddess worship – terracotta figurines, wine cups, and other pottery dating to the sixth century BCE.[1] Around the eighth century BCE Tuscany was settled by (and named for) the Etruscans, who built cities in north and central Italy. They had writing (as yet undeciphered), fine art, and metalwork, traded with the East, and foretold the future from animal entrails and bird flight patterns. Etruscans traced descent matrilineally and raised all children equally. Husbands and wives shared a social life. Contemporaries said that Etruscan women were good-looking, athletic, heavy drinkers, and sexually free. They often had richer tombs than men. The Romans copied Etruscan methods of prognosis, with their arches, vaults, and gladiatorial events, but not their attitude towards women.

Italic peoples had settled Rome and its surrounding hills by the eighth century BCE; two centuries later they overthrew the Etruscans and set up a republic. Roman myth justified this war by a need to avenge an alleged rape by the Etruscan Tarquin of the virtuous Roman wife, Lucretia, who killed herself in shame. Rome was a slave-holding state. Roman history is traditionally divided into two periods: the republic, from around 300 BCE until 30 BCE, and the empire, from 30 BCE until about 500 CE.

The Republic

Ancient Rome was aristocratic; power was held by wealthy landowners who ruled through a Senate after the establishment of a republic. They excluded the poor by not paying public officials. As always until the industrial revolution, wealth came from land, which was passed on in families. Below the nobles was a middle class of traders and weapons manufacturers; small landowners filled the army. The masses of poor and the huge slave class that worked the large estates were treated brutally, worked until they were no longer efficient, then sold to state mines, where conditions were even worse. Rome colonized conquered territories, denying their inhabitants any civil rights and forcing them to pay tribute and accept Roman law.

Unlike the Greeks, however, the Romans were family centred, and women can be powerful within families. Early Roman history celebrated heroic aristocratic women who gloriously saved the city gods or a father's life. The institution of the Vestal Virgins, sometimes attributed to Rhea Silvia (another name for Ilia), suggests an earlier more woman-centred society: it was probably founded to convert family loyalty to state loyalty just as priest-rulers in ancient states included local goddesses in state rites to lure their adherents. Roman families worshipped their own ancestors and hearth; public worship of Vesta, goddess of the hearth, appropriated this devotion for the state. Young girls were selected to guard the sacred fire, a position much vied for by their families. As the only Roman women who were free of paternal or conjugal authority, the Vestal Virgins were required to be chaste. Around thirty, however, they were retired to ordinary life with a pension. Unlike conscripted virgins elsewhere, they were not sacrificed.

The Romans, copying the Greeks, defined women as defective, as *imbecillitas* in law. Seen as *infirmitas sexus, levitas animi* – an infirm, lightminded sex – women were under guardianship for life. In Rome, too, fathers decided whether infants would live or be exposed. Fathers had *patriapotestas* (father-power or absolute power) over the household – the power of life and death and the authority to punish, kill, or enslave. A married woman was under her husband's authority if he held her in manu – "under his hand." If she lacked father and husband, a guardian was appointed over her. In this way, Roman women were more vulnerable than Athenians, whose men could not legally kill them. Athenian women's names were unrecorded, but Roman women had no names at all, only assignments: Julia means "female belonging to Julius"; Cornelia "female belonging to Cornelius." If there were several daughters, they were Agrippina the elder and Agrippina the younger, or first, second, and so on. When they married, their husbands' names were added: Julia Agrippina means Julius' daughter, Agrippa's wife.

Boys too were under *patriapotestas*. If a father died, girls and prepubescent boys became the property of their oldest uncle or brother, who could kill them or sell them into slavery. Older boys were freed at their father's death or – in the oldest Roman law, the Twelve Tables – after he had sold them into slavery three times. In the Republic, women could never be freed.

In most ways, however, Roman women were better off than Athenian women. Speaking only of women from propertied families – the only ones we have knowledge of – it seems likely they complained and agitated, because laws ruling them were changed. Marriage laws were altered to allow a woman to avoid passing under the *manu* of her husband by spending three consecutive nights each year in her father's house. Her father then retained nominal control of her and her dowry. Women chose the form of marriage they wanted, deciding whether their father or their husband was easier to control. They won the right to choose their own guardians and to dismiss intractable ones, and found ways to will their property to their children rather than their uncles. They won the right to inherit from their children. By 300 BCE some noble girls were being educated; by 200 BCE plebeian girls, too, went to school in the Forum until they were twelve or thirteen. By 1 CE many marriage contracts were mutual and voluntary.

Rich women managed to study law, politics, or literature, but they could never practise a profession. Some trained as athletes – hunters, fencers, wrestlers. We can glean some idea of how wealthy Roman matrons lived from the ruins of a Roman villa at Piazza Armerina in Sicily that probably dates to the fourth century BCE. All that remains of the mansion are partial walls and some gorgeous mosaic floors that suggest the nature of the rooms they were designed for. There are many hunting scenes, especially in what is called a "hunting corridor" – a space in which chariot races may have been held. It has cool, warm, and hot pools, baths, massage rooms, and latrines. In its emphasis on water and violence it is totally Roman in ethos – even the children's rooms depict boys killing animals, although the girls are weaving roses into wreaths. One set of rooms functioned as a women's gymnasium. Sicilian guides titter about the uses of the room they coyly call the "bikini girls" room, but it has drains for showers, and mosaics show women hurling the discus, hurdling, playing ball, lifting weights, and winning prizes. No housewife could take care of this house, which needed an army of slaves.[2]

If they could gain their guardians' consent – which was

possible – women could inherit and sell property. Roman couples had a shared social life: they ate, entertained, and visited together. Women were not raised to be inferior to men, and they were not exceptionally younger or less educated than their husbands. They were expected to stay home doing domestic tasks, but they were not confined. Roman wives were respected as supporters of the patriarchy. Literature of the period portrays them as sexually free: divorce and adultery were both common. Some women married and divorced serially, getting richer each time; some registered as prostitutes to avoid prosecution for sexual freedom.

Until the turn of the millennium, Rome was usually at war. War was celebrated in the Roman ethos as it was in the Athenian. Rome conquered Greece, Asia Minor, Egypt, Gaul (France, Belgium, western Germany), and England. War is expensive and it impoverishes a populace, even if it makes certain groups rich. For a long time only landowners were soldiers, and they left their farms in the hands of slaves to join the army. Returning to ruined farms, they sold them to rich farmers, whose estates grew larger and larger, and went to the city. When their money ran out, they joined the mob on the dole. Slaves, who made up most agricultural workers and 80 percent of the shop labour, did almost all the productive work. They were very badly treated and sometimes rebelled. In 135–32 BCE a series of slave revolts erupted in Sicily, and rebellious slaves ravaged the island in 104. In 73 BCE a slave, Spartacus, led a revolt on the mainland: 70,000 slaves repelled government troops for nearly two years. Mobs rose up in cities. The government paid out a dole to freemen and boys and mounted contests pitting hired trained gladiators against prisoners of war and convicts – the "bread and circuses" thrown to the mob. Two brothers of the Gracchi family tried to make democratic reforms, but when aristocrats fought and killed them, the dispute ended in civil war.

Generals with huge armies – Sulla, Pompey, and Caesar – took over the government. In 46 BCE Caesar had himself named dictator for ten years, then extended his term to life. When he was assassinated, three men struggled for dominance – his officers, Lepidus and Marc Antony, and Caesar Octavius, his nephew and heir – each of whom had his own army. Lepidus wisely retired from the competition; Antony went to Egypt, where he allied with (and married) Cleopatra; and Octavius pursued and defeated them at Actium in 31, whereupon Antony and Cleopatra committed suicide. Cleopatra had sent her sixteen-year-old son by Caesar, Ptolemy Caesar, to India for safety, but Octavius tricked him into coming back and had him killed. Octavius became *imperator*, emperor of the world.

The Empire

Octavius needed legitimacy, and he forced the Senate to honour him. In 42 he had Caesar decreed a god, making him the "son of god." He left the law in place, but ruled without it. To placate the plebeians, he raised the dole and threw more circuses. To win the bourgeoisie's support in bridling the old aristocracy, he passed a law allowing family-held land to be sold to pay debts and extended state jurisdiction over acts formerly treated as civil offences. To defuse the huge military establishment, he set up four sets of police to spy on each other and on citizens.

Shakespeare portrayed Octavius as an efficient, ambitious prig. The real Octavius publicized his reforms in a

ATLANTIC

OCEAN

GERMANIA

Rhine R.

Loire R.

GAUL

Rhone R.

ALPS

Danube

Po R.

DALMATIA

Spain

Marseilles

MACED

Rome

Naples

Gadiz

Tangier

MEDITERRANEAN

Carthage

SE

0   1000 miles

THE EXPANSION OF ROME

● Roman territory at the establishment of the Republic, ca. 500 B.C.

Expansion to the beginning of the first Punic War, 264 B.C.

To the end of the Punic Wars, 196 B.C.

To the death of Caesar, 44 B.C.

SARMATIA

BLACK SEA

CASPIAN SEA

ARMENIA

phesus

Tigris R.

Euphrates R.

SYRIA

Persian Gulf

exandria

EGYPT

Thebes

Red Sea

time-honoured way that is still current: as purifications to restore Rome to the moral "good old days." The population had been depleted by war, poverty, and male reluctance to marry, partly because of widespread homosexuality. Believing that nuclear families would undermine the extended aristocratic family, Octavius passed new family laws. The *lex Julia de Adulteriis* (18 BCE) and *lex Papia Poppaea* (9 CE) made marriage compulsory, rewarded parents of three children, and granted majority (legal adulthood) to mothers of three children and to freedwomen (former slaves) with four, enabling them to manage their own property. Barring marriage between classes, he made female adultery a crime against the state, tried by a jury. Wives could not prosecute husbands for it, but husbands had to prosecute unfaithful wives or be prosecuted for pimping. Adulterers were exiled to separate islands for life. Men, forced to marry by twenty-five, could be betrothed to children, fulfilling the law without actually marrying, but girls had to marry right after puberty. Elite women could no longer register as prostitutes.

"Augustus" ("the revered" – another of Octavius' titles) rebuilt temples and revived old priesthoods, although Rome had never been religious: its god was the state; its religion obedience to and respect for authority. He commissioned Horace and Virgil to glorify Roman life and portray him as an emperor who achieved supremacy by defeating a woman, Cleopatra. Virgil's epic, *The Aeneid*, concerns Aeneas, a legendary founder of Rome who escapes from Troy carrying his father on his back and leading his son by the hand – a male trinity. Aeneas's destiny is to found a state, but before reaching Italy he lands in Carthage and falls in love with its queen, Dido. They become lovers, but destiny beckons and Aeneas sails off. Heartbroken, Dido kills herself. Virgil invented the Carthaginian material, which implied that Carthage (which Rome ruined in the Punic Wars) had to be wrecked for Rome to exist. Virgil laments the "tears at the heart of things" *(lacrimae rerum)*, but identifies the defeated state with a female. *The Aeneid* not only justifies the hard-to-justify Punic Wars but pits male against female; especially in its second half, insane, violent, anarchic female figures and forces oppose sane, rational, orderly pious male figures, whose violence is justified by their effort to found a state under the aegis of the male god Jove (the Roman Zeus).

The strong Roman woman had, by degrees, dwindled into a wife, as the Roman image of women shifted from heroic noblewomen to the usual patriarchal ideal – a silent, obedient supporter of husband and state. Biographies idealized women who lived for others: Brutus's wife Portia; who swallowed hot coals on his death, and Cornelia, the accomplished mother of the Gracchi, who devoted herself to her family. Octavia, who had let her brother Octavius use her by marrying her to Antony, was deserted by him for Cleopatra, yet reared his children by his first wife, Fulvia. Roman writers praised the *univira*, the woman who remained faithful to one man by dying young or committing suicide on his death. Assertive women were viragos, enemies of the state.

Yet even as reformist laws were constricting women and an image of docility was being purveyed, some women grew more powerful. Rule by a man involves the women around him. Octavius was deeply influenced by his wife Livia; he freed her from *patriapotestas* and granted her the Right of Three Children when she had only one. Enormously rich, she managed her estate herself and helped run the empire – behind the scenes, the only way a woman could operate. Despite her power, she was never allowed even to enter the

Senate, a male preserve. In his will, Octavius adopted her into the imperial family and she came close to being deified. Her son, Tiberius, who succeeded Octavius, vetoed a Senate resolution to award her the title of *Mater Patriae*, mother of her country, but her grandson, Claudius, proclaimed her a goddess.

It is hard to guess why women in Rome were so indomitable, when women in societies like Japan, China, and Athens were subdued by law and by men's attitudes towards them. Whatever the case, in succeeding centuries woman regularly ran or helped run the empire. And under them, Rome achieved a century of peace.

Because no constitution leashed rulers, they were often unrestrained and capricious. Some emperors were cruel, even insane. Nero burned the hanging bodies of Christians in his garden to light it and forced Christian women to perform in sadistic pornographic spectacles. But historians from Tacitus and Suetonius on blame rulers' brutality and the empire's degeneracy on women. They claim that Livia murdered all other claimants to Octavius' throne to promote her son Tiberius, that Agrippina the Elder cultivated the army to popularize her son Caligula; and that Claudius's third wife, Messalina, committed every imaginable sexual excess and sadistic cruelty. She was eventually executed, but his next wife, Agrippina the Younger, was said to be even worse. They blame Nero's behaviour on his mother's allegedly using sexual wiles on him, yet fail to mention that he had her executed.

Emperors one after another tried to strengthen the empire by granting men more power over women. The law transferred fathers' power over women to husbands and encouraged childbearing, yet it did not stop fathers from abandoning unwanted babies in the streets. It allowed men to take concubines of lower social status, but charged women in sexual relationships with lower-status men of degrading their class and demoted them to freedwoman or slave status. Abortion was a crime if the husband opposed it.

But women's rule kept Rome at peace for nearly a century. Historians attribute the peace to "five good emperors" who ruled for most of the second century, but the sex dominant in government was female. Emperor Trajan's wife Plotina, sister Marciana, and aunt Matidia helped run the state. Plotina, an Epicurean philosopher (the Epicureans studied gender equality), signed a decree in her own name adopting Hadrian after Trajan died; Hadrian married Matidia's daughter Sabina and travelled with her as his adviser, not his consort, for, like many "good" emperors, he was homosexual. Contemporary men acknowledged the impact of honoured women like Faustina, the wife of Marcus Aurelius.

In the third century a contested succession was won by a military leader, Septimius Severus, who had strong female kin. His wife Julia Domna, her sister Maesa, and Maesa's daughters Soemias and Mamaea dominated the next generations. Domna, a philosopher, destroyed all those who challenged her influence on the emperor, even killing one of her sons to seize the throne for the more tractable Caracalla. When Septimius died, she ruled in Caracalla's name. But he also died, and Maesa took command of the army in the name of her grandson, Soemias' son Elagabulus. When troops in battle turned tail in defeat, Maesa and Soemias leaped from their chariots to stop them. Soemias got what Livia and Agrippina had wanted – a Senate seat with power to sign decrees.

Elagabulus believed he was the god whose name he had taken; he married a Vestal Virgin to unite the religion of

Rome with his own and spent his time working wool. He could not rule, and Maesa had him and Soemias killed, then conspired with her daughter Mamaea to promote Mamaea's son, Alexander Severus. When Maesa died, Mamaea out-manipulated her son, took power herself, and established a Senate of Women to complement the male Senate. Alexander abolished it, but it was occasionally restored later.

These women's power was personal and could not be transferred, as is always the case when women's route to power is men. The women described above had to be strong and brilliant to rule imperial Rome, but their accomplishments did not lead to the inclusion of women in the structure. Roman women rulers were not concerned with the rights of women as a caste, and ordinary Roman women were not allowed to vote, run for public office, sit on juries, plead in court, or be legal guardians of their own children until Justinian in the sixth century CE. Only those with the Right of Three or Four Children could manage their affairs.

Meanwhile, common, poor, slave, and illiterate women, who were not given dole money as men were, walked the streets alone dealing with men, earning barely enough to survive. They ground grain and wove textiles, were fullers and butchers, and sold clothes, beans, nails, perfumes, or dyes. At the end of the day, fisherwomen hawked their catch through narrow cobblestone streets. Some owned large brick- and stone-cutting works or small businesses, erected buildings, made pipes, and practised medicine for menial wages. During Rome's power struggles and wars, they continued – resourceful, voiceless, working, drinking, making love, worrying about the children who hung on their legs, in pleasure and in pain.[3]

CHAPTER 10

CHRISTIANITY

A MONG ROME'S CONQUESTS WAS JUDEA, including Jerusalem. A colonized city, fraught with tension, it contained two main political/religious parties: the Sadducees, a priestly elite that valued order and stability and cooperated with Rome, wanting above all to stay in power; and the Pharisees, who opposed foreign control of Judea and resisted Rome, believing a messiah would free them. Both emphasized salvation through ritual observance, but differed on doctrine. Also influential were the Zealots, who wanted to overthrow Rome by force, and the Essenes, ascetic separatists, who renounced the world to achieve mystical atonement with god.

After Octavius died, Tiberius became Roman emperor. During his reign an itinerant Jewish preacher from Galilee, Jesus, began to draw a large following.[1] Probably influenced somewhat by the Essenes, he avoided running foul of the authorities by advocating the separation of religion and state, but he radically promised salvation to all, regardless of rank or wealth. Only rich men could perform temple rituals; they bought small animals and birds to sacrifice, which is why money-changers sat just outside the temple. The priests insisted that this ritual was necessary for salvation, limiting it to the wealthy. Jesus disapproved of Pharisee reliance on ritual, but shared their belief in resurrection, angels, and spirits. The Sadducees rejected these ideas and tried, successfully, to suppress him. Like all colonizers, the Romans were quick to silence dissent, but it was the Sadducees who found Jesus a serious threat.

Jesus dissented from mainstream thought by insisting that women, slaves, and the poor mattered. Institutions (even churches) and governments have almost always considered subversive any attempt to include the poor or the disfranchised. Jesus' male disciples, who were themselves mainly lower class or slaves, marvelled that he lowered himself to talk to a Samaritan woman (John 4: 57), but he always treated both sexes as capable of salvation. The Samaritan woman was the first person to whom he revealed his mission, and he often used women or their work as metaphors in parables. He saved a woman accused of adultery from stoning, healed a bleeding woman (a contaminated figure in Judaism), and took Mary of Bethany as a student. Five women were his constant companions – Mary of Bethany, Mary Magdala, Joanna, Susanna, and Salome – and rich women supported the disciples financially. When Jesus was crucified, his male followers fled, but the women remained praying at his cross, arranged his burial, and returned to find his tomb empty. After the resurrection, he revealed himself to a woman the disciples mocked and dismissed – Mary of Magdala.

Women were important propagators of Jesus' message; of the thirty-six people who founded churches in the Middle East and corresponded with Paul, sixteen were women (see the Epistles). Paul taught with Prisca in Corinth: Thecla of Iconium left her family to travel and teach with him. Paul himself wrote: "There is neither Jew nor Greek, there is neither slave nor free, there is neither male nor female; for you are all one in Christ Jesus." By 100 CE there were Christian churches in Egypt, Syria, Greece, Asia Minor, and Italy, and soon afterward in Europe, Britain, Mesopotamia, and India – a vast network created largely by women.

But Jesus' followers did not share his acceptance of women and omitted them or diminished their role when, from 75 to 100 CE, they wrote gospel accounts of his life. Despite the obliteration of women's letters, sermons, and acts, evidence shows that women vigorously fostered the new religion as missionaries, prophesying and presiding over house churches. Rich Roman women set up house churches, taught Christianity in their own households, and worshipped with their slaves. Following Jewish practice, they endowed charities for women and orphans (who were not included in the Roman dole).

Early Christian communities were free and autonomous. The religion was not yet institutionalized and had no dogma or hierarchy: communities joined in open intellectual discussion. While Irenaeus, bishop of Lyon (c. 130–202), taught that the primary duties of Christians were to fear God and obey the priests, other groups debated doctrine. There were many schools, but none dominated. Prisca of Corinth hypothesized that, in the Second Coming, Jesus would return as a woman. Clement of Alexandria

(c. 150–215), an important theologian, said that women's spiritual capacities were identical to men's; his successor, Origen, castrated himself so women could attend his school without fearing scandal. Second- and third-century churches had women priests and prophets and worshipped a bisexual god. These churches, later called Gnostic and denounced as heretic, were eliminated and their writings censored.

Many women wanted to remain celibate. This choice may puzzle twentieth-century readers, but there were good reasons for it. Marriage in this period put women totally in their husbands' power. People with absolute control are rarely considerate, sexually or otherwise, of those beneath them. Women were forced into early marriage and child-bearing, subject to unrestrained men and what Adrienne Rich labels "compulsory heterosexuality."[2] Phoebe and other members of the Corinth church who repudiated marriage and sex questioned Paul on the subject. He replied:

> For I would that all men were even as I myself.
> But every man hath his proper gift of God, one
> after this manner, and another after that.
> I say therefore to the unmarried and widows, It is
> good for them if they abide even as I.
> But if they cannot contain, let them marry; for it
> is better to marry than burn (Corinthians 7: 7–9).

Virginity let women claim the holiness and closeness to God usually reserved to men: it made women "manly."[3] It defied men's constriction of women within roles – daughter, wife, mother – and the class system that divided women from each other. Single women could control their own lives, spiritual and physical.

For the first time since the establishment of the *naditu* in second-millennium BCE Babylonia, women had an alternative to marriage. They formed communities: virgins, widows, free, and slave. Historical novels (the Apocryphal Gospels) were written about heroines who converted to Christianity just to take vows of chastity. Refusal to marry was disobedience, and fathers or the state often punished it. Stories describe women joining together to defy husbands, parents, or imperial soldiers, forging bonds with their slave-women in prison and facing death together bravely.

Rome's religion was the state: ritual obeisance to Roman gods indicated loyalty to Rome. Because Christians refused to bow to what they considered false gods, Rome tried to suppress the religion and intermittently persecuted Christians, killing 100,000 of them from North Africa to the Rhone Valley. Records show that most victims were women, who were easier to seize and wildly popular with the crowds thronging the arenas to see them killed. A few were later sainted – Agnes, Blandina (taken with her mistress), a slave who maintained her faith through whipping, burning, and encasement in a net. Finally, she was gored to death by a bull. Perpetua, a twenty-two-year-old noblewoman, bonded with her slave, Felicity, in prison as she nursed her baby. She recorded her martyrdom and visions, in one of which she became a gladiator, triumphant, a man. In the arena, the soldier appointed to stab her could not until she guided his sword hand.

Women's religious communities lived free of male regulation. Women died – before the lions or at the stake – alone. This freedom did not please the emerging hierarchy of the new church. "Much as they feared sexual temptation, clergymen feared women . . . withdrawn into a world without men even more."[4] As the church established itself as an institution, it mainly ignored women, their work, and their sacrifices. It adopted an orthodox theology, a male hierarchy, and, in defining doctrine, excluded thought that emerged from inner vision, women's forte. Orthodox writers, like Irenaeus of Lyon, criticized sects in which women prophesied and led rituals. The hierarchy of bishops, priests, and deacons was given authority over an evolving set of sacraments and set above the people, who were now called "laity." They excluded women from every rank but deaconess, and eventually even from that. Clergymen's wives were strictly barred from office; women were told not to debate and to remain either in church or at home. JoAnne McNamara thinks that women accepted such exclusions only after they received private assurances that the church would continue to uphold their right to preserve virginity, cross-class marriage, and loving marriage.[5] Women barred from the church hierarchy still had a voice in framing the religion; they wrote treatises praising married love and affectionate childrearing and opposing the exposure of babies.

When he became emperor in 306, Constantine ended the persecution. There were now too many Christians, and his mother, Helena, was Christian. Helena, Maximian's concubine, was repudiated when he became emperor because concubines could not be empresses, but her son Constantine succeeded Maximian. Constantine converted to Christianity only when he was dying, but he built churches, banned gladiatorial games and animal sacrifice, made divorce more difficult, outlawed pederasty and concubinage, and penalized "illegitimate" birth. His laws had little effect, but his appointments made the imperial bureaucracy a largely Christian body. Over the centuries, Christian precepts seeped into Roman law, limiting men's freedom to abandon wives, granting women the social and economic (not political) rights of citizens, and legalizing marriages between Roman soldiers and provincial lovers.

Helena founded churches and helped build Constantinople, the capital of the eastern Roman Empire. She deposed the bishop of Antioch for his theology. She made so many pilgrimages that she popularized them; she built churches in Bethlehem and the Mount of Olives and the first shrine to Mary, in Nazareth. Throngs of women followed her to the Holy Land to visit churches, where they passionately debated doctrine with friends, lobbied church leaders, gave alms to the poor and to worthy causes, and demonstrated in the streets. Rich noblewomen channelled their wealth to the church and converted their families. Marcella taught Jerome, a theologian who translated the Bible into Latin. Women had intellectual and spiritual relationships with bishops and theologians, contributed money to their causes, and took part in the inner councils of the increasingly hierarchical church. They had a voice in theological issues, church building, appointments to church offices, and patronage for scholars and preachers. Women persuaded churchmen to foster the burgeoning monastic movement.

Women built communities. Macrina formed a community with her mother, brother, former servants, and others (some of them wealthy), and converted her brother Basil (later Saint Basil), who is credited with founding Greek monasticism. Melania the Elder rescued her granddaughter from being sold in marriage to advance her family's dynastic ambitions; Melania the Younger lived in equality with her former slaves. Rich women turned their estates into female communities; Marcella made her home a monastery for aristocratic Roman women to live in and study together. Paula built and managed a monastery in Bethlehem for all classes of women, enabling her daughter Eustochium to avoid marriage. Jerome crowed that Eustochium's virginity ended one of Rome's most ancient houses.

The Monastic Period

After the first century CE, conquered Germanic peoples grew restless and began to invade the south. More and more men entered the church. Middle-class men burdened by taxes became priests or monks so they could live well untaxed. Their removal from the tax roll placed an even greater burden on the peasants, who often became destitute; they too entered monasteries or became soldiers, itinerant day-labourers, thieves, or brigands. Farms fell into ruin. Tax collectors had to be guarded by small armies or risk being killed. Minor but constant peasant and slave revolts drained the armies that were fighting off Germanic tribes sweeping towards Rome. Rome's oppressed classes were undermining the empire from within.

Constantine moved the capital to Constantinople in 330, as wave after wave of Germanic invaders entered Rome's environs and finally sacked the city in 455. They took the western Roman Empire in 476 – the date usually cited for the fall of Rome. Justinian became emperor in 527 and succeeded in reconquering the western empire, but, in the process, devastated Italy and later lost his gains. His recodification of Roman law was more lasting. To marry Theodora, a prostitute, he changed laws and made her joint ruler of the empire, a legal participant in all official functions. Together they revised Roman law massively to fit Christian principles.

They granted women many rights: to control their own property after reaching the age of twenty-five and to leave it to whom they pleased, and to enjoy adult legal rights while single. Marriage became a contract between consenting adults. Theodora tried to use the monastic system to shelter women who started life, as she did, coerced into prostitution. Historians derided her influence on Justinian and her efforts to help prostitutes, but admired her heroism in facing a rebellious city mob and preventing the emperor from fleeing by reminding him that purple, the colour of imperial robes, "makes the best shroud."

In 381 Theodosius I organized the Council of Constantine, which proclaimed the doctrine of the Trinity: Father, Son, and Holy Spirit are of the same substance, consubstantial, one person comprising god. This doctrine went further even than Greek myth in eliminating the female from the godhead. The Christian father-god utters the Word, his son, and procreates through language, entirely without a woman. The Holy Spirit is born from the mutual love of son and father. This creation is not incest because bodies are not involved.

The Trinity, understandably called a mystery, lies at the heart of Christianity. It achieves two major goals: it posits a realm that transcends the physical world, in which reality is made by the word. History is filled with rulers who claimed divinity to justify their superiority, but not until Christianity and the sacralizing of the notion that language creates reality does the debate between appearance and reality begin to pervade Western literature and thought. Increasingly, what is said – the Emperor has new clothes – is called real, while physical reality fades into invisibility or is denied. The Trinity procreates without the female – without body, blood,

ooze, without nature, and superior to it. Generations of clerical writers, wishing that women did not exist, lamented that
this sort of procreation was possible only to god. The church
defined the divine realm in opposition to the earthly one,
celebrating birth through utterance, death as life, the overcoming of sex and body, a realm where nothing changes and
power and justice are one.

People accustomed to the association of godhood with
the male might not have perceived the symbolic import of
the Trinity and saw Christianity as a religion offering a new
freedom and equality. Those most hungry for both these
attributes – women – were the major disseminators of
Christianity throughout Europe. Clothilde, wife of Clovis,
the Frankish king, pressured him until he converted; Queen
Bertha and her daughter Ethelberga converted their husbands Ethelbert of Kent and Edwin of Northumbria. Bertha
corresponded regularly with Pope Gregory I, asking doctri-
nal questions, including one on menstruation. Nature causes this flow, he wrote; women are not at fault, so there is no
reason a menstruating woman should not receive communion. This policy would not endure.

In the late fourth century Emperor Theodosius made
Christianity the state religion, barring indigenous religions.
Over the next two centuries non-Christians were excluded
from the civil service, the army, legal practice, and teaching.
In 529 Justinian destroyed temples, forbade incest, and
ordered pagans to become Christian or face exile and con-
fiscation of property. Although Roman law protected Jews,
Christian mobs destroyed synagogues; in the fifth century
Rome forbade the building of new synagogues, the marriage
of a non-Jew to a Jew, and gradually barred Jews from the
civil service and the army, from practising law or holding

public office. The persecuted had become the persecuters.

By the sixth century life was savage in the western Roman Empire, now Germanic kingdoms, especially for women. Men took many wives, often incestuously. Despite laws penalizing abduction, men often raped and killed women or killed their husbands and seized women on battlefields, forcing them into marriage. The chronicler Bede noted that a whole generation of royal women in Anglo-Saxon England preferred celibate life in a convent to marriage. It was during this time that courageous Romans of faith went to the wilderness to build monasteries.

Late in the third century Christians began to retreat to relatively uninhabited places, like deserts, to establish a regimen based on prayer and fasting. Such a life involved considerable danger, so anchorites built their shelters in clusters, near each other. Fearing sexual temptation, however, they excluded women, who built their communities adjoining male settlements.

In time, they travelled to wildernesses in the north and built shelters for both sexes. Convents of this period were "double monasteries" usually governed by an abbess. Monks and nuns lived by a common rule devised by the monastery itself without episcopal interference. Nuns needed a male community to act as priests and to do heavy labour. Many monasteries were huge estates holding thousands of people; abbesses supervised the religious life of the nuns, monks, and peasants on their land, offered medical attention and education, and mediated disputes. Many abbesses held substantial political power. Hilda of Whitby counselled her royal relatives, trained five bishops, and founded several monastic houses. A meeting held at one, the Synod of Whitby, submitted the English Church to Rome in 644.

Hilda fostered poets and recognized talent in a poor herds-
man, Caedmon, who, instructed by her, became the first
important English poet.

Monasteries were major centres of learning. One of the
greatest scholars of her age was Hroswitha (Hrosvit,
Roswitha) of Gandersheim, a tenth-century nun, who was
admired by Holy Roman Emperor Otto I. She wrote histories, stories, saints' lives, and plays, (she was the only
European dramatist in almost five hundred years). Adopting
the dramatic structures of the misogynistic Roman dramatist
Terence, she made virtuous women heroes. Her regalian
rights (rights of sovereigns of royal monasteries) included
having her own court and knights, coining money, and
attending meetings of the Diet. Otto's daughter Mathilda,
abbess of Quedlinburg, also enjoyed these rights. When
Emperor Otto II was overseeing his domains in Italy, his sister Mathilda ruled for him in the north, presiding over
church councils. When he was in Germany, she held the
powers of a *metropolitana,* overseer of bishops, a role normally reserved for men. Nuns fostered and created art and
literature, producing some of the finest illuminated manu-
scripts of the age; they wrote biographies, narrative, and lyric
poetry.

Laywomen were also powerful in the early medieval
church. Liutprand of Cremona, an Italian monk-historian,
charged that the daughter of the Marquess of Tuscany and
the widow of the Marquess of Ivrea Ermengarde "held the
chief authority in all Italy" by "carnal commerce with everyone, prince and commoner alike."[6] In a common association, he attributed female power to sexual power and called
Italy a "pornocracy" (ruled by prostitutes). In Rome the
Theophylactus family, ruled by Lady Theodora and later her

daughter Marozia, controlled even the papacy. Marozia, mistress to one pope, mother of another, almost united all Italy by marrying its king. Italian women held power because they could inherit money, property, and offices passed through lineages. Barred from holding office themselves, they controlled the men who did. Many ecclesiastics relied on and worked with women.

The great power held by some women in this period intensified the virulent woman-hatred that pervaded Christianity. This vicious misogyny is rooted in its Judaic and Greek sources. In Judaism, woman lures man to disobedience (called "original sin" by the Christian Augustine); in the Greek tradition, woman is an inferior species, a deformed male.[7] The misogynistic pseudo-Paul, whose utterances are conflated with Paul's in the New Testament, ordered women to learn in silent submissiveness, not to teach or have authority over men. Peter too wanted women submissive, modest, and unadorned; the New Testament epistles of Timothy and Titus held that only men could be bishops. Even Clement and Origen found "active" maleness superior to "passive" femaleness. A rabid woman-hater, Tertullian, wrote around 200: "The sentence of God on this sex of yours lives in this age . . . *You* are the Devil's gateway. You are the unsealer of that forbidden tree. *You* are the first deserter of the divine Law. *You* are she who persuaded him whom the Devil was not valiant enough to attack. *You* destroyed so easily God's image, man. On account of *your* desert, that is death, even the Son of God had to die."[8]

When Tertullian wrote this passage, he was considered a heretic; he had earlier vociferously denounced "those women among the heretics" (Gnostic sects), urging their removal. Such denunciations persisted outside mainstream

Christianity for decades. Priests and monks blamed their lust on women's filth and corruption. Not just Eve, but Woman, is weak, frivolous, fallen. Jerome challenged Gregory's judgment that since menstruation was an innocent part of nature, menstruating women could take communion, writing: "Nothing is so unclean as a woman in her periods . . . What she touches she causes to become unclean." By the third century, menstruating women could not approach the altar. By the late sixth century, Christians had adopted the Judaic belief that childbirth was contaminating, requiring priestly purification. Men were lords over women, who should be meek, quiet, gentle, free from anger, and stay at home.

The Greek (eastern) and the Latin (western) branches of the church split. A Roman pope, needing military help in 800, made Charlemagne, a Frankish soldier, emperor of the Holy Roman Empire. Charlemagne "reformed" the church in his domains by excluding women. Clergymen invoked pseudo-Paul to bar women from teaching or holding authority over men: Charlemagne forbade the close association of the sexes in monasteries and ordered nuns and canonesses to be strictly cloistered. Women could no longer assist in mass or give the sacraments; nuns could not teach boys; and abbesses and all conventual affairs were placed under bishops' authority. The major legacy of these reforms after the Carolingian empire (eighth to tenth centuries) collapsed was that nuns educated girls, while boys not destined for the clergy grew up illiterate.

The Defeat of Women in the Catholic Church

In the mid-eleventh century the church tried to bring

secular leaders to heel, with the object of controlling Europe. Popes Gregory VII and Urban II eliminated hostile local church leaders and secular nobles and brought a Holy Roman Emperor literally to his knees. In his campaign for domination of secular government, Gregory promised reform – especially of women and wives of clergy. Priests did not want to be celibate; when, in a tenth-century wave of reform, they were ordered to get rid of their wives, they argued that they could not support themselves and would go hungry and naked without wives. Wives supported husbands who did non-productive work, financially and physically, with their own domestic labour. Some brought dowries to the marriage, adding to church property. But the tenth-century Bishop Atro of Vercelli attacked priests' wives for spending church money, managing church lands, distracting their husbands from their duties, and drawing them into secular disputes.

The attack was taken up by Peter Damian, the thirteenth child of a minor noblewoman. Exhausted by childbearing, she had refused to nurse him. The wife of her parish priest intervened, urging her not to let her baby die. Ironically, as an adult, Peter Damian hysterically campaigned to forbid priests from marrying. He also carried on a flirtatious correspondence with the powerful Empress Agnes, who supported him. His cause was victorious and priests were barred from marrying; afterwards they took concubines who worked as hard as wives and bore children, but had no legal protections and could not claim the men's estates.

The next step in purging women from the church was to bar lay people from influencing the bestowal of church offices – a movement financed mainly by the powerful Beatrice of Tuscany and her daughter Matilda. When

Emperor Henry IV claimed authority over the church, they supported Gregory VII in a power struggle that ended in a dramatic showdown: Henry walked barefoot in the snow to do obeisance to Gregory at Matilda's castle at Canossa. Matilda supported the pope's army until she died and left it extensive Tuscan lands. Women helped to eradicate women's voice in the church.

From the ninth to the eleventh centuries Arab and Viking invaders overran Britain and Europe. Convents were the intruders' favourite target, with their undefended women and wealth. The raiders raped and killed the women, looted the convent, then burned the buildings down. Few were rebuilt. Throughout Europe, independent convents were politically and financially weakened.

In the twelfth century, reform movements and religious enthusiasm inspired men to endow large monasteries. These groups eventually joined together, sharing rule and government. Church officials in charge of the founding of new religious institutions barred women from controlling property like monasteries and from the roles they had performed for centuries – preaching, singing the Gospel, avowing novices, hearing confession, and assisting at Mass. Only a few powerful institutions evaded the new rules by winning a special right to report directly to the pope, bypassing local bishops. Once double monasteries were gone, the few establishments open to women were small and limited to elite women. In England, nunneries took only about twenty upper-class women. Male monastic orders shuddered at the thought of sister establishments – those that accepted them insisted on strict enclosure and supervision by a male prior. But double monasteries remained in Slavic lands, where women were still active in church affairs.

Women wanted to emulate Dominic and Francis (later sainted) in "apostolic life," living in poverty, begging alms, working in and for the community, but neither order would accept women: Dominic even forbade priors to serve women spiritually. So Clare (later sainted) and Diane d'Andalo founded second Franciscan and Dominican orders. The Poor Clares, free of male supervision, were forbidden to beg and supported themselves by spinning and weaving. Even this arrangement required papal dispensation. Several popes, finding Clare's rule too rigorous, imposed debilitating rules on the order. In 1215 the church forbade the founding of new orders. Women who wanted to live independently had to find other ways – in beguinages or communities of anchoresses.

Some women monastics won renown. Hildegard of Bingen (1098–1179) entered a convent as a child and rose to become abbess. At forty, saying god had commanded her, she began to write. She envisioned god as feminine and nurturing, and the universe as an interrelated, harmonious entity. She was erudite and wrote on medicine and natural science. Believing that disease came from disruptions of the body's equilibrium, she explained blood circulation physiologically, wrote on nerve action to the brain, contagion, and links between sugar and diabetes. She taught that women have a greater tendency to miscarry or produce impaired children if they conceive before twenty or after fifty – ideas that were not accepted until centuries later. She wrote allegorical verse and set it to music in a free and original style. Her music, newly discovered in this age, has been recorded and is enjoyed today. Hildegard was enormously influential in her lifetime and, late in her life, she founded a monastery at Rupertsberg.

A nun remembered for her love, not her learning, is Heloise, who was famed in youth for her intelligence. She lived in Paris with her uncle, Canon Fulbert of Notre Dame. Her tutor, the brilliant Peter Abelard, became her lover. They had a son, were secretly married, and fled from the canon, who pursued Abelard and had him castrated. Abelard retired to a monastery and insisted that Heloise do the same. Although not drawn to religious life, she entered it for love of Abelard. She founded an order for women, became its abbess, and tried to fit Benedictine rule to women. The lovers' correspondence has been preserved. Heloise wrote lovingly at first, but Abelard's self-involvement and sternness led her to change her tone to submissive requests for guidance in religious rule.

In 1179 the church/state established cathedral schools, ordering cathedrals to pay for a teacher to instruct, without charge, all boys who wished to learn. At first these schools, intended to train boys as priests, taught only basic skills sufficient to read church offices, but as the church bureaucracy grew, the curriculum expanded to law and administration. Schools began to offer a thorough knowledge of Latin, concentrating on Latin classics. Advanced schools were established in Italy as early as the eleventh and twelfth centuries – Bologna in law, Salerno in medicine. Until about 1200, northern cathedral schools remained primarily clerical, and even men with other goals took holy orders. But as demand increased, secular schools were founded, teaching in the vernacular. These new institutions became the great universities of Paris, Poitiers, Oxford, Cambridge, Salamanca, and Naples, centres of the new learning and seedbeds of new theoretical thinking. Exclusively male, all these northern episcopal schools, except Bologna, barred women from attending as pupils or teaching.

The new learning that emerged in the twelfth century was based largely on logic and mathematics. Excluded from training and work as educators, religious women turned inward to mysticism. In a startling spurt of female mystical writing, Julian of Norwich, Margery Kemp, and Catherine of Siena wrote powerfully of mystical experience in major works of religious literature. The work of women mystics presented a side of experience disregarded by male education, and it is still read by religious students.

The final affront to women in the church came in the late thirteenth century, when it forbade nuns to leave convents or to contact anyone outside the walls. "No nun . . . shall henceforth have or be able to have the power of going out of those monasteries for whatever reason or excuse," Pope Boniface VIII wrote in 1298. Nuns still went on pilgrimages, like Chaucer's Prioress, but, after the Gregorian and later reforms, women had little access to the church hierarchy. Nuns taught girls, but learned nuns vanished. The church that women had worked for and enriched for centuries now barred them from active legitimate participation. The church that women had suffered and died for, that had taught there was no distinction between male and female, decided, after all, that this equality was true only after death.

The powers that abbesses wielded from the seventh to the twelfth centuries were never institutionalized, never granted by law. Women exercised them because no one stopped them, as they had in the Roman Empire and in Hellenistic Greece. But their faith and drive and labour in building and maintaining monasteries was not proof against men's solidarity against women. Women had worked fruitfully in the church for twelve hundred years – far longer than any feminist movement has lasted – yet their voice in the church was utterly silenced.

Everywhere, men base their claim to superiority on a connection with the deity that women lack. During the period of state formation, women lost the right to perform rites of worship. This denial led to the devaluation of female children and the exclusion of women from property rights. Sumer, India, Egypt, Aztec Mexico, Israel, and Christian Europe all began as near theocracies. Over time, transcendent religion in every civilization became a major tool in propagating and in maintaining patriarchy.[9]

CHAPTER 11

ISLAM

UHAMMAD FOUNDED A RELIGION THAT BECAME one
of the major world religions. Starting in small
Arabian cities, it spread to Asia and Africa. In the twentieth
century, Muslim immigrants took it to Europe and the
United States. As Christians use the supposed year of Jesus'
birth to start counting time (BC = before the Christ; AD =
anno domini, the year of our Lord), Muslims use the year
622 CE, the year Muhammad took political control of
Medina. Like Christianity, Islam is a militant religion – it
conquered and converted the Near East and much of Africa,
Asia, India, and Spain – mainly Granada. It was not expelled
from Spain until 1492.

For eons the Arabian Peninsula, a desert, was isolated.
Only nomadic Bedouin camel herders who lived in tents
survived there, following an annual circuit of grazing land.

They were probably matrilineal and male dominated, and materially but not politically equal. Each fiercely independent clan lived, worked, and made decisions collectively. Chiefs (sayyid, sheik) were elected only to lead the almost constant raids. Women went on raids and maintained the clan during men's frequent absences. Subordinate but respected, they had a voice in tribal decisions. Superb poets, they judged poetry contests, which were a favourite tribal pastime. Clans were endogamous, and both sexes had many spouses. No matter whom a woman married, her children belonged to her clan. Charging for sex was acceptable.

Southern Arabia (Yemen) was arable. Even before the first millennium BCE its people had devised a unique irrigation system and strong social organizations that became trading states. They sent myrrh and frankincense – rare costly gum resins extracted from trees that grow only in Yemen and Somalia – by camel caravan to Indian Ocean and Mediterranean ports. Minaeans conquered Sabeans, who had conquered Himyarites; each state left archaeological remains, fortified cities, temples, castles, dams, and written records, mainly codes of property law.

Middle Eastern women were fierce fighters and independent spirits: most Arabs who are remembered are women. The Old Testament queen of Sheba, Bilkis, took Solomon gifts, enchanting him by her flattery and erudition. She returned to Sabea with Judaic knowledge. Christianity was introduced in the first centuries CE, but Himyarite rulers formally adopted the more popular Judaism in 525 CE. Zenobia was queen of Palmyra (now Tadmor in Syria), a city famed for its culture and elegance. She tried to corner the Egyptian grain Rome needed for its wars by invading Egypt in 269, challenging Rome's dominance in the Near

East. Eventually Rome defeated her and Zenobia suffered the humiliation Cleopatra died to avoid – the forced parade through Rome in heavy golden chains. Still, she lived out her days in a comfortable villa in Tivoli.

Arabia was often ruled by queens, who might be priestesses of local goddesses.[1] But Bedouin clans kept few records and, after the fourth century CE, cease to mention female rulers. But poets continued to celebrate strong women and Bedouin graves show rough sexual equality. When Muslim scholars edited Arabian documents centuries later, they erased all references to women, calling the past an "age of ignorance" – *jahilia*. Much of what we know about pre-Islamic Arabia comes from Muhammad's wives, whose utterances were saved only because they were revered.

'Aisha, probably Muhammad's favourite wife, was the source of much information. She said there were four types of marriage, two of which were polygamous (where both sexes had more than one spouse). Either spouse could initiate divorce: the woman did it by waiting for the man to go out, then turning her tent so it faced a different direction. When he returned and saw no door, he knew he had been divorced and did not attempt to enter. Children belonged to the mothers' clan. In some clans women had high status, with rights to divorce and to own and control property.[2]

Early writers described many clans as matrilineal/matrilocal.[3] Clan women with high religious status were judges, mediators, prophets, and priestesses attached to sanctuaries. They took part in battle as warriors, nurses, and cheerleaders. Accounts of male feuds over women and of families' willingness to ransom captured women suggest that seventh-century women were highly valued by clan society, but no longer participated in tribal councils.[4] Among the

Quraish (the dominant clan in Mecca) of that time, governing decisions were made by an all-male Council of Elders, and Quraish men prevented women from expressing opinions outside the private realm. Some began to practise cousin-marriage to keep property within a family.[5]

Women may have lost power and status even before Muhammad, as male-domination spread in the Near and Middle East.[6] Clans became patrilineal, which inevitably entails male-domination. Naming children for fathers is intrinsically an act of force: it reverses natural mother-right. And because it was impossible until recent years to assure paternity, patrilineality requires abuse of women.

Muhammad was born at a time of major social change, as clans were abandoning herding and nomadism for trade and settling in cities like Mecca and Medina. Tribal life is inherently democratic because clans hold property collectively, but collective ownership is not adaptable to city properties. Meccan men were polygynous, and the women monogamous, but women inherited independently, held property, and did business. In Medina, women were sexually free. But the tendency towards patriarchy marched on: some clans buried unwanted female babies alive, many men captured their wives, and most paid women's male guardians for a wife. Women were bought and sold.

Muhammad

Muhammad was born in Mecca around 570 to a minor branch of the Quraish family. His mother, Amna bint Wahb, continued to live with her clan after marriage; her husband, Abdullah, visited her. However, he died before Muhammad was born, and the child lived with his mother's clan. When he was six, Amna died while en route to Medina with him and a female slave, and he was sent to his father's clan under the guardianship of his uncle, Abu Talib.

As a young man Muhammad worked for Khadija, a widow, managing her caravan and carrying goods from Mecca to Syria. Later, she married him. Fifteen years older than Muhammad and wealthy, she proposed to him herself instead of through a male intermediary. She kept him monogamous – he had no other wives while she lived and he exalted her after her death. His later wife 'Aisha once called Khadija "that toothless old woman whom Allah replaced with a better." Muhammad rejoined, "No indeed, Allah has not replaced her by a better. She believed in me when I was rejected; when they called me a liar, she proclaimed me truthful; when I was poor she shared with me her wealth; and Allah granted me her children though withholding those of other women." 'Aisha claimed not to be jealous of any of the prophet's wives but Khadija. A male scholar believes that "without the affection and faith of Khadijah, Mohammed would never have been a prophet; and when death overtook her, Islam lost much of its purity and the Qur'an [Koran] of its dignity."[7]

Judaism and Christianity, both monotheistic religions, were known in Arabia. Muhammad respected them and disparagingly contrasted the behaviour of polytheistic Arabs to monotheistic Arabs. He was a thinking man, a moral man, and, periodically, he would withdraw to a cave in Mount Hira outside the city to ponder Arab morality. There, when he was about forty, he was visited by a heavenly being later identified as the Angel Gabriel. He was disturbed by the vision, but Khadija urged him to trust it and supported him emotionally, intellectually, and financially as the visitations

continued over the years. She depleted her fortune supporting him. Although the Qur'an was not written down until
centuries later, Muslims think that the Qur'an, Islam's holy
book, contains Gabriel's words to Muhammad during his
revelations.

Allah is not the name of a god but the Arabic word for
God; *Islam* means submission to Allah, renouncing all other
gods. Muhammad used the term "Islam" for all monotheists
– Abraham, Lot, Jesus' disciples, Moses – and drew heavily
on Judaic and Christian sources. For him, the Torah and the
New Testament were divinely inspired: he called Christianity and Judaism "religions of the Book," and their adherents "People of the Book." He taught reliance on scripture,
belief in a last judgment, bodily resurrection after death, and
the existence of angels. Banning adultery and infanticide,
which were common in Arabia, he taught that compassion
for others, honesty in business, and care for the poor were
rewarded or punished in an afterlife. He thought that Jesus
was a great prophet, not a god. His own religion, like Judaism, lacked sacraments or priests, and, like Christianity, was
evangelical (aggressive in converting) and universal. His
most important principles were a demand for social justice
and an assertion of human equality.

At first, Muhammad seemed to want to create not a new
religion but a morality for Arabs. Like the great Hebrew
prophets, he offered a simple message: there is one god; faith
and moral rectitude are good, materialism is wicked, and
divine judgment is imminent. Unlike Jesus, he stressed ritual observance – prayer, fasts, and, later, pilgrimages to
Mecca. He made a tactical error when he assailed the morals
of the Quraish and roused their rich businessmen to
persecute him and his followers. To placate them,

Muhammad sanctioned the worship of three Meccan goddesses, "daughters of Allah" – Allat, Manat, and Al-'Uzza. (The verses sanctioning this worship were later called "Satanic Verses," the reference of Salman Rushdie's title for his novel). The accommodation worked until Muhammad revoked the revelation of female deities, saying that if men could have sons, why should God have daughters? Disruption followed, and some of his followers fled abroad.

In 619 the two people most important to Muhammad died – Khadija and Abu Talib, his uncle-protector. Seeking a power base, he met secretly in Aqabah with three Medinans, a man and two women, Umm Umarah and Umm Mani. He made an alliance with them, asking them to swear an oath of allegiance, but he devised separate oaths for men, pledging military help, and for women. Muhammad and his followers made the *hijra* (hegira) to Medina in 622, which became year 1 in the Muslim calendar. The city had been settled by Arab Jews who were later joined by polytheistic Arabs. When he arrived, two Arab tribes vied for control, and the Jews provided a balance of power.[8] Sophisticated secular Medina welcomed Muhammad as a mediator, not a religious leader.

In Medina, Muhammad swiftly changed course politically, taking over as secular ruler of the city. The regulations and laws he issued became part of the Qur'an, rules for a Muslim theocracy. Like contemporary Catholic popes, he relied on military force. But Christian militarism contradicts Christian doctrine, which decrees the separation of church and state ("Render unto Caesar what is Caesar's") and a rhetoric of peace. Muslim militarism, in contrast, fulfils Muslim doctrine, which accepts bellicosity.

But Muhammad longed to return to Mecca, his familial

city, and he raised an army. In 624 he attacked Mecca in the Battle of Badr, in which 300 Muslims defeated 1000 Meccans. Muhammad's followers and many enemies saw this victory as a manifestation of Allah's will. Muhammad seized control of northward caravan routes, but in 625 the Meccans retaliated, again far outnumbering the Muslims. This time, the Meccans won. They wounded Muhammad and killed many of his followers. Muhammad spun this battle into Allah's test of the faithful. In the end, Muhammad won Mecca through conversion and diplomacy, and in 630 he entered the city in triumph. He took control of its ancient holy sites and established an Islamic state. When he died in 632, most of the Arabian Peninsula had adopted Islam.

Women were Muhammad's earliest supporters – Khadija was his first convert, his son-in-law Ali the second, then his aunts Safiyyah, 'Atikah, and Arwa. His aunts supported him despite the hostility of important men in their clan. Ramla (Umm Habiba), an early convert, remained faithful to the prophet and married him even as her father, Abu-Sufyan, led the Meccan opposition to him. Suda bint Kuraiz converted her nephew 'Uthman, and Fatimah her brother 'Umar Ibn al-Khattab, men who would be Muhammad's closest companions and lead Islam after he died. Many Medinan women converted apart from their husbands. Umm Sulaim, who fought at Uhud and Hunain, would not marry Abu Talhaha until he, too, converted.[9]

Women converts were important to Muhammad: he rarely rejected a woman and even broke a treaty with Mecca to oblige a woman. Umm Kulthum, a young literate Meccan, joined Islam during Muhammad's first sojourn there. (At the time, literacy was rare, especially in women, and, as Arab culture was oral, converts memorized the

Qur'an from recitation.) Umm Kulthum followed Muhammad to Medina, the first Quraishite woman to do so, but her brothers pursued her, demanding that Muhammad return her in accord with a treaty he had made with Mecca. Umm Kulthum begged asylum. After a revelation (later used to establish a law banning marriage between Muslims and non-Muslims), Muhammad protected her. Umm Kulthum remained in Medina, successively marrying four of his companions. Women spread Islam much as they spread Christianity.

In later years, men argued over whether Muhammad clasped women's hands during allegiance swearing or dipped his hands in a common bowl of water, as he did with men. This fact shows either that men's attitudes towards women had changed or that Muhammad had always been more accepting of females than had the men of his culture. The women's oath was eventually recorded in this form:

> O thou prophet, when believing women come to thee offering thee allegiance on the basis that they will not associate anything with Allah, will not steal, will not commit adultery, will not kill their children, will not produce a scandal which they have devised between their hands and feet, and will not oppose thee in anything reputable, accept their allegiance and ask Allah to forgive them – Allah is forgiving, compassionate.

Women fought in all the battles of early Islam. At Uhud, 'Aisha and another wife of Muhammad carried water to men on the battlefield, their robes tucked up, showing their anklets. Women carried the wounded and dead from the field. Before a battle with the Quraish, some women repudiated the women's oath and took the men's. In what is called the Pledge of the Tree, they swore not to flee battle, but to fight to the death. Umm 'Umarah (who met Muhammad at Aqaba) seized a tent pole, placed a knife in her girdle, took the men's oath, and cried, "I hope to kill anyone that comes near me!" The fierce Umm 'Umarah always fought beside her husband and sons and was often wounded. She lost a hand fighting in the Battle of Aqabah for Abu Bakr. Newly married Umm Hakim, hearing that her groom had fallen at Marj al-Saffar, wrenched up a tent pole and rushed into battle, killing seven Byzantine soldiers. Muhammad gave women the power to grant asylum to fugitives and enemy refugees, requiring Muslim men to respect it.

Women also fought against Islam. Many female poets opposed Muhammad's doctrines and mocked him. Muhammad especially feared the poet 'Asma bint Marwan and was greatly relieved when a follower executed her: Islam has always taken literature seriously. Hind bint 'Utbah, a prominent Quraish woman married to wealthy Abu-Sufyan, head of the Quraish army, lost her father, uncle, and brother at the Battle of Badr. She wanted revenge, and in 625 at Uhud she was one of fifteen women who led the men into battle, singing, dancing, and playing tambourines. Muhammad's uncle Hamza was killed: she gashed open his chest, tore out his liver, and bit into it. After the Muslims won Mecca in 630, Abu-Sufyan went to their camp to submit; on returning, he urged Meccans to convert. Hind hit him publicly, crying, "Kill this old fool, for he has changed his religion!" She smashed her idols, bewailing her trust in them. A legend claims that Hind was among three or four women whom the Muslims condemned to death and that she saved herself by converting. When she converted, she took the oath defiantly:

> "You shall have but one God,"
> Muhammad declares.
> "We grant you that," Hind responds.
> "You shall not steal."
> "Abu Sufyan is a stingy man. I only stole
> provisions from him."
> "That is not theft. You will not commit adultery."
> "Does a free woman commit adultery?"
> "You will not kill your children"
> [referring to the practice of infanticide].
> "Have you left us any children that you
> did not kill at the battle of Badr?"

Customs at this time granted freewomen considerable freedom of opinion and behaviour, but slavewomen were not allowed to convert against their owners' will. The first Muslim martyr was a slave, Sumayyah bint Khubbat, whose owner persecuted and finally killed her for refusing to give up her new religion. Freewomen too were persecuted for converting; Umm Sharik was tortured by her husband's relatives and exposed to the sun without water for three days, until she was revived by a bucket of water from heaven. The popularity of this unauthenticated tale suggests that people of the era believed that women possessed such courage.[10]

Muhammad married so many women so soon after Khadija's death that scholars suspect she had him sign a marriage contract promising monogamy in her lifetime. After her death, he asked his aunt Khawla, a convert, whom he should marry. She proposed Sawda, if he wanted a non-virgin, and 'Aisha, if he wanted a virgin. He wanted both and sent Khawla to them. Sawda, a convert and widow or divorcee who seemed to have disposal of herself, accepted. But 'Aisha, Abu Bakr's child, was only six. She was outdoors playing when her mother called her in and told her she could no longer play outdoors but must stay indoors. "It fell into my heart that I was married," she recalled, but she did not know to whom. Muhammad visited Abu Bakr's house every day.

Abu Bakr followed Muhammad to Medina. When the prophet's small house (which also served as the mosque) was built, Abu Bakr summoned his family and Muhammad sent for his daughters and Sawda. Each wife had her own "house," a room on the mosque wall, but Muhammad had none; he shared a wife's room each night. When 'Aisha was nine or ten, the prophet visited her. Her mother fetched the child, who was playing on a swing, washed her face, and led her indoors. Muhammad was sitting on a bed with some neighbours. Umm Ruman sat the girl in his lap, saying, "These are your people, God bless you in them and they in you." Everyone rose and left, and "the Prophet consummated the marriage in our house," 'Aisha related. Muhammad, who was over fifty, was very tender with 'Aisha and even played dolls with her. She was his favourite wife and the most famous after Khadija. She grew up assertive, snapping at Muhammad when he claimed Allah allowed him to have more wives than other men: "It seems to me your Lord hastens to satisfy your desire!" After he died, she became a major authority on the early years of the religion, challenging the growing misogyny of Islam. When male leaders barred women as unclean, like dogs and donkeys, from worship in the mosque, 'Aisha scoffed: "You equate us with dogs and donkeys! The Prophet would pray while I lay before him on the bed!"

Three months after marrying 'Aisha, Muhammad married Hafsa, 'Umar Ibn al-Khattab's daughter. 'Umar was Muhammad's most ardent supporter, after Abu Bakr. Muhammad soon revealed that polygyny was allowed: "Marry such of the women as seem good to you, two or three or four." But he did not stop at four: the number of his wives and concubines is unknown. He barred marriage between Muslims and non-Muslims, yet married two Jewish captives, Safiyyah bint Huyayy and Raihanah bint Zaid (both of whom later converted to Islam). He assiduously courted the beautiful but reluctant Umm Salamah, who finally accepted him in 626 and became one of his wisest counsellors. But this old man, powerful enough to fulfil all his desires, may have bitten off more than he could chew. Perhaps unable to control so many women, he began to regulate them.

People sat at Muhammad's feet to learn. In Medina, after the women complained that Muhammad addressed his Qur'anic revelations only to men, he gave them explicitly to both sexes. But the women did the work that supported the group and were often away. They claimed that the men, because they didn't work, knew more of his teachings. Muhammad then set aside a special time for women's instruction. Both sexes attended the mosque and heard Muhammad's public discourses; both took part in religious services on feast days, memorized and recited his teachings, prayed over the dead, and went on pilgrimages. Islam under Muhammad was less misogynist than it became: Muhammad respected women, but was not free from the misogyny of his culture. Islam was not hierarchical, but certain leaders had power: the *imam* (who led the congregation in prayer), the *khatib* (who preached and exhorted the congregation), and the *mu'adhdin* (who summoned the congregation to prayer) had prestige and influence. Muhammad named only two women to these roles – Umm Salamah was imam for women, and Umm Waraqah was imam for her household (including men).

Islamicist Leila Ahmed believes that Muhammad began to restrain women around the time of the battle of Uhud (625), the victory that opened the door to Mecca and that women helped to win. She believes his motivation was jealousy, mainly of 'Aisha, whose behaviour could be as free as her speech. Once, accidentally left behind at a campsite, 'Aisha returned the next morning escorted by a young man. This incident provoked rumours of infidelity. Muhammad withdrew, sullen, resentful; his revelations vanished. After a time he emerged, announcing that heaven had decreed 'Aisha innocent.[11] Other acts triggered possessiveness in the aging man – at meals, male guests' hands might touch his wives' hands, 'Umar's hands might touch 'Aisha's. Nabia Abbott thinks that Muhammad's attitude towards women changed after the scandal about his marriage in 627 to his cousin Zainab bint Jahsh, whom his adopted son Zaid had divorced. Muhammad's effort to seclude his wives occurred soon afterward, driven perhaps by guilt, not jealousy.

This Othello had an Iago, 'Umar, a fierce fanatic who was harsh towards all women and who beat his wives. Pointing out that people who came to consult Muhammad approached his wives to ask for help, 'Umar urged Muhammad to have his wives cloak themselves completely and to seclude them in a *harim*, a taboo part of a household. (The word *harim* [harem] has no sensual connotations for Arabs: it means "forbidden place, sanctuary." Holy sites are harims; a harim is a part of a house off-limits to men who are not close kin. Caliphs and rich men had large harims, but most men, with one wife, and no slave or concubine, had plainly furnished harims where domestic work was done, usually under the supervision of the wife of the eldest male. Harims in wealthy houses were not the bordellos of Western imagination, but rooms furnished with Victorian taste and propriety.) The problem with seclusion was that the women needed to work to support the men: 'Aisha's sister Asma and Muhammad's daughter Fatima both recalled their labours: fetching water, harvesting, lugging vegetables to the compound, grinding corn, and kneading bread. Seclusion was not possible if men were to eat.

The alternative was to envelope women in cloaks. Women have been veiled in many regions of the eastern Mediterranean. Thirteenth-century BCE Assyrians required "respectable" women to veil outdoors. The earliest artistic representation of head-to-foot veiling was in first-century CE bas-reliefs from Palmyra (Zenobia's city in Syria, through which Arab caravans passed). Veiling was known in Rome, and both veiling and seclusion occurred in pre-Islamic Persia and the Byzantine Empire. The Athenians copied the confinement of their women from the Persians, according to the historian Strabo.

Veiling and seclusion have gradations of strictness that vary with place and time. Lady Mary Wortley Montagu wrote that Turkish women in the eighteenth-century Ottoman Empire made sexual liaisons in their veils.[12] In the 1980s a Hindu gentleman I met told me his mother was so strictly confined that she knew her sons-in-law's faces only from photographs and that the only time she ever could chat with her female neighbours was when she (as he put it) "squatted" in the morning. Like other constrictions, veiling and seclusion became status symbols: the only men who imposed it could afford servants to do the work. Rural women who had to work in the fields and fetch water and wood were almost never veiled.

Under pressure from 'Umar (and perhaps internal pressure), Muhammad forbade people from entering his house unless they were invited to a meal, from lingering to chat once they had eaten, and from speaking to his wives without a curtain between them. At first only Muhammad's wives were veiled, but the dictate was later extended to all Muslim women. Veiling rules can be elaborate to the point of absurdity; tradition has the six-year-old 'Aisha veiled from the time of her betrothal to the prophet, even while she played with Muhammad's grandsons.

Muhammad soon barred menstruating women from the mosque, then from praying during their periods. Other restrictions followed: after prayer, women should not lift their heads until the imam lifted his; they must leave the mosque first, while the imam and the men tarried; when they attended prayers, they had to wrap themselves in robes to the point of invisibility. Muhammad remarked that no good came from women assembling, except at funerals and the mosque – a comment that became the basis for later rules barring perfumed women from mosques, forcing women to stand at the back, and denying them entry entirely. Muhammad reportedly said, "There are many perfect men, but there are no perfect women except Maryam bint Imran and Asiya, the wife of the Pharoah" (referring to Mary, mother of Jesus, and the Pharaoh's daughter who saved Moses). Hearing that a queen ruled Persia, he commented that people who place a woman over their affairs are unfortunate, unhappy, or do not prosper.

Muhammad's wives were vocal, especially 'Aisha, so the

complete absence of a response to these new rules suggests suppression. It is likely that they rebelled, because Muhammad withdrew from them for a month and emerged only to present them with an ultimatum: they must submit to his rules or be divorced. If they bowed to rules requiring after all only the simple good conduct expected of a prophet's wives, they would be rewarded in heaven. Traditional explanations for his displeasure naturally lay the blame for this ultimatum at the women's feet. It was said that the wives were greedy for material goods he could not afford; that 'Aisha and Zainab squabbled over shares of a butchered animal; or that Hafsa caught Muhammad with an Egyptian concubine on 'Aisha's scheduled night, Hafsa promised Muhammad she would not tell 'Aisha but she did, 'Aisha confronted Muhammad, and the harim fell to squabbling over the issue. However, such incidents probably occurred regularly in a large harim and do not explain such a serious breach.

The impasse worried the Muslim community: many of Muhammad's marriages had been made to cement alliances with important members of the community in Medina and with tribal leaders outside it. Abu Bakr and 'Umar reproached their daughters severely, siding with Muhammad against them. Muhammad first queried 'Aisha, who chose to stay, knowing her father would not take her back. Muhammad was as much a father as a husband to her. All the wives submitted; they were rewarded by the title Mothers of the Believers and with further restrictions, as Muhammad forbade them to remarry after his death. Men who defend Islam as beneficial to women always cite Muhammad's rule giving women the right to inherit (half as much as men). Yet he bequeathed his modest wealth to charity, leaving his wives – veiled, confined, and forbidden to remarry – penni-less. Abu Bakr even denied Fatima, Muhammad's daughter by Khadija, her inheritance.

In 632 Muhammad fell ill. He lay in his wife Maimuna's room and kept asking where he was due the next day. Finally realizing he was asking when he was to be with 'Aisha, the wives moved him to her room. He died in her arms and was buried in her room, because Abu Bakr recalled his saying a prophet should be buried where he dies. Abu Bakr was later buried there too, as was 'Umar. After his interment, 'Aisha had a partition built between her and the tombs, saying she felt comfortable lying with her husband and father, but not with 'Umar.

The First Century of Islam

Within thirty years of Muhammad's death, Arab Muslims led by Muhammad's four chief male companions – Abu Bakr, 'Umar, 'Uthman, and Ali, called "the righteous caliphs" – conquered the entire Middle East. In these wars, women acted powerfully. Some became leaders opposed to Islam; the Muslims called them "false prophets." The Tamim clan split over Islam; prophet Sajah bint 'Aws led the anti-Islam wing, which was defeated in a civil war. 'Aws left Tamimi territory with her army and went to Yamama, the city of another prophet hostile to Muhammad. Her teach-ings about her god, Rabb al-Sirab (Lord of the Clouds), were not preserved.

Revolts also erupted after Muhammad died: he was both a secular and a religious leader, and many Muslim Arabs had pledged themselves to Muhammad personally. They refused to obey or to pay taxes to other Muslim officials. Abu Bakr, the first caliph *(khalifa resal Allah* means "head of community" or "successor to God's messenger," a secular title), insisted that Muhammad's religion was the foundation of a system of government. He subdued rebellious groups by force. This time, too, women fought on both sides.

Salma bint Malik led a revolt. She had fought Muslims in 628 in her mother's army and lost. The Muslims killed her mother by tying her feet to two beasts sent in different directions, ripping her in two. At that time Salma was captured and given to 'Aisha as a slave. Later, she married a relative of Muhammad. When he died, she returned to her people, determined to avenge her mother's death. On her mother's camel, she led her men into battle; hundreds, including Salma bint Malik, were slain.

The Muslims called one group of women opposed to Muhammad "the harlots of Hadramaut." This title was a slander – they were not prostitutes, but priestesses (some were noblewomen) of a god they hoped to revive once Muhammad died.[13] They lived in a part of southern Arabia hostile to Islam and, when they heard that the prophet was deceased, they gathered to celebrate, sing, and dance. They were not soldiers, but Abu Bakr sent soldiers against them. Men of Kindah and Hadramaut defended them, but the Muslims cut off the women's hands and treated them so cruelly that historians wonder whether they had great religious and political influence or had incited a revolution.[14]

In the two years that Abu Bakr survived his prophet, he subdued rebellions, invaded Iraq and Syria, and gave 'Aisha orders for the Islamic state. 'Umar became caliph. The state had been enriched by foreign conquests and, perhaps shamed by the power of Muhammad's widows, 'Umar gave them a pension. He expelled all non-Muslims from Arabia

and passed new laws. Adultery was now punished by stoning to death, and all women (not just Muhammad's wives)
were confined to the home and barred from mosques
(though 'Umar's wives and a son rebelled against this rule).
He forbade Muhammad's wives to go on pilgrimages and
appointed male imams for both men and women. 'Aisha and
Umm Salamah, who had been imams for women after
Muhammad died, could no longer be so. 'Umar also
expunged the record of women's protests. Women's silences
were now "speaking silences," wrote Ahmed, giving the punishment of the women of Hadramaut as an example. Men
"considered it simply their duty to erase rebellion in women
from the written page of history as ruthlessly as they eradicated it from the world in which they lived."15

'Umar spent years conquering Jerusalem, Iraq, Persia,
and Egypt, but he was assassinated in 644. The next caliph,
'Uthman, rescinded many of 'Umar's "reforms" – he stopped
naming separate imams, let Muhammad's wives go on pilgrimages, and allowed both sexes to worship in the mosques.
He had women tarry until men left at the end of prayers.
But 'Utman, one of the powerful Umayyad clan, gave
important posts to relatives. His nepotism provoked a rebellion and he was killed. 'Aisha rose veiled in the mosque to
deliver a stirring speech demanding vengeance for 'Uthman's
death. Ali Abu Talib, Muhammad's cousin, second convert,
and son-in-law (Fatima's husband), wanted to succeed him.
Ali had disagreed with Abu Bakr and 'Umar about the
nature of Islam, and he set out to establish his own version
of the religion. But 'Aisha mustered an army to fight Ali and
led it on a camel (the Battle of the Camel). Aware of her central importance, Ali had his men cut her camel down to
demoralize her army, which thereupon lost the battle. Ali

treated 'Aisha well, but he ejected her from public life.

Six years later Ali was assassinated by a political opponent and 'Uthman's Umayyad clan seized power. Ali's Shi'a party rose up, and civil war erupted. The split among today's Muslims began with these events. The Shi'a believe the intensely religious Ali was Muhammad's divine successor, and they acknowledge only his descendants as caliphs or authorities in Islam. The opposing Sunni favour the historical development of the caliphate and Muslim customs, believing that Islam ought to evolve with time. They sometimes persecute Shi'ites, who consider themselves the True Believers but are only 10 percent of the world's Muslims.

The first war between Muslims shocked Islam, which blamed a woman. By going into battle, they said, 'Aisha broke Muhammad's rule confining his wives; her defeat proved her wrongness (a charge used to legitimate later Muslim repressions of women). When Muslim scholars list "excellent" women, 'Aisha's name is omitted: most list the Christian Mary, the Egyptian Asiya, Khadija, and Fatima, Muhammad's daughter, who starved herself, lived in great poverty, and worked endlessly. She was his only child to survive him – but not by much. A legend describes Fatima's visit to the dying Muhammad in 'Aisha's house. 'Aisha asked her why, during the conversation, she cried, then laughed. She replied: "The prophet told me that he would die of the illness with which he was then afflicted; then I cried. He whispered that I would be the first of his family to follow him [in death]. Then I laughed."

Most of Muhammad's wives blamed 'Aisha for plunging Islam into civil war. Umm Salamah warned against internecine strife and insisted that Muhammad's wives should be non-political and stay in their houses. She then sent her son (from a prior marriage) to support Ali. After defeating 'Aisha's forces, Ali sent an army to subdue rebels in the Hijaz; Umm Salamah urged them to submit peacefully. Her insistence that women should stay out of politics was a matter of appearance rather than reality.

But many Arabian women remained publicly active. Women fought in all the battles of the Umayyad period, and they joined the *kharijites* (Ali's party) to overthrow the Umayyads. Qatam was held responsible for the murder of Ali (who had killed her father and brother). She told her lover, "Bring me the head of Ali as my dower. If you escape alive, you shall have me as your reward here; if you perish, you shall enjoy better than me above."

The women of Ali's clan were also spirited. His son Hasan had the dubious distinction of being the most married and divorced man of his generation until Jadah, one of his wives, poisoned him. Ali's son Husain, with a party of seventy men, women, and children, was besieged by 4000 Umayyad soldiers. He and his close male kin were killed, except a sick teenaged son. When soldiers came to take the boy for execution, Zainab (Ali's sister and Muhammad's granddaughter) threw herself on him, saying they would have to kill her first. The order was retracted and the prisoners were sent to the caliph in Syria, where Zainab again acted with courage, saving her younger sister Fatimah from enslavement. Zainab's two nieces, Fatima and Sukaina, were also remarkable. Fatima was known for her piety; Sukaina for her beauty and for witty, malicious comments on court poets. The unveiled Sukaina adopted a headdress that was instantly copied by both sexes, though the caliph later banned it for men. Court women were renowned for wisdom or for loyalty to their men: supplicants begged their help in petitioning powerful men, and poets wrote them adoring poems. Some took lovers. Obviously, Islamic rules were not rigid then.

Most wealthy or noble women influenced events behind the scenes, advising caliphs or enthroning their sons and ruling through them. Some killed enemies, or at least were accused of murders. Those who had memorized Muhammad's revelations helped compile a written text of the Qur'an for future generations. All Muhammad's wives, particularly 'Aisha, were regularly consulted about Muhammad's sunna, the sacred law and custom, for the Hadith. 'Aisha revealed that Muhammad helped his wives with the housework, but, for some reason, this piece of knowledge did not become a precedent for later Muslims.

Islam in Later Centuries

Islam and Christianity are both militant proselytizers; they aggressively seek converts through military or missionary action. Under religious banners, Christians invaded Africa, the Americas, and Asia, often wreaking terrible destruction. Like Christianity, Islam is based in principles of compassion and democracy, yet exalts *jihad*, war waged to fulfil the will of Allah or to convert non-believers. Over the centuries, it invaded much of the world in an effort to extend Islam. A century after Muhammad's death, Muslims controlled a huge empire – North Africa, the Arabian Peninsula, Persia, Afghanistan, and India to the Indus River. They conquered Spain (except for the mountainous north), and reached Tours in France, before Charles Martel stopped them in 732. Muslims held Cordoba, Toledo, Granada, and Seville; Spanish Christians gradually regained these cities in the late eleventh and twelfth centuries, recovering Granada in 1492.

Christians protested that Muslims forced conquered peoples to convert to Islam under threat of death, but, in fact, Muslims were usually tolerant because of Muhammad's reverence for "People of the Book." They built an empire through armed force, but rarely coerced conversion in occupied territories. Christianity built its empire mainly by personal conversion of political leaders; it never had a comprehensive policy of armed force. But it used armed force or torture on many occasions: to suppress dissent (e.g., of the Cathars from southern France or the Jews and Moors from Spain), to try to oust Islam from the Middle East (the abortive Crusades), and to suppress dissent among Christians (e.g., the use of torture during the Inquisition). Jesuits bribed and abused Native Americans to force conversion; Columbus in the Caribbean, and Spaniards in Mexico and the Andes, used force and torture to force conversion and to punish dissent.

As colonizers, Muslims remained a discrete ruling class. They discouraged relations with conquered people and barred Muslim ownership of land outside Arabia (a very important difference from other colonial powers). Army chiefs acted as governors; they commanded the army that policed the territory but left civil control to local authorities, avoiding a potential source of conflict. Muslim rulers shared the booty of conquest with all Arabs by granting them an allowance from the state treasury and exemption from taxes, except for a small religious tax for the indigent. The empire was sustained by taxes levied on non-believers, who had to pay poll and land taxes. Many converted to avoid these dues and they eventually outnumbered their conquerors. The converts depleted the treasury, and Arabs were forced to levy a land tax on non-Arab converts. This discrimination caused political unrest.

Over the centuries, different Muslim elites dominated discrete areas. These elites had extremely diverse national backgrounds: the 'Abbasids were non-Arabs descended from the Sasanians; the Almavorids were Berbers; the Ottomans were Turks. The Mamluks, former slaves, overthrew the Egyptian government and created their own dynasty. Turkish Mongols and Persian Muslims created sharply different societies, some of which were splendid. Indian Mughals, Spanish Moors, and Turkish Ottomans produced great art, literature, philosophy, and mathematics. Persians scorned Arabs, but Persian Muslim society was philosophically and scientifically learned and produced an exquisite art and architecture. Muslim tolerance of Jews fostered a brilliant Jewish-Arabic culture: great Jewish thinkers like Moses Maimonides wrote in Arabic. In the East, Arabs adopted local ways: the colonizers overlay Islam on Persian, Turkish, or Indian modes. But western Arabs imposed their culture on the colonized, as in the Alhambra in Granada.

The Umayyad Dynasty, with a capital in Damascus (Syria), ran a regime based on slavery. Arabs had owned slaves before Islam, but Muslims could not enslave Muslims. They sought captives from Russia, Turkey, Persia, Egypt, Greece, and Africa. Slaves might be royal or commoner, but the great difference among them depended on sex. Male and female slaves had unlike experiences. Some men were castrated, despite the high death rate, because eunuchs were in great demand: important men tended to trust them as harem-guards and administrators, thinking that eunuchs would not form personal bonds. Whether eunuch or intact, male slaves could rise by their abilities, prowess, and reliability, and many became powerful in government, households, and the army. The Mamluks (the "owned") took over and founded a slave dynasty.

Female slaves could rise only through sex and reproduction. Sold at public auction as labourers, domestic workers, and entertainers (singers often used as courtesans), slave-women were ranked. Most blacks were given menial tasks; clever or attractive whites might be taught to read, write, sing, dance, or play a musical instrument. Older slave-women were wet nurses, honoured members of households. Some high-ranking slavewomen managed large households. Male owners had sexual rights over female slaves who, if they bore children, were titled Umm Walad (Mother of a Child). They could not be sold or given away and were automatically freed when their owners died. Some of their children were free; indeed, most later Muslim rulers were sons of slavewomen.

Islam's injunction to marry included slaves, and those bought young were often freed in time to marry and bear children. Muslims considered freeing slaves meritorious – men who educate and free slaves are promised a twofold reward in heaven. Owners arranged and paid for slave marriages, usually trying to keep ex-slaves obligated to them. Slavewomen, normally forbidden to veil (veiling was a privilege of free or elite women), could veil if they rose to high rank in rich households. Since they could rise in society, fathers sold daughters into slavery, some to the harims of caliphs and nobles. If a concubine became the favourite of a powerful man, her son could succeed him.

In these circumstances, women had almost the same chances as men. While beauty was a factor, men cherish women for many reasons. Famous consorts like Madame de

Maintenon were noted not for beauty but for wisdom, cleverness, maternality, or animation. Intelligence and administrative ability helped any slave to rise. Women who rose socially and politically could advance their sons. Caliphs preferred concubines to freeborn wives, (perhaps because slaves did not claim equality), and favoured their sons: the last three caliphs of the Umayyad Dynasty had slave mothers. Historians blamed the collapse of the Umayyad Dynasty on slavewomen and concubines with foreign blood and "loose morals," as if slaves could maintain their own moral standards.[16] To please a master, slaves had to exercise qualities the master desired; both men and women were dependent on male owners for preferment and even life. Both men's and women's ascent was tied to a man, but women never ran armies or governments and few exercised power in their own right. Both men and women gained status by relation with a man, but being dependent on a person of the opposite sex has a different effect on self-esteem than dependency on someone of the same sex.

Although elite women held great power at times in some Muslim states, women as a caste were subordinate in all. Muslim society was virilocal – brides lived with their husband's families, and mothers-in-law were the significant figures in their lives. Like Chinese and Indian mothers, Muslim women bind their sons tightly to them. Poor women suffered far worse than poor men – they were married as children to become their husbands' subjects, without freedom of speech, travel, or action. They probably wore a head covering, as Bedouin women still do.

Muslim empires coalesced and, since nature's strictures apply to empires as well as individuals, fell apart. In 751 the Umayyads were overthrown by the 'Abbasids, who set up

ATLANTIC OCEAN

FRANKS

Poitiers

PYRENEES

SPAIN

Toledo

Cordova

Cadiz

Barcelona

Rome

Ravenna

LOMBARDS

AVARS

MAG

BULGARI

Constantine

BYZANTINE

Tangiers

BERBERS

MEDITERRANEAN

SEA

Alex

THE EXPANSION OF ISLAM

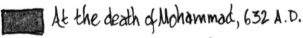

At the death of Mohammad, 632 A.D.

After the death of the first four caliphs, 661 A.D.

After the conquests of the Umayyad caliphs, 750 A.D.

ARAL
SEA

CAUCASUS MTS.

CASPIAN SEA

SEA

E

Antioch

SYRIA

PERSIA

Indus R.

PERSIAN GULF

ARABIA

Medina

Saudi Arabia

RED SEA

Mecca

0   1000
            miles

their own dynasty and moved the capital from Damascus to Baghdad (Iraq), reviving ancient traditions such as veiling and seclusion, which spread to Arab women elsewhere. 'Abbasid rulers, sons of non-Arab slaves, did not trust the Arab elite but maintained power by a strong professional army, efficient bureaucracy, despotism, and great pomp. The 'Abbasid period was later considered a golden age, especially the reign of Harun al-Rashid, whose mother and wife helped make state policy. In his period, trade, agriculture, and the economy expanded, generating intellectual and cultural ferment, a climate that allowed marginal groups like women to enter public life. Women became poets, mystics, teachers, and religious writers; one ran a textile factory. The *Arabian Nights* was set in the time of Harun al-Rashid.

Around 1300 Turks from Anatolia set out to conquer the world; they took Constantinople (renaming it Istanbul), the Balkan states, Syria, Iraq, much of Egypt and North Africa, and, before they were stopped, they reached Vienna. Their empire, called the Ottoman Empire, produced a magnificent court life and lasted into the twentieth century. The Mongol Khans who controlled it treated their wives with great respect and ceremony: women of the Turko-Mongol elite sat on state councils, chose rulers, and ruled as regents. Royal Ottoman women built mosques, hospitals, and public baths in Mecca, Medina, and Jerusalem; they constructed a system to carry water to Mecca for pilgrims, a college for Islamic studies, a sanatorium, travellers' inn, dervish hostel, primary school, soup kitchen, and public bath. They restored and enlarged forts guarding the Dardanelles.

Two generations after Muhammad's death, women vanish from Muslim history. The thirteenth-century Persian historian Rashid ud-Din wrote a history of the world without mentioning women at all until he reached the Mongols.[17] Then he apologized to Muslim readers that it was necessary to discuss women (whom he called *awrat*, meaning "cunts"). Most Muslims argue that Muslim women were subjugated not by Muhammad but by later accretions to the holy books. This is true, but the constraints imposed by later generations grew from woman-hating or woman-fearing rules introduced by Muhammad himself. Later Islam did not misinterpret as much as extend Muhammad's teachings. After the tenth century, women were increasingly subordinated in Christianity and in Judaism too.

The Qur'an and the Hadith

For Muslims, the Qur'an records Allah's revelations to Muhammad, just as Jews and Christians believe that the Torah and the New Testament record the words of their gods. Muhammad's death closed the Qur'an. Another book, the *Hadith*, records the acts and sayings of Muhammad and his companions along with commentaries on Muhammad's practice *(sunna)*. It provided precedents for scholarly discussion of Islamic rule and tradition over the generations. Innovation was allowed only when precedent legitimated it; Barbara Freyer Stowasser believes that hadiths were sometimes faked to enable Muslims to assimilate conquered converts who emerged from varied traditions.[18] Muslims consider the Qur'an, but not the Hadith, infallible, divinely inspired, but both are part of *shari'a*, Holy Law. Both deal with women's conduct and marriage. There were many changes from Muhammad's death in 632 to 1500.

In Muhammad's period, some clans captured their wives, making them little more than slaves; in others, men bought women from guardians or the women themselves, paying them *mahr* or *sadaq*. In such cultures, a man could have as many wives as he could feed and could divorce them at will, so long as he had paid the full mahr, simply by repeating three times a formula of dismissal. Some tribes barred women from owning or managing property and killed female babies. Muslims point out that among such people, the Qur'an improved the lot of women. But not all groups had such customs.

Most ancient marriage contracts were between two men. The Qur'an defines marriage as a contract between a woman and a man, with the groom giving the mahr to the bride. Christian marriage is sacramental, monogamous, and indissoluble: Qur'anic marriage is none of these: women are property, though cherished property – fields a man tills and makes fertile. The Qur'an invests marriage with dignity, as god's gift: both partners must love and comfort each other. Men may have four wives, but must treat them equally. The Qur'an guarantees women rights to inherit and bequeath property and to control their own property, including the mahr, while married and after divorce. Husbands require wives' permission to use their property and must feed and clothe wives properly. The Qur'an also forbids infanticide and eases divorce. Before Muhammad, pronouncement of the formula was the divorce: the wife was immediately turned out. The Qur'an orders a waiting period of three months to see if a repudiated wife is pregnant – if so, reconciliation is advised. The Qur'an also permits *khul*, in which a wife essentially buys a divorce in return for her mahr, a cancelled debt, or extra cash payments; and *tafriq*, a judicial decree of separation after complaints from the wife.[19]

One Surah (section of the Qur'an) reads, "men are a

degree above women" – a statement that is buttressed by others in the Qur'an. The revelation allowing goddess worship (the Satanic Verses) was revoked for strategic reasons, but Muhammad said he withdrew it because it was absurd for Allah to have daughters when even mortals could bear the preferred male sex. Daughters inherit half a son's share and a widow an eighth of her husband's estate, while the husband inherits a fourth of the wife's. Childless widows get a fourth; childless widowers, half. Women's testimony is worth half as much as men's. Women may have one spouse and may not marry non-Muslims.

Surah 4:34 is highly important. It reads: "Men are in charge of women, because Allah hath made the one of them excel the other, and because they spend of their property (for the support of women)." Yet in Muhammad's circle, the women supported the men, as his first wife had supported him. Tenth-century men wanting to legitimate their right to dictate women's behaviour and duties, to discipline and chastise them, used this verse; 350 years later they used it to declare women incapable of and unfit for public office. In the seventeenth century it was cited to deny women positions of religious leadership, to bar them from most religious rites, and to legitimate men's making all decisions for women including those concerning marriage. They claimed that men's economic support and superiority gives them the right to "scourge" wives. Muhammad did not explicity grant men a right to beat wives – he took it for granted they had one – and urged men to resort to it if their wives were disobedient only after remonstration and milder forms of coercion. He forbade them to beat their wives in rage, strike them in the head, or beat them savagely enough to cause fractures, wounds, or serious bruises. There are almost no court records of cases in which wives accused their husbands of violating these rules. However, it is unlikely they were able to bring charges.

Muhammad's rules regarding women were added erratically, the most repressive during his last six or seven years. His early messages appealed to women, who appreciated his banning infanticide, asserting equality, and urging social justice. He promised that both sexes would be rewarded in heaven, but his images of paradise include beautiful female figures to serve men:

> . . . for God's sincere servants
> . . . awaits a known provision,
> fruits – and they high-honored
> in the Gardens of Bliss upon couches,
> set face to face,
> a cup from a spring being passed round to them,
> white, a delight to the drinkers,
> wherein no sickness is, neither intoxication,
> and with them wide-eyed maidens
> restraining their glances
> as if they were hidden pearls (Sura 37).[20]

Islam does not deny women souls, as is often said. In Mamluk society, Muslim women who died in childbirth were martyrs for the faith and were buried in their bloody garments, like soldiers, with the inscription, "May a Fatiha [the opening chapter of the Qur'an] be recited for her soul." The Qur'an asserts spiritual equality of the sexes and holds both men and women accountable for their moral behaviour. Muhammad's version of the Fall and the Expulsion from the Garden of Eden holds Adam and Eve equally responsible. Judgment is sex-blind: thieves and adulterers of either sex were punished similarly (thieves had their hands cut off; adulterers were given 100 lashes). If a husband accuses a wife of adultery and she swears her innocence four times, she had to be believed: he could not punish her. Punishment for adultery requires four eyewitnesses.

The Qur'an also contains an injunction that may be without parallel in religious literature: Muhammad ordered men to be modest!

> Tell the believing men to lower their gaze and be modest. That is purer for them. Lo! Allah is aware of what they do.

The injunction to women, however, is far more elaborate:

> And tell the believing women to lower their gaze and be modest and display of their adornment only that which is apparent, and to draw their veils over their bosoms, and not to reveal their adornment save to the husbands or fathers or husbands' fathers, or their sons or their husbands' sons, or their brothers or their brothers' sons or sisters' sons, or their women or their slaves, or male attendants who lack vigour, or children who know naught of women's nakedness. And let them not stamp their feet so as to reveal what they hide of their adornment.

The question becomes: What, precisely are women's "adornments"? By the tenth century this command was read to mean that women should "lower their gaze so as not to look at what God has forbidden them to look at, and to preserve their private parts from the glances of him who has no right to glance at them, by veiling them with some garment or other." Enjoining women to veil their hair, necks, and ears, the commentator adds:

> Since man has to cover his genitals when praying, and woman has to uncover her face and hands during prayer, but has to cover all else . . . it follows . . . that she has the right to display of her body that which is not pudendal, just as the man has the right to do so.[21]

By the thirteenth century, "adornment" means jewellery, dress, make-up, and the places where they are worn or applied. The commentator orders women to lower eyelids because "the glance is the messenger of fornication." In the most startling injunction in this lascivious objectification of female body parts, women may not display face, hands, or anything else "because the whole body of the free woman is pudendal." That is, women are walking vulvas. They are henceforth required to cover their entire persons, except when giving evidence in court or receiving medical treatment.

Islam is not anti-sex, like Christianity, and it champions marriage, valuing women as highly as horses or perfumes. A man is supposed to give his wife sexual pleasure (yet a successful wedding night is one on which the groom is "pleased by the bride"). Wife rape is forbidden; women's consent to coitus is required, but a woman who rejects her husband will not sleep for the curses of angels descending on her. Men should subjugate wives through kindness, not cruelty, because "woman is like a rib which will snap if one tries to straighten her natural crookedness."

As recorded in the Hadith, Muslim attitudes towards

women hardened simultaneously in Judaism and in Christianity. Jewish women sat with men in synagogues until the tenth century, when they were segregated, and menstruating women forbidden to enter at all. A similar process occurred in Bible reading in Europe over the centuries from Gutenberg to the twentieth century, as male authorities became more blameless and females more blameworthy.[22] Muslim men debated conditions under which women might be excluded from mosques and finally banished them in the tenth century, claiming that dogs, donkeys (unbelievers), and women disrupt prayer just by passing too near a temple. Women are unclean always, not just when they menstruate; baby girls' urine is more polluting than boys'. Women, evil temptresses, cause *fitna* (serious trouble, rebellion, or civil war) in men and make up most of Hell's residents because of infidelity and ingratitude towards their husbands. They are naturally defective in intellect, in moral and religious powers, and in political aptitude. Women who leave the home are sinful; those who "behave and act like men" are cursed. Independent travel by women tormented Hadith writers, who by the fourteenth century forbade them from travelling without their husbands or male guardians.

But law is one thing, practice another. A clear tendency over the centuries is that Qur'anic prescriptions that benefited men were followed; those that did not were ignored. Islamicist Nikki Keddie thinks that most Muslim women did not inherit as the Qur'an decrees unless they married cousins; if they married out of the immediate family, patrilinies loath to part with land and flocks found ways to ignore or evade their inheritance rights.[23] Nor could most women protect their rights: they were confined, without access to men other than husbands and kin, who could threaten and coerce them, or worse. One institution used to evade inheritance laws was the *waqf* (an inalienable endowment similar to an entail), through which a man could ensure that his property would pass only to males. Women also used *waqfs* to benefit themselves. From 1200 to 1850, 25 percent to 40 percent of *waqfs* were established by women, who often made themselves the beneficiaries of the endowments. This outcome suggests that they used *waqfs* to protect their property, which always tended to be less than men's, from male encroachment.[24]

Nikki Keddie thinks that men obeyed the Qur'an when it was convenient. For instance, Qur'anic standards for proof of adultery are almost impossible to meet, and men ignore them: brothers or husbands simply kill suspected women. Muslims assume that any woman who acts without extreme "modesty" (self-effacement) arouses uncontrollable urges in men, and that unauthorized contact between a man and a woman has only one meaning and deserves punishment. In violation of Qur'anic rules, adulteresses are stoned to death – a practice of Jewish origin now identified with Islam. A custom the Shi'a date to the jahilia, but which Muhammad seems to have condoned, is temporary marriage. A man pays a woman to marry him for a period between a few minutes and ninety-nine years, after which the marriage automatically ends; children born of such a union are legitimate. The Sunni forbid this practice as legalized prostitution, but it flourishes at sacred pilgrimage centres, where men go alone.

Birth control was permitted if men using it got consent from free wives, not slave concubines. The most frequent method, *coitus interruptus* (withdrawal of the penis before ejaculation), is undependable. Abortion was practised illicitly. Divorce was rare among Muslims: the substantial payment men made for wives and the fact that most marriages were arranged by parents discouraged divorce. Also, a man had to support a divorced wife for three months after repudiating her. When the three-month waiting period had elapsed, most women returned to their natal families.[25] Divorcees and widows had more voice in later marriages than in the first. Divorce may have varied greatly from one to another culture; for example, for Muslim men in the Ottoman Empire, divorce was common and easy. If men did not want to repay the dowry, they made their wives' lives so miserable that they would leave, forfeiting the dowry.

The sexual ethos of Islam is found in many societies. Men devise a notion of what they call "*family* honour," although it adheres to them alone (men alone comprise the family). In Islam this honour is called *izzat*. It is so essential to a man's status that he must kill anyone who impugns it. Yet the person responsible for maintaining it is the weak, untrustworthy female. She must be pure – not just chaste and faithful, but so rigidly self-effacing she cannot arouse suspicion. Mere public conversation with a non-kin male can impugn honour. Since any girl capable of childbearing is a candidate for bringing "shame" on the family, girls were married off when they reached puberty. Everyone must be perpetually on guard. Women must guard their sexual behaviour: how they move, dress, let their eyes range. Men must keep an eye on women and strange men, who are, of course, capable of anything.

This ethos is a boon to rulers; people obsessed with honour have little energy for other matters. The code of honour gives men a sense they are in control; women also feel in control when they do surveillance of other women. Muhammad created a state structure for ruling a patriarchal class-stratified society.[26] Like Moses melding local differences by positing a universal God with a single set of laws, Muhammad installed religion as the seat of justice and the focus of loyalty. By making the family the organ of control, he undermined tribal cohesion and loyalty. And by placing family rule in male hands and giving men control over women, he bought their loyalty to him, his religion, and his state. That women were thought to cause *fitna*, that *fitna* can mean rebellion or civil war, suggests that women's pivotal position in the political scheme was not lost on early Muslims.

Laws legitimating one form of marriage and outlawing all others dramatically helped in this process.[27] Legitimate marriage was based unambiguously on the assertion of male rights over property, wives, women's bodies, children, and, finally, the right to worship. Islam abolished customs that limited male power, like polyandry, female initiation of divorce, and women's right to child custody in cases of divorce, thereby foreclosing freedoms, activities, and roles that women had formerly enjoyed. Like the other world religions, Islam was instrumental in making patriarchy universal. Muhammad did not impose all the constrictions Muslim women suffer today, but he paved the road to them.[28]

GLOSSARY

acllas (or **mamaconas**) Andean girls taken from their communities by the Inca to be wives of the Sun god. Some were made servants of the gods, remained celibate, and officiated in rituals; others became second wives or concubines of royal or official men; and the most physically and morally perfect were sacrificed in important state rituals.

affines People related by marriage.

anarchy Social organization without a leader. Emma Goldman defined anarchy as liberation of the human mind from the dominion of religion, liberation of the human body from the dominion of property, and liberation from the shackles and restraints of government. For her, anarchy meant a "release and freedom from conventions and prejudice," without denying life and joy.

authority The right, backed by force, to judge others and coerce their behaviour.

ayllus Andean kin-group communities living in traditional egalitarianism.

Bakongo Kongo commoners, culturally distinct from the elite Mwissikongo.

bride-service The work required by a bride's family of a groom to "pay" for her. It occurs mainly in societies that hold land communally.

bride-wealth Wealth required by a bride's family of a groom to pay for her. It occurs mainly in societies that hold land communally.

Buddhism The belief that human life is mere bondage to an illusion that earthly things are real, or matter. Through enlightenment, one can break the chain of desire that recycles souls in rebirths on earth. Souls can break the chain and escape from the cycle by disengagement, education, ethics, and meditation to achieve Nirvana, or heavenly obliteration.

burqa A heavy cloak worn by women. It is draped from the top of the head to the ankles, with a rectangle of netting inserted over the eyes so the woman can see.

cash crops Crops grown to be sold at market, for cash. They are usually inedible items such as tea or coffee or carnations. If the markets fall and the crops cannot be sold, the people starve. Subsistence crops, in contrast, are edible items such as rice or beans, which can keep people alive through the winter.

city-state A city that is a state unto itself, such as Sumerian cities, or Athens, or Sparta.

co-option Traducing the loyalty of selected people by bribery, often in the form of education, advancement, or prestige.

corvée Unpaid, mandatory labour extorted by the state.

curaca The governor or community leader, either female or male, in Andean society.

dhow A single-masted ship used in the Red Sea and the Indian Ocean.

dowry Payment to the groom or his family by a bride's family. It is customary in societies that consider land private property.

endogamy A system in which people must marry within their group or clan.

enfeoffed A form of feudal delegation of power, where a superior grants authority and ownership over lands and people.

entailment A codicil specifying that only males can inherit a property. If a testator's direct descendants were female, the inheritance passed to the nearest male relative. The most famous entailment in fiction appears in Jane Austen's *Pride and Prejudice*; the most famous real one is Vita Sackville-West's loss of her family home.

eugenics The science of improving the human race through breeding. It has favoured sterilization and even extermination of people deemed unfit.

exogamy A system in which people must marry outside their group or clan.

gender-specific laws Laws that apply to only one sex.

harijan "Children of god," Gandhi's name for "untouchables."

hegemony Dominance of a region or confederation by one group or state.

horticulture Farming done with hand tools; farming done by machine is called agriculture.

hypergamy The marriage of a daughter into a higher social group.

izzat A moral system of family honour and pride that is totally dependent on women. This code appears throughout Islam and in Europe, mainly in Italy, Greece, and Spain.

labour intensive Work that requires much human labour, in contrast to machine labour.

levirate marriage If a woman is widowed childless, her husband's family (which has paid a bride-price and "owns" her) has the right to (or must) marry her to the next younger unmarried brother (usually) over ten years of age. If no brother is available, she can be married to her father-in-law, becoming co-wife to her former mother-in-law. The aim is to get children out of her, derive a profit from an investment. Named (in English) for the priestly caste in the Bible, the Levis. Laws (Deuteronomy 25: 5–10) required it of Israelites, but many other peoples practised it.

mahr The dowry in the Ottoman Empire.

manichean Seeing good and evil as utterly separate opposites.

manumission To free from slavery.

matriarchy If it existed, it would be institutionalized female-dominance, a sociopolitical structure in which all women had authority over all men and the right to use force against them.

matricentry A society centred about mothers.

matrifocal Communities focused on the mother.

matrilineality Descent traced through the mother's line.

matrilocality The custom in which a couple lives with the bride's family after marriage.

matronymic Named after ones mother.

monotheism Belief that there is only one god.

Neolithic Age The Neolithic, or New Stone Age, began about 10,000 years ago. Some people maintain Neolithic cultures today.

pale An area delimited by a set of palings set into the ground as a fence. It may be used to keep people out, like the original English Pale in Ireland or the palings around US Army forts in Native American country, or to keep people in, like the fences used by the Soviet bloc.

Paleolithic Age The Paleolithic, or Old Stone Age, is usually dated from the first manufacture of stone implements, 2 to 3 million years ago. Some groups maintained a Paleolithic culture into later periods.

patriarchy Institutionalized male dominance, guaranteed by a set of interlocking structures that perpetuate the power and authority of an elite class of men over all other humans and grant all men power and authority over women of their class.

patrilineality Descent traced through the father's line.

patrilocality A custom in which a couple lives with the groom's family after marriage.

polyandry Having more than one husband.

polygamy Having more than one spouse. Applicable to both sexes, but almost always used (outside this study) to refer to men with multiple wives.

polygyny Having more than one wife.

polytheism Belief in multiple gods.

primogeniture Inheritance of an entire estate by the eldest son.

purdah The veiling and confinement of women.

quern A primitive mill for grinding grain.

statism The belief that the state is supreme, has power over every facet of life, and owns the complete loyalty of all citizens.

status Standing in a society vis-à-vis work, physical being, and rights.

stratification Division of a society into formal "classes" or ranks having different degrees of access to luxuries or even necessities.

subsistence cultures Societies in which people produce only what they need to live.

Taoism and **Neo-Taoism** The belief that ideas are relative and that things exist only as contrasts: there is no good without evil or life without death. Behind everything is the Tao (the Way), a blessed nothingness attainable only through mystical states. Humans should seek naturalness, spontaneity, and disengagement.

Trinity The assertion that the Father, the Son, and the Holy Spirit were of the same substance, consubstantial, "one person" comprising god. The primary "mystery" of the Christian Church.

usufruct rights The right to use a particular piece of land and what it produces. Found mainly in matrilineal societies, which do not believe that humans can own land.

virilocal Same as patrilocal; a couple lives with the husband's family after marriage.

yin-yang theory A theory defining two necessary complementary aspects of existence, touted as teaching interdependence and complementarity. Yin is female, soft, dark, mysterious, cold, moist, receptive, passive, associated with water, death, and decline. Yang is male, warm, bright, dry, hard, creative, assertive, associated with life, growth, and light. A balance of these qualities is considered necessary to ensure cosmic harmony. They are not equally valued and the theory was used to justify male dominance and women's subordination to men and their confinement in the domestic sphere.

NOTES

PREFACE

1 Marilyn French, *Beyond Power: On Women, Men and Morals* (New York: Summit Books, 1985).

2 The phrase comes from Paula Gunn Allen, *The Sacred Hoop: Recovering the Feminine in American Indian Traditions* (Boston: Beacon Press, 1986), 213.

CHAPTER 1

1 For a fascinating comparison of chimpanzees and humans, see Nancy Tanner and Adrienne Zihlman, "Women in Evolution. Part I: Innovation and Selection in Human Origins," *Signs* 1, 3 (1976): 585–608; Adrienne L. Zihlman, "Women in Evolution, Part II: Subsistence and Social Organization among Early Hominids," *Signs* 4, 1 (1978): 4–20; Nancy Tanner, *On Becoming Human* (New York: Cambridge University Press, 1981); Sarah Blaffer Hrdy, *The Woman That Never Evolved* (Cambridge, Mass.: Harvard University Press, 1981). For the theory that changes in the female body triggered hominization, see William I. Thompson, *The Time Falling Bodies Take to Light* (New York: St. Martin's Press, 1981).

2 John Noble Wilford, "2.3 Million-Year-Old Jaw Extends Human Family," *New York Times*, November 19, 1996.

3 John Noble Wilford, "Bones in China Put New Light on Humans," ibid., November 16, 1995.

4 For lively, informative accounts of hominid and early human life, see Helen Fisher, *The Sex Contract* (New York: William Morrow, 1983), and Elise Boulding, *The Underside of History* (Boulder, Col.: Westview Press, 1976).

5 The researchers also claim that *Homo sapiens* evolved into *Homo sapiens sapiens* 80,000 years earlier than fossil evidence suggests. Rebecca L. Cann, Mark Stoneking, and Allan C. Wilson, "Mitochondrial DNA and Human Evolution," *Nature* 325, 6099, January 1, 1987:

31–36; and Rebecca L. Cann, "In Search of Eve," *The Sciences*, September/October 1987: 30–37. Rebecca Cann was a consultant on this project.

6 JoAnn C. Gutin, "Who Peopled the Planet?" *Discover*, November 1992. The scientist was Alan Templeton.

7 Jane Lancaster, *Primate Behavior and the Emergence of Human Culture* (New York: Holt Rinehart & Winston, 1975); Nancy Chodorow, *The Reproduction of Mothering* (Berkeley: University of California Press, 1978).

8 See A.R. and T.B. Gardner, "Teaching Sign Language to a Chimpanzee," *Science* 165 (1969): 664–72. Experimenters attempting to teach chimpanzees or to see if they acquire knowledge usually use female animals. In one experiment in Japan, researchers tossed fruit on a beach frequented by chimps. The fruit became too sandy to eat. A young female chimpanzee realized that she could wash the fruit off in the sea; soon, other young females, then older females, then young males followed her example. The older male chimps stubbornly refused to adopt the new practice.

9 For example, the people of Vanatinai in Papua New Guinea. See John Noble Wilford, "Sexes Equal on South Sea Isle," *New York Times*, March 29, 1994.

10 Richard Lee and Marjorie Shostak studied the !Kung. Richard B. Lee, "Population Growth and the Beginnings of Sedentary Life among the !Kung Bushmen," in *Population Growth: Anthropological Implications*, ed. Brian Spooner (Cambridge, Mass.: MIT Press, l972); *Kalahari Hunter Gatherers*, ed. Richard B. Lee and Irven deVore (Cambridge, Mass.: Harvard University Press, 1976). Marjorie Shostak, *Nisa: The Life and World of a !Kung Woman* (Cambridge, Mass.: Harvard University Press, 1981), is an in-depth portrait, in her own words, of a modern !Kung woman.

11 Colin Turnbull, *The Forest People* (New York: Simon & Schuster, 1961), and *The Human Cycle* (New York: Simon & Schuster, 1983).

12 Richard A. Gould, *Yiwara: Foragers of the Australian Desert* (New York: Schribner, 1969).

13 Diane Bell, "Desert Politics: Choices in the Marriage Market," in *Women and Colonization*, ed. Mona Etienne and Eleanor Leacock (New York: Praeger, 1980).

14 Ibid. See also Catherine H. Berndt, "Interpretations and 'Facts' in Aboriginal Australia," in *Woman the Gatherer*, ed. Frances Dahlberg (New Haven, Conn.: Yale University Press, 1981); and Phyllis M. Kaberry, *Aboriginal Women, Sacred and Profane* (London: Routledge and Kegan Paul, 1939).

15 Information about early calendars and women's invention of them comes from Alexander Marshack, *The Roots of Civilization: The Cognitive Beginnings of Man's First Art, Symbols and Notation* (New York: McGraw Hill, 1972); and Elise Boulding, *The Underside of History* (Boulder, Col.: Westview Press, 1976).

16 Today, most Bari are dominated by Westerners, who brought them private land ownership, a money economy, and class distinctions. For Westerners, normalcy is a nuclear family supported by a wage-earning man, and they hire men only, teach Bari men to sell surplus goods, choose chiefs, own land, and vote. Westerners import goods that can be obtained only with money, but only Bari men have money, and women are forced to depend on men for such goods. Westerners teach new fishing techniques, but only to men – so fishing is no longer a communal activity. With native male help, foreign men build small new houses in which the Bari live – no longer communally. Boys are sent away to be educated, and women have been eliminated as healers. Worst of all, Westerners took Bari land and, with the territory so limited, the Bari have become sedentary: the women can no longer gather and the people are undernourished and obese. Women no longer participate in the singing feasts. And all this change was ostensibly done for the Bari's own good! Elisa Buenaventura-Posso and Susan E. Brown, "Forced Transition from Egalitarianism to Male Dominance: The Bari of Colombia," in Etienne and Leacock, eds., *Women and Colonization.*

17 Nan Rothschild, "Sex, Status, and Social Complexity: An Analysis of Six Midwestern Sites," in *Northwestern University Author Papers*, Occasional Series. Rothschild was a consultant for this project.

18 Rothschild, personal communication.

19 Eleanor Burke Leacock, *Myths of Male Dominance: Collected Articles on Women Cross-Culturally* (New York: Monthly Review Press, 1981).

20 George Bancroft, *History of the United States of America, From the Discovery of the Continent* (Port Washington, NY: Kennikat, 1967), vol. 1.

21 Eleanor Leacock, "Women in Egalitarian Societies," in *Becoming Visible*, ed. Renate Bridenthal, Claudia Koonz, and Susan Stuard (Boston: Houghton Mifflin, 1987); and Judith K. Brown, "Economic Organization and the Position of Women among the Iroquois," *Ethnohistory* 17 (1970).

22 Eleanor Leacock, "Myths of Male Dominance," in Etienne and Leacock, eds., *Women and Colonization.*

23 Near the villages of Bhimbetka, Lakhajoar, Bhonrawli Hill, Kathotia, Kharwai, and Jaora.

24 Erwin Neumayer, *Prehistoric Indian Rock Paintings* (Delhi: Oxford University Press, 1983).

25 The site is Bhimbetka.

26 Kumkum Roy, who provided most of the information used in this section, was a consultant on this project.

27 The sites are Kathotia, Bhimbetka, and Kharwai.

28 André Leroi-Gourhan, "The Evolution of Paleolithic Art," *Scientific American* (February 1968); Mary Leakey, "Preserving Africa's Ancient Art," *Science Digest* 92, 8 (1984): 57–81; Thompson, *The Time Falling Bodies Take to Light.*

29 Catal Hüyük was discovered in 1961 and excavated by James Mellaart, who has written several books about it: *Catal Hüyük: A Neolithic Town in Anatolia* (New York: McGraw-Hill, 1967); *Earliest Civilizations of the Near East* (London: Thames and Hudson, 1965); and *The Neolithic of the Near East* (London: Thames and Hudson, 1975). More recent studies of Catal Hüyük are Anne Barstow, "The Uses of Archaeology for Women's History: James Mellaart's Work on the Neolithic Goddess at Catal Hüyük," *Feminist Studies* 4, 3 (1978): 7–18; Riane Eisler, *The Chalice and the Blade: Our History, Our Future* (San Francisco: Harper & Row, 1987); and Monica Sjöö and Barbara Mor, *The Great Cosmic Mother: Rediscovering the Religion of the Earth* (San Francisco: Harper & Row, 1987).

30 Edward DeMarco, "New Dig at a 9000-Year-Old City Is Changing Views on Ancient Life," *New York Times*, November 11, 1997.

31 Mary Voigt was a consultant on this project. See Voigt, *Hajji Firuz Tepe, Iran: The Neolithic Settlement* (Philadelphia: University of Philadelphia Museum Monographs 50, 1983); "Village on the Euphrates," *Expedition* 27, 1 (1985): 10–24; and review essay on *The*

Hilly Flanks and Beyond: Essays on the Prehistory of Southwestern Asia, ed. T. Cuyler Young Jr., Philip E.L. Smith, and Peder Mortensen (Chicago: Oriental Institute of the University of Chicago, 1983) in *Paléorient* 12 (1986): 101–9. Voigt describes several categories of figurines. First, very worn, dilapidated figurines of cheap materials were children's toys; found in groups, they vary in form (some had carefully detailed anatomies) and may have been used to initiate young people in sexual behaviour. Second, objects representing people, animals, or designs may have been used in rituals beseeching intervention from a deity – asking for rain or a child, the end of rain, or healthy crops – and were almost always made of cheap materials and deliberately broken before they were discarded. Third, religious figures, used as symbols or objects of worship, were usually anthropomorphic and sometimes made of precious materials or marked with iconographic symbols. They were not thrown out with the ordinary garbage but disposed of in some special way.

32 Marija Gimbutas, *Gods and Goddesses of Old Europe* (Berkeley: University of California Press, 1974); and *The Language of the Goddess* (San Francisco: Harper & Row, 1989). The villages include Vinca, Petresti, Butmir, and Cucuteni.

33 See Peter Steinfels, "Idyllic Theory of Goddesses Creates Storm," *New York Times*, February 13, 1990.

34 Louise Levathes, "A Geneticist Maps Ancient Migrations," ibid., July 27, 1993.

35 Michael Dames, *The Silbury Treasure* (London: Thames and Hudson, 1976), and *The Avebury Cycle* (London: Thames and Hudson, 1977). A book that focuses more on art but also describes Avebury is Lucy Lippard, *Overlay* (New York: Pantheon Books, 1983). See also Sjöö and Mor, *Great Cosmic Mother*.

36 McGuire Gibson, "By Stage and Cycle to Sumer," in *The Legacy of Sumer*, ed. Denise Schmandt-Besserat, *Bibliotheca Mesopotamica* 4 (1975): 51–58.

37 Mohenjo-daro and Harappa were beautifully laid out cities of 35,000–40,000 people, with well-built brick houses, some three stories high with bathrooms and a drainage system. Mohenjo-daro was stratified and had a public realm, huge buildings in a town centre, paved stone roads, an elaborate system of irrigation, and megaliths along the roads into town. The people worshipped the Mother Goddess: their artifacts depict women, animals, and fertility symbols.

They had writing, sculpture, and other arts, but the culture disappeared about 1600 BCE, destroyed by floods, earthquakes, or an invasion of semi-nomadic Aryans. Its oblivion was so complete that no one had any idea it existed until archaeologists stumbled upon it early in the twentieth century.

38 The information on Crete is derived from several sources: Jon-Christian Billigmeier, who was a research consultant on this project; Ruby Rohrlich-Leavitt, "Women in Transition: Crete and Sumer," in *Becoming Visible*, ed. Renate Bridenthal, Claudia Koonz, and Susan Stuard (Boston: Houghton Mifflin, 1977); Sjöö and Mor, *The Great Cosmic Mother*, Eisler, *The Chalice and the Blade*.

CHAPTER 2

1 Erich Fromm, *Love, Sexuality, and Matriarchy: About Gender* (New York: Fromm International Publishing, 1997), 42, names Georg Groddeck as "probably the first to note . . . the male's envy of the female and particularly his 'pregnancy envy.'"

2 Carol Beckwith and Angela Fisher, *African Ceremonies II* (New York: Harry N. Abrams Inc., 1999).

3 Compare chapter 1.

4 Robert S. McElvaine, *Eve's Seed* (New York: McGraw-Hill, 2001).

5 Before the establishment of the Kingdom of Israel under David, the Hebrews were organized into matrilineal clans. To qualify as a Jew, it is still necessary to have a Jewish mother, but not a Jewish father. Scholars who claim that Israel was named for Sarah also believe that the original priests – the tribe of Levi – were named for Leah. See Julian Morgenstern, "*Beena* Marriage (Matriarchat) in Ancient Israel and Its Historical Implications," *Zeitschrift für die Altestamentische Wissenschaft* 47 (1929); and David Bakan, *And They Took Themselves Wives* (San Francisco: Harper & Row, 1979).

6 Peggy Reeves Sanday, *Female Power and Male Dominance: On the Origin of Sexual Inequality* (New York: Cambridge University Press, 1981); *Sexual Meanings: The Cultural Construction of Gender and Sexuality*, ed. Sherry B. Ortner and Harriet Whitehead (Cambridge: Cambridge University Press, 1981); and *Woman, Culture, and Society*, ed. Michelle Rosaldo and Louise Lamphere (Stanford, Cal.: Stanford University Press, 1974).

7   For Greek myths, see Robert Graves, *The Greek Myths* (Baltimore, Md.: Penguin Books, 1966); Jane Harrison, *Themis: A Study of the Social Origins of Greek Religion* (New York: Meridian Books, 1962); and for the origins of Athene and Hera, Marija Gimbutas, *Gods and Goddesses of Old Europe* (Berkeley: University of California Press, 1974), 148–50. On Sumerian and Babylonian myths, see Ruby Rohrlich and June Nash, "Patriarchal Puzzle: State Formation in Mesopotamia and Mesoamerica," *Heresies* 4, 1, issue 13 (1981): 60–65; and Alexander Heidel, *The Babylonian Genesis* (Chicago: University of Chicago Press, 1951). For Norse myths, see Kevin Crossley-Holland, *The Norse Myths* (New York: Pantheon, 1973). For Aztec myth, see Rohrlich and Nash, above; Ferdinand Anton, *Woman in Pre-Columbian America* (New York: Abner Schram, 1973); and Burr Cartwright Brundage, *The Fifth Sun* (Austin: University of Texas Press, 1979).

8   "Social charter" myths were given their name by Joan Bamberger in "The Myth of Matriarchy: Why Men Rule in Primitive Society," in Rosaldo and Lamphere, *Women, Culture, and Society.*

CHAPTER 3

1   Graham Connah, *African Civilizations: Precolonial Cities and States in Tropical Africa: An Archaeological Perspective* (Cambridge: Cambridge University Press, 1987).

2   The terracing invented by ancient Andean peoples has recently been rediscovered and has amazed modern archaeologists and agronomists. Dr. Clark Erikson excavated fields near Lake Titicaca, planted from 1000 BCE through 1400 CE, and found a system of raised platforms of earth surrounded by canals. The platforms were about 1 metre high, from 4 to 10.5 metres wide, and 10.5 to 106 metres long. The canals were the same length, width, and depth. Crops were planted on the platforms and watered from the canals. This system enabled crops to withstand drought and frost – the canal water raised the temperature around the fields – and yielded more than any modern system of terracing, without chemical fertilizer or machinery. It was probably lost under the Incas or before.

3   Irene Silverblatt was a consultant on this project, and most of the information on the Andean peoples comes from her. See her *Moon, Sun, and Witches: Gender Ideologies and Class in Inca and Colonial Peru*

(Princeton: Princeton University Press, 1987). Gisela Schue, a research assistant on the project, also contributed useful material.

4 Silverblatt, *Moon, Sun, and Witches.*

5 Roderigo Hernandes Principe, "Mitologia Andina" [1621], Inca 1 (1923): 24–68, cited by Silverblatt, *Moon, Sun, and Witches.*

6 Barbara Lesko, *The Remarkable Women of Ancient Egypt* (Providence, RI: B.C. Scribe Publications, 1987), and "Women of Egypt and the Ancient Near East," in Renate Bridenthal, Claudia Koonz, and Susan Stuard, *Becoming Visible: Woman in European History* (Boston: Houghton Mifflin, 1987).

7 Lesko, "Women of Egypt and the Ancient Near East."

8 Dominique Valbelle, *Les oeuvriers de la tombe: Deir el Médineh à l'Époque Ramesside* (tome 46, Bibliotheque d'Étude, Cairo: Institut français d'archiéologie orientale du Caire, 1985), 240. I am grateful to Barbara Lesko for this reference.

9 Sir William Tarn, writing in the *Cambridge Ancient History*, vol. 10 (London: Cambridge University Press, 1970), 110.

10 Sarah B. Pomeroy, *Women in Hellenistic Egypt: From Alexander to Cleopatra* (New York: Schocken Books, 1984).

11 Stella Maloof did research for this section. Other sources are Bierbrier Morris, *The Tomb Builders of the Pharaohs* (London: British Museum, 1982); *The Cambridge Ancient History*, vol. 2, part 2 (Cambridge: Cambridge University Press, 1975); William F. Edgerton, "The Strikes in Ramses III's Twenty-ninth Year," *Journal of Near Eastern Studies (JNES)*10, 3 (1951): 139–45; Marianne Galvin, "The Priestesses of Hathor in the Old Kingdom and the 1st Intermediate Period," PhD dissertation, Brandeis University, 1981; P.W. Pestman, *Marriage and Matrimonial Property in Ancient Egypt* (Leiden: Papyrologica Lugduno-Batava no. 9, 1961); Christine N. Qunta, *Women in Southern Africa* (London: Allison and Busby, 1987); Donald B. Redford, *History and Chronology of the Eighteenth Dynasty* (Toronto: University of Toronto Press, 1967); Julia Samson, *Nefertiti and Cleopatra* (London: Rubicon, 1985); Steffan Wenig, *The Woman in Egyptian Art* (New York: McGraw-Hill, 1969).

12 It has long been believed that the temples were dominant in early Sumerian city-states. This idea has been challenged by Marc van de Mieroop of Columbia University, who argues that the early states were ruled by secular princes whose power was based on control of the

great temple estates. His argument appears in *Women's Earliest Records from Ancient Egypt and Western Asia*. ed. Barbara Lesko (Brown Judaic Studies Series 166; Atlanta, Geo: Scholars Press, 1989).

13 Nancy Huston, "The Matrix of War: Mothers and Heroes," *The Female Body in Western Culture: Contemporary Perspectives*, ed. Susan Suleiman (Cambridge, Mass.: Harvard University Press, 1986).

14 Rivkah Harris, "Biographical Notes on the Naditu Women of Sippar," *Journal of Cuneiform Studies (JCS)*16 (1962): 1–12; "The *Naditu* Laws of the Code of Hammurapi in Praxis," *Orientalia* 30 (1961): 163–69; "The Organization and Administration of the Cloister in Ancient Babylonia," *Journal of the Economic and Social History of the Orient (JESHO)* 6, 1 (1963): 121–57; "The *Naditu*-Woman," in *Studies Presented to A. Leo Oppenheim* (Chicago: University of Chicago, Oriental Institute, 1964); Elizabeth C. Stone, "The Social Role of the Naditu Woman in Old Babylonian Nippur," *JESHO* 25, 1 (1982): 50–70.

15 George Dorsey, *Man's Own Show: Civilization* (New York: Harper & Brothers, 1931).

16 Lesko, "Women of Egypt and the Ancient Near East."

17 Women in many parts of the world do not possess the rights to deny a husband sex, to use birth control, to abortion, and to have sex as they please, whether they are married or not – a right men have always retained for themselves. Beyond this, men everywhere rape and murder women for no reason except that they are women.

18 J.S. Cooper, "Heilige Hochzeit," *Reallexicon der Assyriologie* 4: 259–69.

19 The section on Mesopotamia draws on a great many materials. Binnum Ercem did research on the subject. Beyond the sources mentioned in the text are Bernard Batto, *Studies on Women at Mari* (Baltimore, Md.: Johns Hopkins University Press, 1974); Elinor C. Burkett, "Indian Women and White Society: The Case of Sixteenth-Century Peru," in *Latin American Women*, ed. Asuncion Lavrin (Westport, Conn.: Greenwood Press, 1988); J.A. Brinkman, "Forced Labourers in the Middle Babylonian Period," *JCS* 32, 1 (1980): 17–22; J.J. Finkelstein, "Sex Offenses in Sumerian Laws," *Journal of the American Oriental Society (JAOS)* 86, 4 (1966): 355–72; Benjamin Foster, "A New Look at the Sumerian Temple State," *JESHO* 24, 3 (1981): 225–41; I.J. Gelb, "The Ancient Mesopotamian Ration System," *JNES* 26, 3 (1965): 230–43, and "Prisoners of War in Early

Mesopotamia," *JNES* 32, 1–2 (1973): 70–98; McGuire Gibson, "By Stage and Cycle to Sumer," in *The Legacy of Sumer*, ed. Denise Schmandt-Besserat, *Bibliotheca Mesopotamica* 4 (1975). Cyrus H. Gordon, "The Status of Women Reflected in the Nuzi Tablets," *Zeitschrift für Assyriologie*, Neue Folge, Band 9 (1936): 147–69; Samuel Greengus, "The Old Babylonian Marriage Contracts," *JAOS*, 89 (1969): 505–32; K. Grosz, "Dowry and Brideprice in Nuzi," *Studies on the Civilization and Culture of Nuzi and the Hurrians* 1: 166–67; W.W. Hallo, "Women of Sumer," in Schmandt-Besserat, *The Legacy of Time*; Alexander Heidel, *The Babylonian Genesis* (Chicago: University of Chicago Press, 1951), 10–14; S.N. Kramer, "The Women in Ancient Sumer: Gleanings from Sumerian Literature," and W.G. Lambert, "Goddesses in the Pantheon," in *La Femme dans le Proche-Orient Antique*, ed. Jean-Marie Durand (Paris: Éditions Recherche sur les Civilisations, 1987); Kazuya Maekawa, "Female Weavers and Their Children in Lagash," *Acta Sumerologica* 2 (1980): 81–125; Piotr Michalowski, "Royal Women of the Ur III Period, Part I," *JCS* 28, 3 (1976): 169–72; P.R.S. Moorey, "What Do We Know about the People Buried in the Royal Cemetery?" *Expedition* 20 (1977); Guity Nashat, "Women in the Middle East: 8000 BC to AD 1800," in *Restoring Women to History* (Bloomington, Ind.: Organization of American Historians, 1988); David Owen, "Widow's Rights in Ur III Sumer," *Zeitschrift für Assyriologie und vorderasiatische Archaologie (ZA)* 70 (1981): 170–84; Jonathan Paradise, "A Daughter and her Father's Property at Nuzi," *JCS* 25 (1980):189–207; Ruby Rohrlich and June Nash, "Patriarchal Puzzle: State Formation in Mesopotamia and Mesoamerica," *Heresies* 4, 1 (1981): 60–65; W.H.P. Romer, "Frauenbriefe uber Religion, Politick und Privatleben in Mari," *Alter Orient und Altes Testament* 12 (1971); Jack Sasson, "Biographical Notices on Some Royal Ladies from Mari," *JCS* 25, 2 (1973): 59–78; Claudio Saporetti, "The Status of Women in the Middle Assyrian Period," *Sources and Monographs on the Ancient Near East* 2, 1 (1979): 1–20.

CHAPTER 4

1 The Paleolithic, or Old Stone Age, is usually dated from the first man-ufacture of stone implements, 2 to 3 million years ago, to about 10,000 years ago, when the Neolithic, or New Stone Age, began. But certain groups maintained a Paleolithic culture into later periods, and some people maintain Neolithic cultures today.

2 Norman Girardot, *Myth and Meaning in Early Taoism* (Berkeley: University of California Press, 1983).

3 K.C. Chang, *The Archaeology of Ancient China* (New Haven: Yale University Press, 1977).

4 Marcel Granet, *Chinese Civilization* (London: K. Paul, Trench, Trubner & Co., 1930).

5 Ibid.

6 The date of the Bronze Age in China may have been as early as 2000 BCE, 1500 years later than in the Middle East, or as late as 1000 BCE.

7 Anne Holmes, personal communication. Anne Holmes was a consultant for this project.

8 Granet considers this a perversion of an earlier rite: the river god's name originally belonged to the river goddess. Similar usurpations occur among the Greek gods.

9 The approximate dates of the dynasties are as follows:

Zhou Dynasty	1122/1027 BCE to 221 BCE
Qin Dynasty	221 BCE to 213 BCE
Han Dynasty	206 BCE to 220 CE
Six Dynasties	221 to 589
Sui Dynasty	581 to 618
Tang Dynasty	618 to 906
Five Dynasties	906 to 960
Song Dynasty	
(Northern)	960 to 1126
(Southern)	1126 to 1279
Yuan Dynasty	
(Mongol)	1279 to 1368
Ming Dynasty	1368 to 1644
Qing Dynasty	
(Manchu)	1644 to 1911

(these last two periods together are called the late imperial era)

10 Susan Mann, "Historical Change in Female Biography from Song to Qing Times: The Case of Early Qing Jiangnan," *Transactions of the International Conference of Orientalists in Japan* 30 (1985): 65–77, and "Widows in the Kinship, Class, and Community Structures of Qing Dynasty China," *Journal of Asian Studies* 46, 1 (1987): 37–56.

11 Sharon L. Sievers, "Women in China, Japan, and Korea," in *Restoring Women to History*, ed. Renate Bridenthal, Claudia Koonz, and Susan Stuard (Bloomington, Ind.: Organization of American Historians, 1988).

12 Foreign historians blindly repeat the Chinese vilifications: so Arthur F. Wright, *Buddhism in Chinese History* (Stanford: Stanford University Press, 1959), describes the "typical northern woman" as "harsh, puritanical, a fanatical monogamist, a sharp and economical household manager," "meddlesome, vindictive, and insanely jealous."

13 Ge Hong; his words were translated and cited in Beatrice Spade, "The Education of Women in China during the Southern Dynasties," *Journal of Asian History* 1, 13 (1979): 15–41. Cited by Mann, "Historical Change."

14 Tang Souyu, an eighteenth-century scholar who married into a distinguished scholarly family with an extensive library, compiled a history of women artists, *The Jade Terrace History of Painting*. For biographies and examples of the work of these artists, see *Views from Jade Terrace: Chinese Women Artists, 1300–1912*, by Marsha Weidner, Ellen Johnston Laing, Irving Yucheng Lo, Christina Chu, and James Robinson (Indianapolis, Ind.: Indianapolis Museum of Art; New York: Rizzoli, 1988).

15 Cited in Howard S. Levy, *Chinese Footbinding: The History of a Curious Erotic Custom* (New York: Walton Rawls, 1966).

16 Anne Holmes, Susan Mann, and Karen Gottschang were consultants for this project: Holmes provided material on early China, Mann on China after 200 BCE, and Gottschang on early myth. I have also drawn on *The Cambridge History of China*, ed. John K. Fairbank (Cambridge: Cambridge University Press, 1978); Richard W. Guisso and Stanley Johannesen, eds., *Women in China: Current Directions in Historical Scholarship*, Historical Reflections Series 3 (Youngstown, NY: Philo Press, 1981); R.H. van Gulik, *Sexual Life in Ancient China* (Leiden: E.J. Brill, 1961); Edward H. Schafer, *The Divine Woman: Dragon Ladies and Rain Maidens* (San Francisco: North Point Press, 1980); Marina H. Sung, "The Chinese Lieh-nü Tradition," in Guisso and Johannesen, *Women in China; and Women in Chinese Society*, ed. Margery Wolf and Roxane Witke (Stanford: Stanford University Press, 1975).

CHAPTER 5

1 The script remains undeciphered.

2 A.S. Altekar, *The Position of Women in Hindu Civilization* (Banaras, India: Motilal Barnarsidass, 1956), 190.

3 Veena Oldenburg was a consultant to this project, dealing with India in later periods.

4 Wendy Doniger O'Flaherty, *Women, Androgynes, and Other Mythical Beasts* (Chicago: University of Chicago Press, 1980).

5 Conversation hymns and marriage hymns.

6 Sarama, the dog goddess, undertook to find stolen cattle in return for their milk for her children and succeeded against severe obstacles.

7 Kumkum Roy was a consultant for this project, contributing information on India up until the rise of Buddhism.

8 The Maruts are called bridegrooms with a lovely spouse; the Asvins use gifts to court Surya, daughter of the Sun, who agrees to marry them.

9 Pusan, a pastoral god, is his sister's lover and his mother's suitor, and neither arrangement is condemned.

10 Each caste was divided into hierarchically arranged *jatis*, which are further subdivided into lineages or clans called *gotra*.

11 In Chinese myths, formerly female deities transformed into men are accompanied by wives – the former deities. Those who appear alone are paralyzed on one side or crippled, incomplete.

12 The *Therigatha*, ed. F.L. Woodward, trans. Caroline A.F. Rhys Davids (London: Pali Text Society, 1948). *Attha Katha*, a commentary with biographical sketches of the sisters, appeared in the fifth or sixth century CE but reflects earlier times. Both recount women's experience – their reasons for renouncing the world, their monastic lives, their support for each other, and their struggles. Despite their female point of view and subject matter, their German editor, Karl Neumann, claimed that men wrote these texts. The translator comments on Neumann's claim: "Not often since the patriarchal age set in has woman succeeded in so breaking through her barriers as to set on lasting record the expression of herself and of things as they appeared to her...I make no counter assumption that gifted Theris had a hand in the compilation of the Brothers' Psalms. I would only ask English

readers to avail the appearance of those, and note the interesting differences in idiom, sentiment, and tone between them and the Sisters' Psalms. Even the 'common stock' of refrains is different"(xxiii).

13 Most nuns came from the elite: they were Brahmans (the priestly caste), of Buddha's clan, the royal family, or of other respectable clans. But three were courtesans and several had been poor – one, a domestic slave.

14 The *Ramayana* of Tulsidas.

15 Veena Oldenburg, personal communication, 1987.

16 Kalidasa's plot and characters, slightly altered, still haunt modern Indian films.

17 Sita, the beautiful wife of Rama, is abducted by a demon king. After her rescue, she is suspected of infidelity and unjustly cast out and maligned by her husband. She suffers but remains faithful. Her ending is not rosy, however.

18 Eroticism is a strong element in Indian art, too, which portrays women as incredibly voluptuous, with heavy thighs and breasts, miniscule waistlines, and thick lips.

19 Sacred texts recognize eight forms of marriage:

1 Brahma or *kanya dan*, the gift of the virgin: a bride's family chooses her husband, gives her away with a dowry, and enters a long ceremonial and ritual relationship with the groom's family, the main burden of which falls on them.

2 *Daiva*: a man gives his daughter to a priest as part payment for a sacrifice.

3 *Arsa*: marriage with a token bride-price instead of a dowry.

4 *Prajapatya*: marriage with no financial transactions, neither bride-price nor dowry.

5 *Gandharva*: a love-match between two consenting people with no accompanying ritual, solemnized by plighting troth, often secret – an elopement. It was not fully approved, since most people who practised it mated in a socially unacceptable way – a Brahmin girl with a lower-caste boy, or a very rich and a very poor person.

Other forms with even less social approval are named after demons – *Asura*, marriage by purchase (since many approved forms involve payment, one wonders why explicit purchase is considered worse);

Rakshasa, marriage by capture; and *Pasisaca,* having sex with a girl who is asleep, deranged, or drunk (all really rape).

20 Another source for this chapter was Barbara N. Ramusack, "Women in South and Southeast Asia," in *Restoring Women to History,* ed. Renate Bridenthal, Claudia Koonz, and Susan Stuard (Bloomington, Ind.: Organization of American Historians, 1988).

CHAPTER 6

1 June Nash, "The Aztecs and the Ideology of Male Dominance," *Signs* 4, 2 (1978): 349–62, and "Aztec Women: The Transition from Status to Class in Empire and Colony," in *Woman and Colonization,* ed. Mona Etienne and Eleanor Leacock (New York: Praeger, 1980); Nash, with Ruby Rohrlich, "Patriarchal Puzzle: State Formation in Mesopotamia and Mesoamerica," *Heresies* 13, 4, 1 (1981): 60–65.

2 Jonathan Kandell, *La Capital: The Biography of Mexico City* (New York: Random House, 1986).

3 Frederick A. Peterson, *Ancient Mexico* (New York: G.P. Putnam's Sons, 1959), 85.

4 The structure of their religious hierarchy was the same as their political hierarchy, the royal council of Tenochtitlan.

5 Burr Cartwright Brundage, *The Fifth Sun* (Austin: University of Texas Press, 1979), 33.

6 *Columbia History of the World,* ed. John A. Garraty and Peter Gay (New York: Dorset Press, 1985), 651.

7 Contributors to the section on Mexico were Irene Silverblatt, who specializes in Andean life and on theories of state formation, and Christine Gailey, who also focuses on state formation and was very helpful. Binnum Ercem, Stella Maloof, and Gisela Schue did research. Sources not mentioned in the text were Marysa Navarro, "Women in Pre-Columbian and Colonial Latin America," in *Restoring Women to History,* ed. Renate Bridenthal, Claudia Koonz, and Susan Stuard (Bloominton Ind.: Organization of American Historians 1988); Ferdinand Anton, *Woman in Pre-Columbian America* (New York: Abner Schram, 1973).

CONCLUSION: AN ANALYSIS OF THE STATE

1 See Marilyn French, *Beyond Power: On Woman, Men, and Morals* (New York: Summit Books, 1985).

2 As late as 1943, Erich Fromm could write an essay lamenting women's total sexual dependency on the male penis, an essay thought worthy of reprinting in 1997. See Erich Fromm, *Love, Sexuality, and Matriarchy: About Gender* (New York: Fromm International Publishing, 1997).

3 Although the theory of the rise of the state that is offered here is my own, my thinking has benefited from the work of many scholars. My citing them here does not mean they agree with me, only that I am indebted to them.

A major contributor to theories of state formation is anthropologist Christine Gailey. Some of her more accessible major works are *Kinship to Kingship: Gender Hierarchy and State Formation in the Tongan Islands* (Austin: University of Texas Press, 1987), *Power Relations and State Formation*, ed. Thomas C. Patterson and Christine W. Gailey (Washington, DC: American Anthropological Association, 1987), "Evolution of Gender Hierarchy," in *Analyzing Gender*, ed. Beth Hess and Myra Ferree (Newbury Park, Cal.: Sage Publications, 1988), "Putting Down Sisters and Wives," in *Women and Colonization*, ed. Mona Etienne and Eleanor Leacock (New York: Praeger, 1980), and "The State of the State in Anthropology," *Dialectical Anthropology* 9, 1–2 (1985): 65–89.

Other important theorists are Rae Lesser Blumberg, "A General Theory of Gender Stratification," *Sociological Theory*, ed. Randall Collins (San Francisco: Jossey-Bass, 1984); Eleanor Leacock, *Myths of Male Dominance* (New York: Monthly Review Press, 1981); Sherry Ortner, "Is Female to Male as Nature Is to Culture?" in *Woman, Culture and Society*, ed. Michelle Rosaldo and Louise Lamphere (Stanford, Cal.: Stanford University Press, 1974), and "The Virgin and the State," *Michigan Discussions in Anthropology* 2 (1976): 1–16; Rayna Rapp, "Anthropology: A Review Essay," *Signs* 4, 3 (1979): 497–513; Rayna Rapp Reiter, "The Search for Origins: Unraveling the Threads of Gender Hierarchy," *Critique of Anthropology* 2, 9–10 (1977): 5–24; *Toward an Anthropology of Women*, ed. Rayna Rapp Reiter (New York: Monthly Review Press, 1975); Gayle Rubin, "The Traffic in Women," ibid.; Karen Sacks, "State Bias and Women's Status," *American Anthropologist* 78, 2 (1976): 565–69.

CHAPTER 7

1   George Mendenhall, "The Hebrew Conquest of Palestine," *Biblical Archaeologist* 25 (1962): 66–87.

2   See, for example, Julian Morgenstern, "*Beena* Marriage (Matriarchat) in Ancient Israel and Its Historical Implications," *Zeitschrift für die Altestamentische Wissenschaft* 47 (1929): 47, 91–110; and David Bakan, *And They Took Themselves Wives* (San Francisco: Harper & Row, 1979), 71.

3   See Phyllis Trible, *God and the Rhetoric of Sexuality* (Philadelphia: Fortress Press, 1978), 33–39.

4   Carol Meyers was a consultant on this project. See her "Gender Roles and Genesis 3: 16 Revisited," in *The Word of the Lord Shall Go Forth: Bulletin of the American Schools of Oriental Research* (1983), "Of Seasons and Soldiers: A Topological Appraisal of the Premonarchic Tribes of Galilee," ibid. (1983), and "Procreation, Production, and Protection: Male-Female Balance in Early Israel," *Journal of the American Academy of Religion* 51, 4 (1983): 569–93.

5   Meyers, personal communication.

6   Gerda Lerner, *The Creation of Patriarchy* (New York: Oxford University Press, 1986).

7   See A.D.H. Mates, "Judges," *Journal for the Study of the Old Testament* (1985).

CHAPTER 8

1   Plutarch, "Lycurgus," *Lives of Illustrious Men* (London: Chatto and Windus), I, 81.

2   Eva C. Keuls, *The Reign of the Phallus: Sexual Politics in Ancient Athens* (New York: Harper & Row, 1985).

3   John Noble Wilford, "Ancient Graves of Armed Women Hint at Amazons," *New York Times*, February 25, 1997.

4   For example, Phoebe "gives" her birthdate, home, and name to "Phoebus" Apollo in the opening scene of Aeschylus' *Eumenides*. Athena induces the Furies, ancient defenders of mother-right, to stop punishing Orestes for killing his mother. She persuades them to support Athens' new male-dominated laws by arguing that, because she was born of a male without a female, the father is the true parent, and the mother only a vessel.

5 Marylin Arthur, "From Medusa to Cleopatra: Women in the Ancient World," in *Becoming Visible,* ed. Renate Bridenthal, Claudia Koonz, and Susan Stuard (Boston: Houghton Mifflin, 1977).

6 Sarah Pomeroy, *Goddesses, Whores, Wives and Slaves: Woman in Classical Antiquity* (New York: Schocken Books, 1975).

7 Ibid., 63. Pomeroy derives her figures on longevity from J. Lawrence Angel's studies of skeletal remains.

8 The writer was Lysias; the fourth-century orator was Lycurgus; the second orator was Hyperides. The most famous proclamation about women's invisibility comes from Pericles' funeral oration.

9 Husbands called their wives *gyne* – "woman," literally, childbearer. Women past childbearing age were called *graus,* "old woman."

10 M.I. Finley, *The World of Odysseus* (New York: Meridian Press, 1959), 128–29, describes competitions in poetry and dramatic composition. The Greek obsession with competition is pointed out by John Huizinga, *Homo Ludens* (Boston: Beacon Press, 1955), 73.

11 Philip Slater, *The Glory of Hera* (Boston: Beacon Press, 1971), 36.

12 Thomas F. Scanlon has demonstrated that young girls participated in footraces, perhaps as a prenuptial rite. As in the men's contests, the winner was crowned with an olive wreath and awarded a portion of the sacrificial cow at the final festival. Surprisingly, they ran in chitons. Thomas F. Scanlon, "Virgineum Gymnasium," *The Archaeology of the Olympics,* ed. Wendy J. Raschke (Madison: University of Wisconsin Press, 1988).

13 Keuls, *The Reign of the Phallus.*

14 Pomeroy, *Goddesses, Whores, Wives and Slaves.*

15 See Eva Stehle Stigers, "Sappho's Private World," in *Reflections of Women in Antiquity,* ed. Helene P. Foley (New York: Gordon and Breach Science Publishers, 1981).

16 Brunilde Ridgway, "Ancient Greek Women and Art," *American Journal of Archaeology* 91 (1987): 399–409.

17 Amy Swerdlow, "The Greek Woman in Attic Vase Painting," *Women's Studies* 5 (1978): 267–84.

18 Like Arete of Cyrene or the hated Artemisia, who commanded a ship brilliantly and fought them in the battle of Salamis. Plato had female

students; seventeen women were Pythagoreans. Athenians saw Spartan women and knew about Sauromatian women, who had to kill an enemy before they could marry and who, Aristotle said, looked like men beside Spartan women. He also wrote that the most warlike races were ruled by women.

19 Ethlie Ann Vare and Greg Ptacek, *Mothers of Invention* (New York: William Morrow, 1988). Robert French did research on Greece. Sources not mentioned above are Sarah Pomeroy, *Women in Hellenistic Egypt* (New York: Schocken Books, 1984); W.K. Lacey, *The Family in Classical Greece* (Ithaca, NY: Cornell University Press, 1968); and J. Vogt, *Ancient Slavery and the Ideal of Man* (Oxford: Blackwell, 1974).

CHAPTER 9

1 Eric Pace, *New York Times*, April 30, 1985.

2 The builder and any owners of the house are unknown, but scholars have guessed that it was the country estate of an emperor or an imperial administrator. Other highly placed administrators have been named as possible owners, but because the house is in Sicily, not Rome, it was probably a country house.

3 Jo Ann McNamara was a consultant on this period. See her *"Matres Patriae/ Matres Ecclesiae*: Women of the Roman Empire," in *Becoming Visible*, ed. Renate Bridenthal, Claudia Koonz, and Susan Stuard (Boston: Houghton Mifflin, 1977). Robert French was a research assistant for this section. Other sources were Marylin Arthur, "From Medusa to Cleopatra," in *Becoming Visible*; J.P.V.D. Balsdon, *Roman Women* (London: The Bodley Head, 1962); David Herlihy, "Land, Family, and Women in Continental Europe 701–1200," *Women in Medieval Society*, ed. Susan Mosher Stuard (Philadelphia: University of Pennsylvania Press, 1976); Charles Seltman, *Women in Antiquity* (London: Thames and Hudson, 1956); Sarah Pomeroy, *Goddesses, Whores, Wives and Slaves: Women in Classical Antiquity* (New York: Schocken Books, 1975); *Reflections of Women in Antiquity*, ed. Helene Foley (New York: Gordon and Breach Science Publishers, 1981); C.A. Robinson, *Ancient History* (Toronto: Macmillan, 1967); E.A. Thompson, "Peasant Revolts in Late Roman Gaul," in *Studies in Ancient Society*, ed. M.I. Finley (London: Routledge and Kegan Paul, 1952).

CHAPTER 10

1   The discussion of Christianity is based on Jo Ann McNamara, *"Matres Patriae/Matres Ecclesiae*: Women of the Roman Empire," in *Becoming Visible*, ed. Renata Bridenthal, Claudia Koonz, and Susan Stuard, and *A New Song* (New York: Haworth Press, 1983); and, with Suzanne F. Wemple, "The Power of Women through the Family in Medieval Europe: 500–1100," in Clio's *Consciousness Raised*, ed. Mary S. Hartman and Lois Banner (New York: Harper & Row, 1974).

2   Adrienne Rich, "Compulsory Heterosexuality and Lesbian Existence," *Signs* 5, 4 (1980): 631–60.

3   The ideology of asceticism held that manliness was acquired through training and discipline. Women were considered capable of these qualities as well as men. "Virginity wiped out gender differences and turned women into men by giving them independence and the authority to pursue a lofty spiritual calling . . . Indeed, the Fathers of the church enjoyed the rhetorical strategy of praising virile women at the expense of effeminate men." See Jo Ann Kay McNamara, *Sisters in Arms: Catholic Nuns through Two Millennia* (Cambridge, Mass.: Harvard University Press, 1996), 3.

4   Ibid., 7.

5   Jo Ann McNamara, personal communication.

6   Suzanne F. Wemple, "Sanctity and Power: The Dual Pursuit of Early Medieval Women," in *Becoming Visible*, ed. Bridenthal, Koonz and Stuard.

7   For an in-depth study of woman-hatred in the early Christian church, see David F. Noble, *A World without Women: The Christian Clerical Culture of Western Science* (New York: Random House, 1992).

8   Cited by Bonnie S. Anderson and Judith P. Zinsser, *A History of Their Own* (New York: Harper & Row, 1988), 79.

9   Sources not mentioned in the text are Susan Stuard, "The Dominion of Gender: Women's Fortunes in the High Middle Ages," in *Becoming Visible*, ed. Bridenthal, Koonz, and Stuard; Anderson and Zinsser, *A History of Their Own*; Robin Lane Fox, *Pagans and Christians* (New York: Alfred A. Knopf, 1987); Elaine Pagels, *The Gnostic Gospels* (New York: Random House, 1979).

CHAPTER 11

1 Nabia Abbott lists twenty-four queens over 1600 years. Nabia Abbott, "Women and the State in Early Islam: I," *Journal of Near Eastern Studies (JNES)* 1 (Jan. 1942): 106–25, and "Women and the State in Early Islam: II," *JNES* 1 (July 1942): 341–68.

2 Abbot, "Early Islam, I"; Gertrude Stern, "The First Women Converts in Early Islam," *Islamic Culture* 13, 3 (1939): 290–305.

3 W. Robertson-Smith, *Kingship and Marriage in Early Arabia* (London, 1903).

4 Jane I. Smith, "Women, Religion, and Social Change in Early Islam," in *Women, Religion, and Social Change*, ed. Y. Haddad and E. Findly (Albany: State University of New York Press, 1985), 19–37.

5 Cousin-marriage (widespread outside Islam) allows inheritance exclusively in the male line and has contradictory consequences for women: they remain within their family group, with its emotional, material, and physical support, but are disinherited and watched by the entire group. Stern thinks that cousin-marriage increased after Islam, though it is a debated point. See Germaine Tillion, *Le harem et les cousins* (London: Zed Press, 1983). Some families married women to cousins on the fathers' side to bypass female inheritance rights.

6 Smith, "Woman, Religion, and Social Change."

7 Sprenger, *Leben*, I, 355, quoted by Leila Ahmed, "Women and the Advent of Islam," *Signs* 11, 4 (1986): 665–691.

8 The tribes were the Aus and the Khazraj.

9 See Stern, "The First Woman Converts," for a long list of other early female supporters.

10 Smith, "Woman, Religion, and Social Change," 19–37.

11 Ahmed, "Woman and the Advent of Islam."

12 Mary Wortley Montagu, *The Complete Letters of Lady Mary Wortley Montagu*, vol. I, ed. Robert Halsband (Oxford: Clarendon Press, 1965).

13 A.F.L. Beeston, "The So-Called Harlots of Hadramaut," *Oriens* 5 (1952): 16–22.

14 Smith, "Woman, Religion, and Social Change," offers the first hypothesis, Ahmed the second.

15 Ahmed, "Woman and the Advent of Islam."

16 Abbott, "Woman and the State."

17 For a twentieth-century example, see William McNeil, *A World History* Oxford: Oxford University Press, 1967) which mentions only one woman, once – Queen Elizabeth I of England.

18 Barbara Freyer Stowasser, "The Status of Women in Early Islam," in *Muslim Women*, ed. Freda Hussain (London: Croom Helm, 1984), and *Women in the Muslim World*, ed. Lois Beck and Nikki Keddie (Cambridge, Mass.: Harvard University Press, 1978).

19 Judith Tucker, who was a consultant to this project, found considerable evidence of *khul* and a few of *tafriq* in nineteenth-century Egypt and eighteenth- and nineteenth-century Palestine.

20 Translations in A.J. Arberry, *The Koran Interpreted* (New York: Macmillan, 1955). The word translated as *maidens* has recently been questioned.

21 "Pudendal," from the Latin *pudeo*, "to be ashamed," refers to external genitals, but I have never seen it applied to male organs – which really are external.

22 Ruth B. Bottigheimer, *The Bible for Children: From the Age of Gutenberg to the Present* (New Haven: Yale University Press, 1996), traces changes in readings on women, showing how, over the ages, they are silenced, made powerless, and portrayed as more evil, while readings about fathers became more favourable: "fathers should, and therefore could, do no wrong, and that seems to have been the mandate that drove the rewritings of many stories."

23 Nikki Keddie was a consultant for this project.

24 Leslie Pierce, who was a consultant for this section, believes that urban women were more likely than rural or nomadic women to obtain inheritances because urban property did not rest mainly in land, so was divisible.

25 Keddie, personal communications.

26 Ibid.

27 Ahmed, "Woman and the Advent of Islam."

28 Veena Talwar Oldenburg and Judith Tucker were also consultants for this section. Sources of information on Islam not cited above include

Julia Pardoe, *The City of the Sultans and Domestic Manners of the Turks in 1836* (Philadelphia: Carey, Lea & Blanchard, 1837); and Denise Spellberg, "The Politics of Praise: Depictions of Khadija, Fatima, and 'A'isha in Ninth Century Muslim Sources" (unpublished paper).

BIBLIOGRAPHY

Abbott, Nabia. "Women and the State in Early Islam: I." *Journal of Near Eastern Studies* 1 (Jan. 1942): 106–25.

__ "Women and the State in Early Islam: II." *Journal of Near Eastern Studies* 1 (July 1942): 341–68.

Ahmed, Leila. "Women and the Advent of Islam." *Signs* 11, 4 (1986): 665–91.

— "Women of Egypt." *Women's Review of Books*, 5, 2 (Nov. 1987). Review article.

Allen, Paula Gunn. *The Sacred Hoop: Recovering the Feminine in American Indian Traditions.* Boston: Beacon Press, 1986.

Altekar, A.S. *The Position of Women in Hindu Civilization.* Banaras, India: Motilal Barnarsidass, 1956.

Anderson, Bonnie S., and Judith P. Zinsser. *A History of Their Own.* New York: Harper & Row, 1988.

Anderson, Karen. "Commodity Exchange and Subordination: Montagnais-Naskapi and Huron Women, 1600–1650." *Signs* 11, 1 (1986): 48–62.

Anton, Ferdinand. *Woman in Pre-Columbian America.* New York: Abner Schram, 1973.

Bakan, David. *And They Took Themselves Wives.* San Francisco: Harper & Row, 1979.

Balsdon, J.P.V.D. *Roman Women.* London: The Bodley Head, 1962.

Beeston, A.F.L. "The So-Called Harlots of Hadramaut." *Oriens* 5 (1952): 16–22.

Billigmeier, Jon-Christian, and Judy A. Turner. "The Socio-Economic Roles of Women in Mycenean Greece: A Brief Survey from Evidence of the Linear B Tablets." *Women's Studies* 8 (1981): 3–20.

Blumberg, Rae Lesser. "A General Theory of Gender Stratification." *In Sociological Theory*, ed. Randall Collins. San Francisco: Jossey-Bass, 1984.

Bottigheimer, Ruth B. *The Bible for Children: From the Age of Gutenberg to the Present.* New Haven: Yale University Press, 1996.

Boulding, Elise. *The Underside of History: A View of Women Through Time.* Boulder, Colorado: Westveiw Press, 1976.

Bridenthal, Renate, Claudia Koonz, and Susan Stuard. *Becoming Visible: Women in European History.* Boston: Houghton Mifflin, 1987.

Brinkman, J.A. "Forced Laborers in the Middle Babylonian Period." *Journal of Cuneiform Studies* 32, 1 (1980): 17–22.

Brown, Judith K. "Iroquois Women: An Ethnohistoric Note." *Toward an Anthropology of Women*, ed. Rayna R. Reiter. New York: Monthly Review Press, 1975.

Brundage, Burr Cartwright. *The Fifth Sun.* Austin: University of Texas Press, 1979.

Burkett, Elinor C. "Indian Women and White Society: The Case of Sixteenth-Century Peru." In *Latin American Women*, ed. Asuncion Lavarin. Westport, Conn.: Greenwood Press, 1988.

Chadwick, John. *The Myceanean World.* New York: Cambridge University Press, 1976.

Chang, K.C. *The Archaeology of Ancient China.* New Haven: Yale University Press, 1977.

Connah, Graham. *African Civilizations: Precolonial Cities and States in Tropical Africa: An Archaeological Perspective.* Cambridge: Cambridge University Press, 1987.

Cooper, J.S. "Heilige Hochzeit." *Reallexicon der Assyriologie* 4: 259–69.

DeMarco, Edward. "New Dig at a 9000-Year-Old City Is Changing Views on Ancient Life." *New York Times*, November 11, 1997.

Dorsey, George. *Man's Own Show: Civilization.* New York: Harper & Brothers, 1931.

Edgerton, William F. "The Strikes in Ramses III's Twenty-ninth Year." *Journal of Near Eastern Studies* 10, 3 (1951): 139–45.

Etienne, Mona, and Eleanor Leacock. *Women and Colonization.* New York: Praeger, 1980.

Finkelstein, J.J. "Sex Offenses in Sumerian Laws." *Journal of the American Oriental Society* 86, 4 (1966): 355–72.

Finley, M.I. *The World of Odysseus.* New York: Meridian Press, 1959.

Foley, Helene P. *Reflections of Women in Antiquity*. New York: Gordon and Breach Science Publishers, 1981.

Foster, Benjamin. "A New Look at the Sumerian Temple State." *Journal of the Economic and Social History of the Orient* 24, 3 (1981): 225–41.

Fox, Robin Lane. *Pagans and Christians*. New York: Alfred A. Knopf, 1987.

Fromm, Erich. *Love, Sexuality, and Matriarchy: About Gender*. New York: Fromm International Publishing, 1997.

Galvin, Marianne. "The Priestesses of Hathor in the Old Kingdom and the 1st Intermediate Period." PhD dissertation, Brandeis University, 1981.

Gelb, I.J. "The Ancient Mesopotamian Ration System." *Journal of Near Eastern Studies* 26, 3 (1965): 230–43.

—"Prisoners of War in Early Mesopotamia." *Journal of Near Eastern Studies* 32, 1–2 (1973): 70–98.

Gibson, McGuire. "By Stage and Cycle to Sumer." *In The Legacy of Sumer*, ed. Denise Schmandt-Besserat. *Bibliotheca Mesopotamica* 4 (1975): 51–58.

Gimbutas, Marija. *Gods and Goddesses of Old Europe*. Berkeley: University of California Press, 1974.

— *The Language of the Goddess*. San Francisco: Harper & Row, 1989.

Girardot, Norman. *Myth and Meaning in Early Taoism*. Berkeley: University of California Press, 1983.

Gordon, Cyrus H. "The Status of Women Reflected in the Nuzi Tablets." *Zeitschrift fur Assyriologie*, Neue Folge, Band 9 (1936): 147–69.

Gould, Richard A. *Yiwara: Foragers of the Austrailian Desert*. New York: Schribner, 1969.

Granet, Marcel. *Chinese Civilization*. London: K. Paul, Trench, Trubner & Co., 1930.

Greengus, Samuel. "The Old Babylonian Marriage Contracts." *Journal of the American Oriental Society* 89 (1969): 505–32.

Grosz, K. "Dowry and Brideprice in Nuzi." *Studies on the Civilization and Culture of Nuzi and the Hurrians* 1 (1981) 166–67.

Gutin, JoAnn C. "Who Peopled the Planet?" *Discover*, Nov. 1992.

Hallo, W.W. "Women of Sumer." In *The Legacy of Sumer*, ed. Denise Schmandt-Besserat Malibu, Cal.: Bibliotheca Mesopotamica, 1976.

Harris, Rivkah. "Biographical Notes on the *Naditu* Women of Sippar." *Journal of Cuneiform Studies* 16 (1962): 1–12.

—"The *Naditu* Laws of the Code of Hammurapi in Praxis." *Orientalia* 30 (1961): 163–69

—"The Organization and Administration of the Cloister in Ancient Babylonia." *Journal of the Economic and Social History of the Orient* 6, 1 (1963): 121–57.

—"The *Naditu*-Woman." In *Studies Presented to A. Leo Oppenheim.* Chicago: University of Chicago, Oriental Institute, 1964.

Hayden, Dolores. *Seven American Utopias: The Architecture of Communitarian Socialism.* Cambridge, Mass.: MIT Press, 1975.

Heidel, Alexander. *The Babylonian Genesis.* Chicago: University of Chicago Press, 1951.

Herlihy, David. "Land, Famiy, and Women in Continental Europe, 701–1200." In *Women in Medieval Society*, ed. Susan Mosher Stuard. Philadelphia: University of Pennsylvania Press, 1976.

Huston, Nancy. "The Matrix of War: Mothers and Heroes." In *The Female Body in Western Culture: Contemporary Perspectives*, ed. Susan Suleiman. Cambridge, Mass.: Harvard University Press, 1986.

Kandell, Jonathan. *La Capital: The Biography of Mexico City.* New York: Random House, 1986.

Keuls, Eva C. *The Reign of the Phallus: Sexual Politics in Ancient Athens.* New York: Harper & Row, 1985.

Lacey, W.K. *The Family in Classical Greece.* Ithaca, NY: Cornell University Press, 1968.

Lambert, W.G. "Goddesses in the Pantheon." In *La Femme dans le Proche-Orient Antique*, ed. Jean-Marie Durand Paris: Éditions Recherche sur les Civilisations, 1987.

Lee, Richard B. "Population Growth and the Beginnings of Sedentary Life among the !Kung Bushmen." In *Population Growth: Anthropological Implications*, ed. Brian Spooner. Cambridge, Mass.: MIT Press, 1972.

Lerner, Gerda. *The Creation of Patriarchy.* New York: Oxford University Press, 1986.

Lesko, Barbara S. "Women of Egypt and the Ancient Near East." In *Becoming Visible*, ed. Renate Bridenthal, Claudia Koonz, and Susan Stuard. Boston: Houghton Mifflin, 1987.

Levathes, Louise "A Geneticist Maps Ancient Migrations." *New York Times*, July 27, 1993.

Levy, Howard S. *Chinese Footbinding: The History of a Curious Erotic Custom*. New York: Walton Rawls, 1966.

Maekawa, Kazuya. "Female Weavers and Their Children in Lagash." *Acta Sumerologica* 2 (1980): 81–125.

Mann, Susan. "Historical Change in Female Biography from Song to Qing Times: The Case of Early Qing Jiangnan." *Transactions of the International Conference of Orientalists in Japan* 30 (1985): 65–77.

—"Widows in the Kinship, Class, and Community Structures of Qing Dynasty China." *Journal of Asian Studies* 46, 1 (1987): 37–56.

Marshack, Alexander. *The Roots of Civilization: The Cognitive Beginnings of Man's First Art, Symbols and Notation*. New York: McGraw-Hill, 1972.

Mates, A.D.H. "Judges." *Journal for the Study of the Old Testament* (1985).

McNamara, Jo Ann. "*Matres Patriae/Matres Ecclesiae*: Women of the Roman Empire." In *Becoming Visible*, ed. Renata Bridenthal, Claudia Koonz, and Susan Stuard. Boston: Houghton Mifflin, 1987.

—*A New Song*. New York: Haworth Press, 1983.

—*Sisters in Arms: Catholic Nuns Through Two Millennia*. Cambridge, Mass: Harvard University Press, 1996.

—and Suzanne F. Wemple. "The Power of Women through the Family in Medieval Europe: 500–1100." In *Clio's Consciousness Raised*, ed. Mary S. Hartman and Lois Banner. New York: Harper & Row, 1974.

Mellaart, James. *Catal Hüyük: A Neolithic Town in Anatolia*. New York: McGraw-Hill, 1967.

Mendenhall, George. "The Hebrew Conquest of Palestine." *Biblical Archaeologist* 25 (1962): 66–87.

Meyers, Carol. "Gender Roles and Genesis 3: 16 Revisited." In *The Word of the Lord Shall Go Forth: Bulletin of the American Schools of Oriental Research* (1983).

—"Of Seasons and Soldiers: A Topological Appraisal of the Premonarchic Tribes of Galilee." *Bulletin of the American Schools of Oriental Research* (1983).

—"Procreation, Production, and Protection: Male-Female Balance in Early Israel." *Journal of the American Academy of Religion* 51, 4 (1983): 569–93.

Michalowski, Piotr. "Royal Women of the Ur III Period, Part I." *Journal of Cuneiform Studies* 28, 3 (1976): 169 –72.

Montagu, Mary Wortley. *The Complete Letters of Lady Mary Wortley Montagu,* Vol. 1, ed. Robert Halsband. Oxford: Clarendon Press, 1965.

Moorey, P.R.S. "What Do We Know about the People Buried in the Royal Cemetery?" *Expedition* 20 (1977).

Morgenstern, Julian. "*Beena* Marriage (Matriarchat) in Ancient Israel and Its Historical Implications." *Zeitschrift für die Altestamentische Wissenschaft* 47 (1929).

Muller, Viana. "Kin Reproduction and Elite Accumulation in the Archaic States of Northwest Europe." In *Power Relations and State Formation*, ed. Thomas C. Patterson and Christine W. Gailey. Washington, DC: American Anthropological Association, 1987.

Nash, June. "The Aztecs and the Ideology of Male Dominance." *Signs* 4, 2 (1978): 349–62.

Nashat, Guity. "Women in the Middle East: 8000 BC to AD 1800." In *Restoring Women to History,* ed. Renata Bridenthal, Claudia Koonz, and Susan Stuard. Bloomington, Ind: Organization of American Historians, 1988.

Noble, David F. *A World without Women: The Christian Clerical Culture of Western Science.* New York: Random House, 1992.

Noel, Jan. "New France: Les Femmes Favorisées." *Atlantis* 6, 2 (1981): 80–98.

O'Flaherty, Wendy. *Doniger Women, Androgynes, and Other Mythical Beasts.* Chicago: University of Chicago Press, 1980.

Owen, David. "Widow's Rights in Ur III Sumer." *Zeitschrift für Assyriologie und vorderasiatische Archäologie* 70 (1981): 170–84.

Pagels, Elaine. *The Gnostic Gospels.* New York: Random House, 1979.

Paradise, Jonathan. "A Daughter and Her Father's Property at Nuzi." *Journal of Cuneiform Studies* 25 (1980): 189–207.

Pardoe, Julia. *The City of the Sultans and Domestic Manners of the Turks in 1836.* Philadelphia: Carey, Lea & Blanchard, 1837.

Pestman, P.W. *Marriage and Matrimonial Property in Ancient Egypt.* Leiden: Papyrologica Lugduno-Batava no. 9, 1961.

Peterson, Frederick A. *Ancient Mexico.* New York: G.P. Putnam's Sons, 1959.

Plutarch. "Lycurgus." In *Vitae parallelae. Lives of Illustrious Men*, vol. 1. Translated from the Greek. 2 vols. London: Chatto and Windus, 1876.

Pomeroy, Sarah B. *Women in Hellenistic Egypt: From Alexander to Cleopatra.* New York: Schocken Books, 1984

—Goddesses, Whores, Wives and Slaves: Woman in Classical Antiquity. New York: Schocken Books, 1975.

Qunta, Christine N. "Outstanding African Women, 1500 BC–1900 AD." In *Women in Southern Africa*, ed. Christine Qunta. London: Allison & Busby, 1987.

Ramusack, Barbara N. "Women in South and Southeast Asia." In *Restoring Women to History*, ed. Renate Bridenthal, Claudia Koonz, and Susan Stuard. Bloomington, Ind.: Organization of American Historians, 1988.

Redford, Donald B. *History and Chronology of the Eighteenth Dynasty.* Toronto: University of Toronto Press, 1967.

Rich, Adrienne. "Compulsory Heterosexuality and Lesbian Existence." *Signs* 5, 4 (1980): 631–60.

Ridgway, Brunilde. "Ancient Greek Women and Art." *American Journal of Archaeology* 91 (1987): 399–409.

Robertson-Smith, W. *Kingship and Marriage in Early Arabia.* London, 1903.

Rohrlich, Ruby, and June Nash. "Patriarchal Puzzle: State Formation in Mesopotamia and Mesoamerica." *Heresies* 4, 1 (1981): 60–65.

Romer, W.H.P. "Frauenbriefe uber Religion, Politick und Privatleben in Mari." *Alter Orient und Altes Testament* 12 (1971).

Rubin, Gayle. "The Traffic in Women." In *Toward an Anthropology of Women*, ed. Rayne Rapp Reiter. New York: Monthly Review Press, 1975.

Samson, Julia. *Nefertiti and Cleopatra*. London: Rubicon, 1985.

Sanday, Peggy Reeves. *Female Power and Male Dominance: On the Origin of Sexual Inequality*. New York: Cambridge University Press, 1981.

Saporettei, Claudio. "The Status of Women in the Middle Assyrian Period." *Sources and Monographs on the Ancient Near East* 2, 1 (1979): 1–20.

Sasson, Jack. "Biographical Notices on Some Royal Ladies from Mari." *Journal of Cuneiform Studies* 25, 2 (1973): 59–78.

Scanlon, Thomas F. "Virgineum Gymnasium." *The Archaeology of the Olympics*, ed. Wendy J. Raschke. Madison: University of Wisconsin Pres, 1988.

Schafer, Edward H. *The Divine Woman: Dragon Ladies and Rain Maidens*. San Francisco: North Point Press, 1980.

Schemandt-Besserat, Denise, ed. *The Legacy of Sumer*. Malibu, Cal: Undera, 1976.

—*Ancient Persia: The Art of an Empire*. Malibu, Cal.: Undera, 1980.

Seltman, Charles. *Women in Antiquity*. London: Thames and Hudson, 1956.

Sievers, Sharon L. "Women in China, Japan, and Korea." In *Restoring Women to History*, ed. Renata Bridenthal, Claudia Koonz, and Susan Stuard. Bloomington, Ind.: Organization of American Historians, 1988.

Smith, Jane I. "Women, Religion, and Social Change in Early Islam." In *Women, Religion, and Social Change*, ed. Y. Haddad and E. Findly. Albany: State University of New York Press, 1985.

Smole, W.J. *The Yanomama Indians: A Cultural Geography*. Austin: University of Texas Press, 1976.

Spade, Beatrice. "The Education of Women in China during the Southern Dynasties." *Journal of Asian History* 1, 13 (1979):15–41.

Steinfels, Peter. "Idyllic Theory of Goddesses Creates Storm." *New York Times*, February 13, 1990.

Stern, Gertrude. "The First Women Converts in Early Islam." *Islamic Culture* 13, 3 (1939): 290–305.

Stigers, Eva Stehle. "Sappho's Private World." In *Reflections of Women in Antiquity*, ed. Helene P. Foley. New York: Gordon and Breach Science Publishers, 1981.

Stone, Elizabeth C. "The Social Role of the Naditu Woman in Old Babylonian Nippur." *Journal of the Economic and Social History of the Orient* 25, 1 (1982): 50–70.

Stowasser, Barbara Freyer. "The Status of Women in Early Islam." In *Muslim Women*, ed. Freda Hussain. London: Croom Helm, 1984.

—*Women in the Muslim World*, ed. Lois Beck and Nikki Keddie. Cambridge, Mass.: Harvard University Press, 1978.

Sung, Marina H. "The Chinese Lieh-nü Tradition." In *Women in China: Current Directions in Historical Scholarship*, Historical Reflections, Directions Series, 3 ed.

Swerdlow, Amy. "The Greek Woman in Attic Vase Painting." *Women's Studies* 5 (1978): 267–84.

—"Ladies' Day at the Capitol: Women Strike for Peace versus Huac." *Feminist Studies* 8, 3 (1982): 493–520.

Tarn, Sir William. *Cambridge Ancient History*, vol. 10. London: Cambridge University Press, 1970.

Thompson, E.A. "Peasant Revolts in Late Roman Gaul." In *Studies in Ancient Society*, ed. M.I. Finley. London: Routledge & Kegan Paul, 1952.

Thompson, William I. *The Time Falling Bodies Take to Light*. New York: St. Martin's Press, 1981.

Trible, Phyllis. *God and the Rhetoric of Sexuality*. Philadelphia: Fortress Press, 1978.

Valbelle, Dominique. *Les oeuvriers de la tombe: Deir el Médinehá l'Époque Ramesside*. Bibliotheque d'etude, tome 46. Cairo: Institut français d'archiéologie orientale du Caire, 1985.

Van Gulik, R.H. *Sexual Life in Ancient China*. Leiden: E.J. Brill, 1961.

Van Kirk, Sylvia. *Many Tender Ties: Women in Fur Trade Society in Western Canada, 1700–1850*. Winnipeg: Watson & Dwyer, 1980.

Vogt, J. *Ancient Slavery and the Ideal of Man*. Oxford: Blackwell, 1974.

Voigt, Mary. *Hajji Firuz Tepe, Iran: The Neolithic Settlement*. Philadelphia: University of Philadelphia Museum Monographs 50, 1983.

Wenig, Steffan. *The Woman in Egyptian Art.* New York: McGraw-Hill, 1969.

Wilford, John Noble. "Sexes Equal on South Sea Isle." *New York Times,* March 29, 1994

—"Skull in Ethiopia Is Linked to Earliest Man." *New York Times,* March 31, 1994.

—"Bones in China Put New Light on Humans." *New York Times,* November 16, 1995.

—"2.3 Million-Year-Old Jaw Extends Human Family." *New York Times,* November 19, 1996.

—"Ancient Graves of Armed Women Hint at Amazons." *New York Times,* February 25, 1997.

Wright, Arthur F. *Buddhism in Chinese History.* Stanford: Stanford University Press, 1959.

Date Due

MAR 0 2	2004		
APR 6	2004		
MAY 0 7	2004		
NOV 2 4	2004		
DEC 1 3	2004		

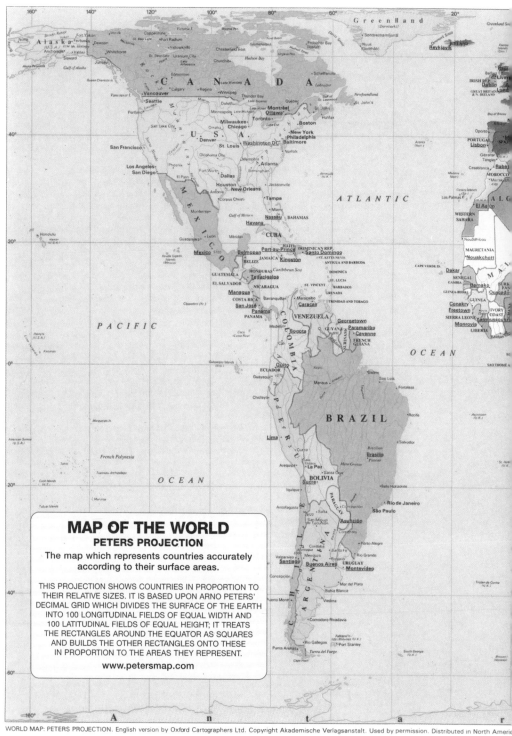

MAP OF THE WORLD
PETERS PROJECTION
The map which represents countries accurately
according to their surface areas.

THIS PROJECTION SHOWS COUNTRIES IN PROPORTION TO
THEIR RELATIVE SIZES. IT IS BASED UPON ARNO PETERS'
DECIMAL GRID WHICH DIVIDES THE SURFACE OF THE EARTH
INTO 100 LONGITUDINAL FIELDS OF EQUAL WIDTH AND
100 LATITUDINAL FIELDS OF EQUAL HEIGHT; IT TREATS
THE RECTANGLES AROUND THE EQUATOR AS SQUARES
AND BUILDS THE OTHER RECTANGLES ONTO THESE
IN PROPORTION TO THE AREAS THEY REPRESENT.

www.petersmap.com